Fetal Rights, Women's Rights

Fetal Rights, Women's Rights

Gender Equality in the Workplace

Suzanne Uttaro Samuels

THE UNIVERSITY OF WISCONSIN PRESS

The University of Wisconsin Press
114 North Murray Street
Madison, Wisconsin 53715

3 Henrietta Street
London WC2E 8LU, England

1   3   5   4   2

Printed in the United States of America

Library of Congress Cataloging-in-Publication Data
Samuels, Suzanne Uttaro.
Fetal rights, women's rights: gender equality in the workplace /
Suzanne Uttaro Samuels.
238 p.   cm.
Includes bibliographical references and index.
ISBN 0-299-14540-9.   ISBN 0-299-14544-1 (pbk.)
1. Pregnant women—Employment—United States. 2. Prenatal
influences—Government policy—United States. 3. Women's rights—
United States. 4. Fetus—Legal status, laws, etc.—United States.
5. Women—Employment—United States. 6. Sex discrimination in
employment—United States. I. Title.
HD6067.2.U6S25   1995
331.4'4—dc20   94-40267

Dedicated to the memory of my father,
Ralph T. Uttaro

Contents

Preface

The proliferation of fetal protection policies in the 1980s raised difficult and fascinating questions about the role of women in society and about our government's commitment to equal employment opportunity and occupational safety and health. These policies, which were promulgated by private employers and barred fertile women from jobs that might expose an embryo or fetus to certain toxins, severely limited women's employment opportunities and may have placed at risk occupational safety and health.

The debate about fetal protection policies touched upon several highly charged issues. Fetal protection policies allowed employers to bar women from jobs solely out of concern about fetal health. As a result, these policies had grave implications for women's ability to find jobs. The policies were almost always confined to male-dominated occupations, which tended to pay more and provide better benefits and more opportunities for advancement. Thus, fetal protection policies reinforced the existing sex segregation of the work force and impaired women's ability to achieve economic equality.

Fetal protection policies also implicated the abortion debate, which intensified in the middle to the late 1980s and early 1990s. These policies placed the fetus's "right" to be free from exposure to maternally transmitted harm above the woman's right to choose her employment. This balancing approach paralleled that adopted by the Supreme Court in *Roe v. Wade.* In this landmark case, the Supreme Court held that the woman's right to choose abortion was paramount in the first and second trimesters, while the state's interest in fetal health, and by implication, the fetus's right to life, became dominant in the third trimester. The balancing of fetal rights against women's rights has been a recurrent theme in the debate about fetal protection policies, and one that has often been overlooked in analyses of these policies.

My interest in the issue of fetal protection policies was sparked in an employment discrimination seminar given at the University at Buffalo Law School in the spring of 1989. Initially, I was interested in this topic because I thought that fetal protection policies bridged the gap between abortion and employment rights: "protecting" fetuses imbued them with rights independent of the mother, and served to undermine women's reproductive and employment rights. It was this conception of fetal protection policies that prompted me to undertake this project. Clearly, my views on the abortion controversy and the importance of equal employment opportunity provided the frame of reference for my re-search on these policies. At the outset, I assumed that fetal protection policies were subtle devices employed to reinforce sex segregation in employment. The whole concept of fetal "protection" policies seemed to be nothing so much as a clever public relations ploy: Who would argue with the employer's motive of protecting fetuses? On their face, these policies appeared to be benign measures taken by employers seeking to eliminate fetal exposure to occupational toxins. While these policies may have protected fetuses from certain occupational hazards, however, they were not benign. Any employment policy that bars women from certain jobs on the basis of their procreative capacity undermines their ability to compete effectively in the workplace.[1]

Only after I had begun my research did I understand that these policies also implicated policies concerned with occupational safety and health. In fact, in workplaces that pose significant health hazards to both male and female workers, these policies seemed to provide the prover-bial "half a loaf" for individuals concerned with occupational safety.

Underlying the debate about these policies is the question of whether fetuses have rights independent of women. Moreover, where workplaces are not safe and cannot be made safe for fetuses without significant cost to both employers and to the public, the issue is one of determining who should decide whether these fetuses should be exposed to occupational toxins.

Prohibiting women from certain jobs to protect the welfare of the race has Orwellian overtones. At the root of these policies is the belief that the individual rights of women may be subjugated to the larger interests of the society. The conception of women as "vessels" for child-bearing would seem to be more properly the stuff of fiction. In fact, *The Handmaid's Tale,* by Margaret Atwood, chronicles a distopia in which women's sole function is to bear children. In one eerie passage, one with significance for both fetal protection policies and state protective legislation of the early twentieth century, a high government official explains why the new system is preferable to the old. He states that in the old system "[m]oney was the only measure of worth . . . [and] women got no respect as mothers." As a result, he says, women chose not to become pregnant. In the new society women are barred from participating in the workplace. The result, the official states, is that "[women] are protected, [and] they can fulfill their biological destinies in peace . . . [w]ith full support and encouragement."[2] Similarly, fetal protection policies "pro-tected" women and their offspring from exposure to hazardous toxins. Like the distopia in Atwood's *The Handmaid's Tale,* a society that allows employers to adopt fetal protection policies reifies women's procreative role while denigrating their other contributions. In such a society, women can never be the equals of men.

My thanks to Stephen C. Halpern, for his help at all stages of this project. Thanks also to Karen Maschke, Susan Mezey, Carin Clauss, and Dale Bauer for their careful readings of the manuscript and thoughtful suggestions, and to Stacey Donohue, Lori Rhodebeck, Donald B. Rosen-thal, Isabel Marcus, Jo Renee Formicola, and Mary Boutilier for their support throughout the writing and revision process. Finally, my special thanks to Steven C. Samuels for his unwavering support from the begin-ning of this project through the final draft.

Fetal Rights, Women's Rights

1. Introduction: Fetal Protection Policies and Gender Equality

In the late 1970s and throughout the 1980s, many private sector employers formulated policies that restricted fertile women, defined as women of childbearing age who had not undergone surgical sterilization, from jobs that might pose a risk to an embryo or fetus. These policies, which employers termed "fetal protection policies," typically barred all women between the ages of 15 and 50 from hazardous jobs unless the women could establish that they had been sterilized. According to estimates, two-thirds of working women fell within this age category and were potentially at risk of exclusion.[1] In 1991, the Supreme Court held that these policies were prohibited under Title VII of the 1964 Civil Rights Act; nonetheless, the policies appear to have had a significant impact upon women's attempts to achieve equality in both the workplace and the larger society. Most particularly, these policies implicated both equal employment opportunity and occupational safety and health, since fetuses were presumed to be at risk of harm through maternal, but not paternal exposure to occupational toxins. All three branches of government had statutory responsibility for regulating these policies. This book assesses both how governmental institutions responded to the proliferation of fetal protection policies in the 1980s and the extent to which each branch fulfilled this duty.

The American government has evinced a surprising ambivalence in dealing with gender-related issues in the past. Beginning with the state protective laws of the early 1900s, decision-makers have revealed that they are unable to distinguish between sex, which is based on biological characteristics, and gender, which is socially constructed. Throughout the twentieth century, American administrators, legislators, and judges have confused gender with sex, often permitting gender-based distinctions to stand despite statutory mandates to eliminate gender discrimination.

Perhaps equally surprising, the American people, and American theorists in particular, have demonstrated a willingness to allow such distinctions. The governmental response to fetal protection policies in the late 1980s and early 1990s may be viewed as another manifestation of this ambiguity. These policies brought to the forefront fundamental questions about women's "basic nature," responsibility for reproduction of the species, and control over pregnancy and contraception. Much of the ongoing debate among feminists about the contours of equality analysis and about the need for special treatment of women in the workplace, especially with regard to pregnancy benefits, may be discerned in the fetal protection controversy. Furthermore, the abortion controversy, which raged throughout the 1980s, also played out in the debate about fetal protection policies. In a sense, the fetal protection issue is a microcosm of the ongoing debate in American society about the ordering of sex roles and about the perceived conflict between women's responsibility for wage-earning and for propagation of the species.

Even apart from their wider ramifications for gender equality, fetal protection policies were significant in their own right. These policies were adopted in a large number of workplaces, and their long-term impact on sex segregation in the workplace and on occupational safety and health has yet to be determined.

The Prevalence of Fetal Protection Policies

The adoption of fetal protection policies was not isolated to a few random workplaces. In fact, a large number of employers in a variety of workplaces used these policies in the 1980s and early 1990s. There has been no definite accounting of the number of women barred from jobs as a result of these policies, but one estimate suggested that as many as twenty million women were at risk of exclusion.[2] In 1985, the Office of Technological Assessment (OTA), an organization that gathers information for Congress, estimated that at least fifteen of the Fortune 500 companies and a significant number of hospitals utilized fetal protection policies.[3]

Moreover, recent findings suggest that these policies were even more widespread than earlier statistics had indicated. A survey conducted in Massachusetts in 1989 suggested that upwards of 20 percent of chemical and electronics firms barred certain groups of employees from jobs on the basis of reproductive health hazards; and another 13 percent offered voluntary transfers to employees concerned about reproductive dangers.[4] All of these employers except one framed their policies with regard to reproductive risks to women alone: even where scientific evidence indicated that a substance posed a danger to both the male and female reproductive systems, women alone were restricted or offered transfers.[5] The results of this survey strongly suggest that the use of exclusionary policies has been grossly underestimated.

The number of jobs from which fertile women were actually excluded was much larger than the number from which they were formally excluded. Because many of the affected workplaces were unionized, women were excluded not only from the hazardous jobs, but from any jobs that might lead to these positions in the lines of progression specified by union contracts.[6] The express exclusion from one job on the basis of reproductive hazards effectively foreclosed access to many other jobs that may not have posed a danger to reproductive health.

Fetal protection policies were most widely utilized in the lead industry, where there was abundant scientific evidence that exposure to lead posed risks to fetuses and embryos at the earliest stages of development. Since 1976, the Lead Industries Association publicly opposed the employment of women in jobs where they would be exposed to lead, and it is estimated that women were excluded from almost one million jobs in this industry alone.[7]

While these policies were often used in the lead industry, they were also adopted by many companies outside of this industry. Among those companies known to have barred fertile women from certain job categories were the Olin Corporation, American Cyanamid, Union Carbide, General Motors, Bunker Hill, Allied Chemical, B.F. Goodrich, Monsanto, St. Joe's Minerals, ASARCO, Sun Oil, and Delco-Remy.[8] It also bears noting that corporate interest in the issue of fetal protection policies intensified in the late 1980s and early 1990s. In late 1985, the Deputy General Counsel for the National Association of Manufacturers stated that concern about fetal hazards in the workplace was "an emerging issue" with companies.[9] Thus, at the same time that the Supreme Court held that fetal protection policies were prohibited under Title VII, a significant number of employers had either adopted a fetal protection policy or were contemplating such a policy.

Not all industries utilizing or producing reproductive toxins, however, chose to adopt fetal protection policies. These policies were more common among large firms with male-intensive or evenly proportioned male/female work forces than they were among small companies or those with female-intensive work forces.[10] In fact, companies that excluded broad classes of women, such as all women or fertile women, were much more likely to have male-intensive work forces than those that did not.[11]

Even more significantly, many women in traditionally "female" jobs, like operating room nurses, flight attendants, beauticians, workers in dry cleaners, lab technicians, health care workers, dental technicians, hygienists, and pottery painters, are exposed on a routine basis to materials that may harm a developing fetus; however, these women were not barred from working in these occupations.[12] For example, operating room nurses are exposed to waste anesthetic gases, which result in an increased incidence of spontaneous abortion and miscarriage; airline flight attendants are exposed to increased radiation levels, which may result in an increased incidence of miscarriage; beauticians are exposed to halogenated hydrocarbon hair spray propellants, which are known abortifacients, and to mutagenic and carcinogenic hair dyes; and workers in the dry-cleaning industry are exposed to tetrachloroethylene, which is a mutagen.[13]

Some commentators have contended that reproductive hazards to women in female jobs have been downplayed in an effort to keep women in these jobs. For example, prolonged use of video display terminals (vdt's) has long been suspected of increasing the risk of miscarriage. One researcher claims that this risk has been ignored by both employers and the federal government, in large part because these terminals are used in clerical jobs that are overwhelmingly filled by women.[14]

The selective exclusion of women from jobs that have been traditionally male, and for which replacements were readily available, strongly suggests that women have been excluded from workplaces in which they were "marginal" workers, i.e., where they occupied jobs that were traditionally male jobs and that were, for the most part, still occupied by men.[15] This selective exclusion is often cited as evidence that employers did not bar women solely out of a desire to protect them from reproductive injury and their offspring from developmental harm. Moreover, the corporate response to data indicating that a substance poses a threat to the male reproductive system, but not to that of the female, suggests that an employer's motivation in adopting these policies was not always benevolent. In 1977, the pesticide dibromochloropropane (DBCP) was found to cause sterility in male workers exposed to it. Rather than barring male workers from jobs that might expose them to the substance, DBCP was banned. While women have been replaced with men because of reproductive hazards associated with certain workplace toxins, in the case of DBCP no one suggested that the male workers should be similarly replaced.

Thus, it appears that fetal protection policies were adopted in certain types of industries, typically by corporations engaged in heavy industry with work forces predominantly composed of men. In addition, these workplaces were usually unionized.[16] The content and rationale for these policies, however, varied widely. As the OTA concluded in its 1985 report, some policies were based upon extensive epidemiological and toxicological data about particular substances; others were tentative with regard to suspected hazards. Similarly, some were carefully written and meticulously documented; others were more informal.[17] According to the OTA, the policies were usually announced to both the union and the employees in large manufacturing companies, while policies were adopted in an ad hoc fashion in smaller organizations.[18]

Employers contended that they adopted these policies for benevolent, or at least benign, reasons. Typically, employers relied upon two rationales for justifying their adoption of a fetal protection policy.[19] The first of these rationales focused on the employer's moral concerns about the welfare of its workers' offspring; the second focused upon the employer's desire to limit its liability for occupational exposure to hazardous materials.

Nearly all employers contended that they adopted these policies out of a concern about the effects of occupational exposure upon the health of the fetus. Typically, the employer alleged that it was morally obligated to protect the fetus from workplace toxins and that fetal protection policies were the only means of eliminating exposure to these toxins. The employer contended that workplace toxins were transmitted to the fetus principally through the mother; the employer largely ignored the effects of paternal exposure on fetal health.

This lack of concern about paternal transmission may have stemmed from an abundance of scientific data demonstrating the link between developmental harm and female transmission, and from a corresponding paucity of research about male-mediated effects.[20] The scientific data on reproductive hazards have been in flux in recent years. In addition, the employer's absolute disregard of paternally transmitted harm, coupled with its selective "protection" of the fetuses of women working in predominantly male jobs and its lack of concern about the offspring of women working in female occupations, weakened the employer's argument that the policies had been adopted solely to protect fetal health. The second rationale, that of limiting employer liability, was more likely the driving force for the employer's action than was the concern about fetal health.

The basis of this second rationale is that concerns about potential tort liability drove the employer to adopt these essentially preventative policies. The much bemoaned "explosion" in tort litigation throughout the 1980s was used as the backdrop for this argument. Unlike an adult, a child who is injured in utero as a result of exposure to occupational hazards, or whose injuries have led to death, is not required to exhaust those remedies available under the workers' compensation statute before bringing a tort suit against the employer. Employers adopting fetal protection policies contended that a tort suit based upon injury in utero could result in astronomical awards, the size of which could lead to bankruptcy.[21]

The problem with this rationale was that there were no records of any lawsuits having been brought by the children of women exposed to occupational toxins. Because of the speculative nature of this justification, it was rejected by a number of analysts, and by several courts that considered fetal protection policies.[22] In spite of this rejection, employers continued to assert that concerns about tort liability compelled them to adopt these policies.

By focusing on this seemingly benign concern about liability, employers were able to dodge concerns about the discriminatory effects of fetal protection policies. While it is impossible to know for certain why an employer chose to adopt a fetal protection policy, the available evidence suggests that employers adopted these policies for less than benevolent reasons. Perhaps the most feasible explanation is that employers adopted fetal protection policies as an alternative to the more costly task of eliminating occupational hazards: by utilizing these policies, the employer fostered the illusion that the workplace was safe for all employees and their offspring. The employer may have believed, with good reason, that by adopting these exclusionary policies, further governmental regulation of the workplace could be forestalled and existing regulations could be largely circumvented.[23]

It is also possible that, by framing the discussion about fetal hazards in terms of maternal transmission of harm, the employer sought to eliminate the possibility of tort liability for paternally-mediated harm. Since there is an abundance of data about maternal transmission and a corresponding dearth of scientific data about paternal transmission, employers may have been more concerned, some think quite justifiably, about limiting women's exposure than they were about limiting men's. An employer concerned about tort liability may have believed that by excluding women from the workplace, the likelihood of a judgment against him or her in a tort case arising from fetal harm would be substantially reduced.

Thus, the exclusion of women appears to have served certain employer objectives: it demonstrated commitment to occupational safety and health, and it diminished the likelihood of tort liability for both maternal and paternal exposure to toxins. Furthermore, the elimination of women from whole plants and lines of production served to decrease the employer's insurance costs. In particular, an employer who offered insurance benefits to his or her work force was relieved of the obligation to offer maternity benefits. Since there were male employees readily available to replace the women, the costs of implementing a fetal protection policy were meager.[24]

The Impact of Fetal Protection Policies

By the close of the 1980s, the proliferation of fetal protection policies had had a profound impact on women's attempts to achieve economic and social equality. These policies contributed to the existing sex segregation of the work force and to the pay disparity that exists between men and women. At present, over 50 percent of women working outside the home are in occupations that are more than 70 percent female. In fact, sex segregation is so extensive that it is estimated that to achieve an integrated work force more than 10 million men and women would need to switch jobs.[25]

In jobs where most of the workers are female, the pay is substantially lower, and there are fewer fringe benefits and opportunities for advancement.[26] Sociologists explain this phenomenon by reference to the "crowding thesis."[27] Since women are concentrated in a few occupations, the influx of women into the paid labor market results in too many women seeking too few jobs. As a result of the forces of supply and demand, the wages of women in these occupations are driven down.

The exclusion of women from jobs traditionally held by males, and that, for this reason, were better paying, further aggravated the existing sex segregation of the workplace. Through the operation of fetal protection policies, women were barred from entire areas of production and were restricted to a few, traditionally female, occupations. Furthermore, since "women's work" tends to pay much less than "men's work," with women earning 66 cents for every dollar earned by men, these policies threatened to worsen the existing wage gap. The impact of fetal protection policies upon the existing discrepancies should for these reasons not be underestimated: by barring pregnant or fertile women from a large number of jobs, the existing sex segregation of jobs became even more pronounced, and with it, the wage gap likely widened.

In addition to exacerbating the sex segregation of the work force and increasing the wage disparity between men and women, fetal protection policies may also have had a negative impact on occupational safety and health. These policies only addressed the risk of maternal transmission, even where the scientific data indicated that a fetus could be harmed by paternal exposure to toxins. As a result, the policies ignored the effects of paternal exposure to occupational toxins upon fetal health. In this sense, fetal protection policies were underinclusive because they failed to eliminate reproductive hazards.

Fetal protection policies also created "hidden" health risks: they excluded women from more lucrative jobs, which were higher paying and frequently provided medical insurance benefits. It is conceivable that this loss of income and benefits resulted in poorer nutrition and health care for the offspring of excluded workers. As a result, these offspring may have been exposed to even greater health risks than those apparent in the workplace.

Moreover, fetal protection policies were problematic not only because of their impact upon job segregation and occupational safety and health, but because they were based upon certain assumptions about women's proper role in the workplace and in society at large. In particular, fetal protection policies fostered what has been termed a "new gender stereotype." This stereotype encouraged the perception that women should be primarily concerned with childbearing and childrearing and only secondarily concerned with work-force participation. These policies classified women according to their capacity to become pregnant, and, in doing so, equated women solely with their reproductive functions. The new gender stereotype was that all women become pregnant, and that all women are at constant risk of becoming pregnant.

This new gender stereotype viewed women as pregnant virtually all of their working lives and encouraged a view of women as marginal workers.[28] Moreover, since this stereotype identified women solely by reference to their procreative capacity and parcelled out jobs on the basis of this capacity, it threatened to nullify existing legislation barring discrimination on the basis of sex and pregnancy. Again, the basis of this new gender stereotype was the belief that occupational toxins could be transmitted to the fetus only through the mother, and that an embryo or fetus could not be harmed by pre-conception paternal exposure.[29]

Thus, fetal protection policies have likely had a significant impact not only upon occupational safety and health, but also on women's attempts to achieve economic parity and social and political equality. The emergence of a new gender stereotype, one that reified women's procreative role while denigrating their contribution in the workplace, reinforced the existing sex segregation of the work force. Women's economic role was marginalized, and the view of women as secondary workers for whom an income is of limited importance was reinforced.[30]

The debate over fetal protection policies was extremely strident, in large part because it was seen by many as a referendum on the proper role of women in American society. Since the debate was framed in such a way that it required the rank ordering of women's roles in society, i.e., worker, childbearer, mother, it brought to a head a number of issues and concerns that continue to simmer below the surface in American society. At the heart of the debate about fetal protection policies is this question: Should individual women be allowed to weigh the costs and benefits of employment against the possibility of harm to a developing fetus? Fetal protection policies are conditioned on the assumption that fetal health and safety should be placed above the employment goals of individual women.

Some of the individuals and groups that supported these policies believed that fetal health was of paramount importance, and that a woman's employment prospects were to be limited to pursuits that did not threaten a potential fetus, if indeed such a thing is possible. Many of the groups and individuals opposing the policies rejected this argument, contending that it was based upon the belief that biology is destiny and that a woman's reproductive capacity should govern the most critical aspects of her life. Both supporters and opponents of fetal protection policies were extremely active in getting this issue on the public agenda. In addition, when the issue did reach the agenda of a number of governmental institutions, among these Congress, the courts, and the administrative agencies, these groups were very active in voicing their support or opposition.

Given both the impact of these policies on occupational segregation and health and safety, and the ominous connections between fetal protection policies and the abortion controversy, the governmental response to the increased use of fetal protection policies in the 1980s becomes critically important. A significant aspect of this response concerns the manner in which governmental institutions, most notably the courts, Congress, and the administrative agencies, responded to the view of women as marginal, potentially pregnant workers that was at the heart of these policies.

In the past, the response of the American government to gender-related issues has been troubling. The American people and their government evince a surprising ambiguity about the nature of sex differences and the role of gender in allocating societal resources, especially jobs. Throughout the twentieth century, American decision-makers have had a great deal of difficulty in responding to gender-related issues. In particular, courts and legislatures have frequently confused gender and sex, and have been willing to allow gender-based classifications to stand. The debates in the early twentieth century over state protective legislation, and over the Equal Rights Amendment and the male-only draft in the 1970s and 1980s, have demonstrated that decision-makers are willing to distinguish between the sexes in a myriad of situations, many of which have little to do with primary sex characteristics.

While decision-makers throughout the twentieth century have been called upon to assess the legality of gender-based classifications, including state protective laws, the ERA, and the male draft, fetal protection policies in modern American society were unprecedented. Never in the late twentieth century had women been barred from the workplace solely out of a concern about fetal well-being. Fetal protection policies, unlike other employment policies and practices that discriminated against female employees, had nothing to do with the employee's ability to perform the job in question: the sole basis for exclusion was reproductive capacity.

Governmental agencies should have had very little difficulty in responding effectively and efficiently to these policies. By their very nature, fetal protection policies were sex-based: since only women can conceive, only women were affected by the policies. Title VII of the 1964 Civil Rights Act bars sex-based discrimination in employment, and it would have seemed that governmental agencies like the Equal Employment Opportunity Commission would have readily found these policies in violation of the act. Similarly, since these policies were predicated on the employer's belief that the workplace was unsafe for fetuses, it would have seemed that agencies like the Occupational Safety and Health Administration and the Environmental Protection Agency would have responded to the increased use of the policies. Furthermore, even when these administrative agencies faltered, it would have seemed that Congress, which is responsible for the oversight of these agencies, would have regulated the policies. Strangely, however, neither Congress nor the administrative agencies crafted an adequate response to these policies.

Despite what seems to have been a clear statutory mandate to regulate these policies, Congress and the administrative agencies dodged the issue and effectively opted out of the debate about fetal protection policies for much of the 1980s and early 1990s. Instead, regulation of fetal protection policies was left to the courts, and, in particular, to the federal courts, with profound repercussions. In the vacuum left by the inactivity of Congress and the administrative agencies, the federal courts have engaged in the grossest form of policymaking and have shown themselves to be no better at settling issues involving gender differences and sex roles than have the other branches of government. In nearly all the fetal protection cases, the courts reached out beyond settled Title VII caselaw to permit these policies and relied upon the judges' own conceptions of gender roles to justify this deviation. In many cases, judges contended that the fetal protection policy implicated issues far beyond the scope of Title VII. They argued that the violation of Title VII could be justified by the employer's concerns about its employees' potential offspring. In essence, the courts, like other decision-makers, have shown themselves to be unable to distinguish between biological and socially constructed differences with regard to men and women.

Relying on the courts to craft a governmental policy for regulating fetal protection policies has been problematic for other reasons as well. The courts, unlike the regulatory agencies or research arms of Congress, have had difficulty understanding the scientific method, especially when called upon to decipher complicated studies involving teratogenicity and exposure to occupational toxins. In addition, the adjudication process itself has confounded attempts to address both the use of fetal protection policies and the existence of occupational hazards. By its very nature, adjudication encourages an either/or solution. It does not allow for a comprehensive evaluation of these policies and so was unable to encourage a solution that would have effectively responded to the many issues involved in the debate.

For various reasons, then, governmental decision-makers throughout the 1980s and early 1990s failed to respond effectively to the increased use of fetal protection policies. In many ways, this failure was predictable: throughout the twentieth century, governmental entities have demonstrated a startling ambiguity about whether primary sex characteristics should determine one's place in society. The debate over fetal protection policies fully exposed this ambiguity. Questions about gender equality and the role of women in industrial society and cultural images of motherhood and pregnancy were at the heart of the governmental response to fetal protection policies.

The difficulty faced by policymakers attempting to craft an effective response to fetal protection policies in the 1980s was compounded by the close symbolic connection between fetal protection policies and abortion. The debate over abortion intensified in the 1980s and permeated all branches of federal and state government.[31] Fetal protection policies were purported to be based on fetal rights, and disagreement about how to reconcile the rights of fetuses with those of women mirrored the ongoing abortion controversy. This uncertainty about gender, coupled with the close identity between fetal protection and abortion, undermined the resolve of policymakers to regulate these policies under existing statutes or caselaw.

More often than not, governmental actors simply opted out of the debate about these policies. Where the governmental entity was compelled to respond to the use of these policies, as in court cases, the response was invariably colored by its opinion of both the importance of gender differences and the nature of sex roles. The conception of gender equality embraced by decision-makers is as apparent in government's response to these policies as it is in its non-response. Even where decision-makers tried to dodge consideration of these policies, they were effectively reinforcing certain notions about the role of women in society and about women's responsibilities for childbearing.

1
Equality Analysis

Equality is a concept about which there has been vigorous public debate throughout much of our nation's history.[1] In the last century, women's demands for political, social, and economic equality have grown in intensity as women have continued to enter the sphere of paid employment. There has been much resistance to the full integration of women into American society, and, in particular, into the American work force. Debate about this integration has focused on the issue of whether women have "special" roles by virtue of their ability to bear children, and whether these roles should determine their work-force participation. Over the last 100 years, this "special-role" has been invoked repeatedly to justify the disparate treatment of women. The use of fetal protection policies and the response of policymakers to these policies can be seen as further manifestation of this continuing pattern.

2. Gender and the American Mind

At this point in our technological development, only women are able to bear children. Much of the debate about gender equality focuses upon this biological capacity. Many individuals believe that men and women are fundamentally different by virtue of their different reproductive functions, and that a woman's reproductive role has ramifications beyond the bearing of a child. These individuals claim that there are immutable differences between the sexes which are manifested in their emotional, physical, and intellectual traits. A significant number of these analysts would applaud the use of fetal protection policies because they would perceive these policies as enabling women to fulfill their childbearing function. These individuals would contend that the disparate treatment of women based upon their reproductive roles should not only be permitted but encouraged.

In the opposite camp are those who contend that the sexes are far more alike than different, and that reproductive function is not determinative of emotional makeup or intellectual or physical capacity. Many of these individuals would, and indeed have, opposed the use of fetal protection policies, arguing that sex characteristics do not determine one's capacity to do certain types of work. These analysts reject the implicit assumption that women are differentially susceptible to workplace toxins, and that fetuses are more vulnerable to the transmission of these toxins through maternal than paternal exposure.

In sum, at the core of the debate over fetal protection policies are

questions about the nature of sex differences. These policies have implicated the most divisive of issues in gender politics, among these being
the question of how to reconcile women's role in the procreative process
with their needs and aspirations in the economic sphere. There is little
consensus about the importance of reproductive or biological differences between the sexes, even among those groups of which one would
expect solidarity on the issue, such as feminists.

Women and Men as Fundamentally Different: Darwin, Craniology, and Biological Determinism

American equality analysis has a long history, going back to the mid-
nineteenth century, when women were viewed as the physical and intellectual inferiors of men. While the modern debate is framed in terms of
less mutable characteristics than muscle mass and brain size, much of
this debate bears at least a semantic resemblance to that of the past.

During the middle to the late nineteenth century, biologists and
physicians found strong "scientific" evidence that women and men differed in fundamental ways. Charles Darwin, who developed the theory
of evolution through natural selection, later used this theory as support
for his contention that women were less evolved than men, and that
women were the intellectual and physical inferiors of men.[2] In the late
nineteenth century, craniology, the study of brain size and skull forma-
tion, also provided evidence of male superiority.[3] It was believed that
since women had smaller heads and smaller brains they could never be
the intellectual equals of men. Nineteenth-century physicians and biologists utilized this scientific information as evidence that women were of a
different class than men.

During the 1800s, there was widespread agreement that women's
primary function in society was the bearing and rearing of children. As a
result, women were prohibited from engaging in any activity believed to
impair their reproductive capacity. The uterus and ovaries were believed
to be extremely sensitive organs that required a great deal of rest in
order to function properly. For this reason, after young girls began to
menstruate, they were kept away from school, to prevent the intellectual
exertion from causing "their uteruses and ovaries to shrivel and the
human race [to] die out."[4] If a woman did not fulfill her role as wife and

mother, she was viewed as violating some higher law that decreed this to be her natural function.[5]

Moreover, women were viewed as the physical, intellectual, and social inferiors of men. Women, especially middle-class women, were responsible for the home and family and so were strongly discouraged from entering the work force. This conception of a "sexual division of labor" formed the basis for nineteenth-century society. The differentiation in roles, which relegated women to the home and men to the outside world, was acceded to by much of American society. While at least one wing of the women's suffrage movement that emerged in the mid-nineteenth century was a notable exception to this, it was not until the nineteenth amendment was passed in 1920 that a widespread public debate about the principles of equality and sexual difference arose.

Social Darwinism and craniology might be seen as just an interesting footnote to the nineteenth century if their central premise, which was that primary sex characteristics should determine one's role in society, had been totally abandoned. In truth, however, this premise has re-emerged in the latter part of the twentieth century. Beginning in the 1970s, there has been a resurgence of studies alleging to prove scientifically that women are inherently better at childcare and homemaking, and that men are innately better suited to compete in the workplace.[6]

The proponents of these studies, who have become known as sociobiologists, contend that our culture is shaped by biological adaptation. Women's reproductive functions are determined by biological factors, and these factors in turn affect all aspects of their social lives.[7] To sum up their theory in what are perhaps oversimplified terms, sociobiologists argue that women alone are capable of bearing children: since they alone can bear children, it follows that the responsibility for childbearing and childrearing should fall exclusively upon them. In this view, any jobs women might have outside the home are merely temporary or marginal jobs, since their primary function is that of wife and mother. Thus, discrimination in the work force has a seemingly valid basis: since women's primary sphere is the home, subordination in the workplace is both understandable and acceptable.

Some sociobiologists contend that the scientific data also establish male supremacy.[8] This view appears to be a logical corollary to the theory that women are best suited for childcare and home. Michael Levin, a well-known sociobiologist, contends that "innate gender differences express themselves as differences in the typical preferences of men and women."9 As long as people are permitted to act freely, socio-biologists like Levin believe, sexism and inequality will continue to exist.

Much like the scientists of the nineteenth century, Levin and other sociobiologists contend that women cannot compete with men in the workplace because of their physical inferiority. These theorists claim that a lack of testosterone renders women unable to compete successfully. Moreover, they assert that parenting is woman-centered not because the culture has come to expect it, but because women like to care for children more than men do. The sociobiologists claim that even if men were socialized differently they still would not be as good at parenting as are women.10 These theorists conclude that men and women's roles in society are the result of the innate biological differences between men and women; they reject any claim that the status of women in the home and in the workplace is the result of "environmental" factors like social-ization or employer discrimination.

The extremism of sociobiologists is indeed disturbing; however, even more troubling is the fact that neoconservatives and members of the New Right are using the "data" assembled by the sociobiologists as support for their contention that women and men are different, and have distinct roles in the family and in society. The New Right and neoconser-vatives claim that a woman's "nature" imposes certain inherent and unchangeable limitations upon her ability to compete in the workplace, and upon her ability to achieve economic and social equality.11

Some theorists, among them Zillah Eisenstein, contend that the present discourse among neoconservatives and members of the New Right about sexual difference is the result of certain socioeconomic conditions. Eisenstein claims that discussion about sexual difference arises when men's and women's lives look like they are becoming more similar. Moreover, it appears that this discourse is most pronounced during conservative eras, when certain individuals and groups "react to the threatened boundary lines between the sexes."12 During these eras, certain groups within the polity focus on the differences between men and women in an attempt to ensure that men and women are not viewed as more similar than different. Thus, the discourse about sexual differ-ence that arose during the 1970s and 1980s coincided with the call for women's equality in the workplace, in the home, and in society.

Men and Women as Fundamentally the Same: Socialization and Workplace Discrimination

As might be expected, many analysts reject biological determinism and its emphasis upon physical sex characteristics. These individuals contend that while males and females are initially differentiated by their physical sex characteristics, socialization magnifies the effect of this initial differentiation.[13] For example, economist Victor Fuchs contends that socialization for the roles of wife and mother can negatively affect women's occupational opportunities by limiting the choices that women make in school and in the workplace, thus limiting their earning power. Fuchs contends that even when women do resist the effects of socialization, they encounter difficulties in the labor market "simply because they are women and are often evaluated and treated according to gender norms."[14] Thus, even though the market is neutral, in that it sets no internal bar to the participation of women, women's earning capacity is undermined by insidious cultural and social conceptions of women's place in society.[15]

While biological determinists believe that one's role in society is shaped by his or her sex characteristics, their opponents contend that biological and social differences cannot be clearly distinguished.[16] Although women bear children, this is less important today than it was several decades ago, when women bore more children and were unable to work outside the home for substantial blocks of time. At present, it appears that while biology does affect human development, changes in science, technology, and culture may be rendering biological determinism obsolete, or at least much less important.[17]

In fact, the sex of the worker is significant in only a few jobs. As one commentator has noted, "[T]he only jobs for which sex . . . is crucial are semen donor and wet nurse."[18] Moreover, it appears that secondary sex characteristics, like strength and size, are becoming less important as technology becomes more integral to the production process. Thus, many analysts believe that socialization, rather than biology, is most responsible for differences in job participation between men and women.

While men and women are initially differentiated by their physical characteristics, what makes these characteristics important in the workplace is the significance that society derives from them. A number of analysts contend that sex differences are of consequence because of the political, economic, and social benefits or disadvantages that adhere to them.[19] Sex differences are stressed because sex is directly linked to social and political status and political participation. Thus, sex is more important because of the ramifications that derive from it than it is in its own right.

Opponents of biological determinism also contend that the scientific research upon which biological determinism is alleged to be based is not methodologically sound. As one analyst has claimed, "Scientists and physicians have asked scientific questions from a male-supremacist perspective, with the conscious or unconscious intention of proving that a woman's place in society derives naturally from her biological being."[20] These theorists, among them Kate Millett, contend that scientific research on sex differences generally assumes that psycho-social distinctions between the sexes can be explained by sex differences.[21]

There is a substantial body of literature dealing with the concept of "difference" in sex research.[22] Zillah Eisenstein, who has authored a number of books and articles on this subject, contends that "the female body is most explicitly said to be 'different' from the male when the equality of men and women is being denied."[23] According to Eisenstein and many other feminists, the male is perceived to be the standard; any deviations from this standard, such as childbearing capacity, are seen as creating an inherently inferior distinction. These analysts argue that because of this the debate about equality is imbued with certain assumptions about the superiority of men.

The disagreement between biological determinists and some feminists about the significance of primary sex characteristics is understandable. What is unexpected is the widespread dissension among feminists about the relevance of sex-based characteristics, and of the reproductive function in particular. Some feminists believe that men and women should be treated identically, regardless of their reproductive functions, others contend that these differences should be accounted for by allowing pregnant women to receive "special" benefits that no other workers receive.

Warring Feminists: The Debate Over "Special Treatment" versus "Equal Treatment"

The disagreement among feminists about whether women should be treated differently when their childbearing capacity is implicated first emerged in the early 1920s, when the National Women's Party rejected the use of state protective labor legislation and, for this reason, broke from the rest of the women's movement. This debate was resurrected in the early 1980s, when states and private employers began formulating special plans designed to give pregnant women more generous leave benefits than were required by the 1976 Pregnancy Discrimination Act. Feminists who believe that women should be treated differently with regard to pregnancy, who have become known as proponents of "special treatment," vehemently disagree with "equal treatment" proponents, who assert that women should not be treated differently even when pregnant.

The controversy over special versus equal treatment reached a boiling point during the litigation of *California Federal Savings and Loan Association v. Guerra.*[24] This case involved a provision of the California Fair Employment and Housing Act, which required an employer to grant an employee "reasonable" leave to have a child, and then required that the employee be offered her job back at the end of her leave. The relevant section of the act provided that:

> It shall be an unlawful employment practice unless based upon a bona fide occupational qualification . . . for any employer to refuse to allow a female employee affected by pregnancy, childbirth, or related medical conditions . . . to take a leave on account of pregnancy for a reasonable period of time; provided, such period shall not exceed four months.[25]

At issue was whether this state provision, which required that an employer treat pregnant women differently than it treated other workers who were similarly disabled, was preempted by the Pregnancy Discrimination Act, an amendment to Title VII of the Civil Rights Act.[26] A number of organizations, among them the National Organization of Women, the American Civil Liberties Union, and the Department of Justice, filed amicus curiae, or "friend of the Court" briefs with the U.S. Supreme Court, asserting that the state law did violate Title VII, since it required preferential treatment in violation of Title VII.[27] In 1985, the Court of Appeals for the Ninth Circuit heard *California Federal* and held that the Pregnancy Discrimination Act (PDA) provided a "federal floor," or minimum standard, for maternity benefits.[28] An employer was not permitted to go below this standard; however, a state was permitted to mandate additional benefits.

In its 1987 decision, the Supreme Court agreed with the Ninth Circuit and upheld the California state law. In a majority opinion by Justice Thurgood Marshall, the Court held that while the PDA did not require employers to give special consideration to pregnant women, it also did not prohibit the preferential treatment of these workers. According to the majority, the state statute was not inconsistent with Title VII, nor was it preempted by it.[29]

The California statute and Title VII had the same objective. Both were intended to ensure equal employment opportunities by removing barriers that had previously served to discriminate against women. The majority asserted that Congress did not intend to bar all favorable treatment of women under the Pregnancy Discrimination Act. Thus, states were not barred from requiring employers to provide protections beyond those ensured under Title VII.[30]

In his dissenting opinion, Justice Byron White argued that the California law violated Title VII, since the PDA prohibits the preferential treatment of pregnant women.[31] In addition, he repeated the concerns of amici who argued that the law, and the majority's interpretation of it, would reinvoke nineteenth-century stereotypes about women and would ultimately prevent women from being able to have both jobs and families.[32]

As *California Federal* wound its way through the federal judiciary, feminists began to line up on either side of the debate about preferential treatment. Special treatment advocates claimed that the preferential policies were acceptable since the capacity to become pregnant was an immutable sex characteristic. In fact, special treatment advocates began drawing on an expanding literature that suggested women were, after all, different than men by virtue of their intrinsic characteristics. This body of writings, which has become known as relational feminism, was strongly influenced by the work of Carol Gilligan, whose controversial book, *In A Different Voice*, suggests that there are real sex-based differences between men and women which go beyond their differing reproductive roles. Gilligan contends that men and women perceive the world differently and have differing conceptions about the nature of relationships and rights.[33] Gilligan and other relational feminists claim that men and women are inherently different, and that society has not accounted for these differences. According to these analysts, gender inequality "stem[s] less from denial of opportunities available to men than from devaluation of the functions and qualities associated with women."[34] These feminists argue that men and women are different in many ways, including their reproductive functions, and that society should seek to celebrate, rather than eliminate, these differences.

The fact that men and women differ with regard to reproduction became the crux of the argument between those feminists who called for special treatment of pregnancy and those who insisted upon the equality of treatment of all potentially disabling condition.[35] Special treatment advocates contend that the reality of in utero pregnancy colors all discussions about gender equality: pregnancy and childbirth are unique, and for this reason they cannot be treated like any other illnesses. For this reason, special treatment proponents argue, society should allow, and in many cases encourage, the preferential treatment of pregnant women.[36]

In fact, many feminists who advocate the special treatment approach echo statements made by biological determinists about women's capacity not only for childbearing, but childrearing as well. For example, one analyst contends that "[t]he maternal role *is* more closely connected to parental responsibility than the paternal one, and neither talents nor conditioning nor tastes enter into it."[37] Here women are considered to be more responsible for parenting, and to be better parents, simply because they bear the children.

A number of scholars who advocate special treatment have proposed alternative legal structures for dealing with gender discrimination. Elizabeth Wolgast asserts that, since men and women are different and have different interests, egalitarianism (equal treatment) will not sufficiently protect the interests of both. Wolgast argues that we need a bivalent form of thinking to adequately represent the interests of women.[38] Similarly, Lucinda Finley rejects traditional egalitarianism, contending that its ideal of homogeneity "has legitimated much invidious discrimination throughout our history [and] consequently [has] marginaliz[ed], disempower[ed], and render[ed] invisible those such as women, who have seemed most unlikely to ever melt into the white male model of homogeneity."[39] For these reasons, Finley alleges that equality analysis is incapable of eradicating the gender discrimination that pervades American society.[40]

Thus, special treatment feminists argue that the attempt to treat all individuals equally, i.e., without regard for gender-related differences, will undermine the "special" interests of women.[41] At present, only women can become pregnant, and this central fact is often ignored by proponents of egalitarianism. Special treatment proponents contend that women have unique interests, and that legislation or private employer policies that take these interests into account should be not only permitted, but also encouraged. These feminists contend that ignoring pregnancy in the workplace or treating it as a disability unfairly penalizes women.

Unlike advocates of special treatment, equal treatment feminists emphasize that "special" treatment is harmful because it establishes the principle that women workers are incapable of competing in the workplace and require certain provisions to enable them to remain in the workplace. Proponents of equal treatment reject the "special treatment" approach, often branding it "protectionism."[42] Moreover, egalitarians contend that in the past a woman's "specialness," her reproductive function, justified paternalistic laws that restricted women's presence in the workplace and forced them back to the home.[43]

In fact, egalitarians often point out the parallels between the protectionism of the 1980s and that of the early 1900s and 1910s. These individuals argue that in the 1980s, as in the early 1900s, people became attracted to protectionism out of concerns about expedience. Egalitarians contend that while it may not be possible to alter society's conceptions of sex fundamentally in the near future, it is possible to wrest from society certain concessions that help women to balance home and work. As Wendy Williams, who is perhaps the best-known proponent of the equal treatment approach, has said,

> It has always been easier to wrench from the jaws of the political system special provisions for women in the name of motherhood than general provisions aimed at the realignment of sex roles in the family and restructuring of the workplace.[44]

In the early twentieth century, the seemingly intractable problems of long hours, poor wages, and hazardous working conditions compelled progressives to use sex-based protective labor legislation; similarly, in the 1980s and 1990s, the continuing difficulties inherent in women's full-time employment in the workplace seem to militate in favor of special laws intended to benefit women.

Equal treatment advocates contend that these special provisions are never benign. One analyst contends that the "perils of modern domesticity" are already apparent in the judiciary's handling of discrimination claims. Joan C. Williams focuses on the Seventh Circuit's 1988 decision in *E.E.O.C. v. Sears, Roebuck and Co.*, which found that the retail giant had not discriminated against women despite the underrepresentation of women in commission sales positions, since women as a group "lacked interest" in these positions.[45] According to Williams, the language of difference articulated by special treatment feminists was employed by Sears and Roebuck to justify the segregation of women in lower paying non-commission sales positions. In a strange twist, relational feminism is used as a justification for the view that women are not competitive and do not have an interest in high pressure sales jobs. Since women as a class were held to lack interest in these positions, Sears and Roebuck was found not responsible for integrating women into these positions.

Equal treatment advocates also argue that giving women "special" protections out of concern about their reproductive role reinforces the view of women as secondary workers whose commitment to employment is questionable and whose primary responsibility remains that of childcare and homemaking.[46] The special treatment approach has established a "separate but equal female norm," that ensures special maternity benefits or "mommy-track" jobs, and thus "implicitly endorse[s] the view of women as weaker, secondary workers."[47] Perhaps even more disturbingly, this special treatment reinforces differentiations that are often cultural, rather than biological, in origin. The special treatment approach, which provides women with certain benefits solely because they are women and are capable of bearing children, encourages the view that the sexes are to be distinguished not only by biology, but by cultural norms.

While proponents of special treatment emphasize the uniqueness of pregnancy, egalitarians stress the analogy of pregnancy to illnesses or other conditions.[48] Equal treatment feminists contend that pregnant women should be treated the same as workers with disabling or potentially disabling illnesses. These individuals argue that pregnancy does not create a class of individuals requiring "special" needs; instead, it exemplifies basic health care needs.[49] If these needs are not met through an employer's health care plan, pregnant workers join the larger class of male and female employees for whom basic fringe benefits are inadequate. According to these analysts, the solution is to require adequate fringe benefits for all workers, rather than special benefits for pregnant workers.[50] Equal treatment is intended to "normalize" pregnancy, rather than treating it as a distinct condition requiring a unique health care approach. Egalitarians contend that, in most cases, pregnancy should not be treated any differently than other nondisabling conditions. Where pregnancy becomes disabling, it should be treated as disabling illnesses are, and the benefits given to other disabled workers should also accrue to pregnant workers.[51]

Furthermore, egalitarians contend that equal treatment is part of a larger strategy "to get the law out of the business of reinforcing traditional, sex-based family roles."[52] Egalitarians point out that the special treatment approach puts feminists in bed with the New Right by stressing the differences rather than the commonalities between men and women.[53] Advocates of equal treatment contend that men and women are more similar than different, and they attempt to deal with pregnancy in the same manner they would adopt for other medical conditions.

Thus, during the 1980s, feminists became divided over the issue of sexual difference, and in particular, over the question of how to apply the principles of equality when dealing with certain physical conditions, like pregnancy, childbearing, and nursing, that are unique to women.[54] Feminists were not the only individuals, however, examining the relationship between sex difference and equality. During the 1970s and 1980s, a number of theorists have attempted to assess whether sex-based characteristics should determine one's ability to function competitively in the workplace.

Two major divisions have emerged among these groups. On the one side, biological determinists and special treatment feminists contend that biology must be taken into account when assessing women's workplace participation. On the other side, cultural determinists and egalitarian feminists assert that socialization and employer discrimination largely explain the widespread discrimination and sex segregation of the work force that exists in the workplace.

The ongoing debate about the importance of gender in determining one's capacity to compete in the industrial work force is based in large part upon a disagreement about the relevance of sex-based characteristics to job performance. Biological determinists, like nineteenth-century scientists, physicians, and philosophers, contend that women are less capable of competing in the workplace simply because of their sex. Special treatment feminists agree with this assessment; however, they contend that women are not inherently less capable of competing, only that the nature of the American workplace renders them less capable of competing. Equal treatment feminists agree with this conclusion but disagree with the solution offered by special treatment feminists. Egalitarian feminists assert that equality, i.e., the equal treatment of similar individuals, should govern; special treatment feminists adopt an approach that would give women certain benefits because of their reproductive role.

One commentator has noted that "American equal protection doctrine has drawn heavily on [the] Aristotelian tradition, which define[s] equality as *similar treatment for those similarly situated*."[55] Much of the difficulty inherent in the debate about the nature of equality stems from the fact that men and women are not similarly situated with regard to their capacity for childbearing. As a result, men and women cannot be seen as functional equals in situations where reproductive differences are at issue. Thus, the most difficult, yet most significant question raised in the debate about equality is this: If men and women differ with regard to reproductive roles, how should they be treated in other areas that bear, however tangentially, upon procreative capacity? The answer to this question has great significance not only for gender-based laws and regulations but for fetal protection policies as well.

There is widespread disagreement about how important sex-based differences are, or should be. Much of the conflict among biological determinists, neoconservatives, New Rightists, and special treatment and equal treatment feminists centers upon how important reproductive capacity is, or should be, in determining one's economic rights, and this is precisely the issue implicated by fetal protection policies. Fetal protection policies view women who have not been sterilized as belonging to a separate class of workers, whose work-force participation must be restricted solely because of their reproductive capacities. Fetal protection policies are based upon a conception of "equality" that focuses on biological difference.

The manner in which our government interprets its mandate to provide equal protection determines the extent to which it will respond to gender-based policies like fetal protection policies. In the past, our government has adopted a concept of equality that has focused on sexual difference and, in so doing, has permitted gender-based statutes and policies. The American people and their government have shown themselves quite willing to adopt different policies for men and women, even where these policies are based upon socially constructed views of gender roles rather than sex-based characteristics. In fact, an examination of the governmental response to gender-based statutes in the twentieth century, in particular state protective laws, the Equal Rights Amendment, and the male-only draft, reveals that American decision-makers have a pattern of interpreting sex differences to encompass not only biological characteristics but socially constructed ones as well. Most significantly, the history of our government's response to gender-based distinctions establishes a pattern that recurs in its response to fetal protection policies in the 1980s and early 1990s.

3. Gender Discrimination
Past and Present: State
Protective Laws, the ERA,
and the Male-only Draft

The proliferation of fetal protection policies in the late twentieth century was troubling not only because of the immediate impact on affected workplaces, but because it highlighted the fragility of equal employment opportunity and the willingness of employers to view fully one half of the potential employee pool as secondary, marginal workers. To some, the proliferation of fetal protection policies seemed monstrous, an obvious "wrong turn" on the inexorable path to sexual equality. These individuals, hopeful that the women's liberation movement had begun a trend toward gender egalitarianism, could not understand how or why these policies should erupt onto the scene in the late 1970s and early 1980s, when much of the hard work of sexual politics seemed to have already been completed.

A closer look at the history of gender equality in the U.S., however, especially during the twentieth century, reveals that the emergence of fetal protection policies was not anomalous. Moreover, much could have been predicted about the government's response to these policies by examining its handling of other gender-based laws and policies enacted throughout the twentieth century. During this period, governmental decision-makers have consistently viewed women's primary responsibility as that of childbearing and childrearing. The governmental response to fetal protection policies may, in fact, best be viewed as part of an ongoing pattern. In the twentieth century, federal and state governments enacted a variety of statutes intended to "protect" women's childbearing capacity and "special characteristics," often at the expense of women's full integration into American society. In addition, the balancing of fetal rights and women's rights, so pervasive in the abortion controversy, presaged the balancing approach employed by governmental decision-makers in the debate over fetal protection.

State Protective Laws: Progenitors of Fetal Protection Policies

It is sometimes said that "the past is prologue," and this is certainly true in the case of fetal protection policies. Employer fetal protection policies bear a striking resemblance to the protective legislation passed in many states some sixty to seventy years previous. These state laws barred women from certain occupations, restricted the number of hours and days that women were allowed to work, and set minimum hourly wages for female employees. The Progressive Movement lobbied aggressively in the state legislatures for enactment of these laws. The men and women who belonged to this political movement believed that the harsh working conditions of the late nineteenth and early twentieth centuries were detrimental to the health of the female worker and to her ability to produce healthy offspring.

During this period, the government, and in particular, the judiciary, viewed men and women as differentially susceptible to occupational harm. For example, in the 1905 case, *Lochner v. New York*, the U.S. Supreme Court struck down a New York State law that regulated the number of hours bakers could be employed, finding that the law violated the due process rights of the employee.[1] In the early 1900s, most, if not all, bakers were men. In this case, the Supreme Court held that the state regulation constituted unlawful interference with an individual's right to contract with his employer about his hours of employment. The Court held that there was no reason for restricting the hours of employment for a baker: according to the Court, this occupation was not sufficiently hazardous to necessitate regulation and bakers were capable of determining for themselves how many hours they should work.[2] In dicta that had significance for later cases on work restrictions, the Court held that "[t]here is no contention that bakers as a class are not equal in intelligence and capacity to men in other trades or manual occupations, or that they are not able to assert their rights and care for themselves without the protecting arm of the State . . . They are in no sense wards of the State."[3] Since bakers were considered fully capable of deciding how many hours they should work, the state was barred from substituting its judgment by restricting work hours.

Three years later, the Supreme Court was called upon to evaluate a corresponding law that regulated the number of hours that female employees could work. By the time *Muller v. Oregon* reached the Court in 1908, 26 states had laws either restricting the hours that women could work or barring women from working at night.[4] Fourteen states had laws in place that restricted women from working in certain jobs. These state laws were based upon the "scientific evidence" that continuous standing, stretching or repetitive movements weakened the procreative capacities of women.[5] As a result of the Court's 1905 holding in *Lochner v. New York,* however, states were barred from placing similar restrictions upon the employment of males. The issue before the Court in *Muller* was whether women were sufficiently different, and by implication, sufficiently inferior, to necessitate the use of hours restrictions.

By 1908, the courts had already adjudicated a number of cases arising from these statutes, and had upheld the laws. For example, in its 1873 decision in *Bradwell v. Illinois,* the Supreme Court upheld Illinois's decision not to allow a female attorney to be admitted to the state bar.[6] In his concurring opinion, Justice Joseph Bradley articulated what has come to be known as the "separate spheres" doctrine:

> The natural and proper timidity and delicacy which belongs to the female sex evidently unfits it for many of the occupations of civil life . . . [T]he paramount destiny and mission of woman are to fulfill the notable and benign offices of wife and mother.[7]

The Court held that women should not be permitted access to certain occupations because to do so would be a violation not only the civil law of the states, but of some higher natural law as well.

In 1906, the Oregon Supreme Court found Curt Muller, the owner of a laundry, guilty of violating Oregon's 10-hour law. Muller appealed the decision to the Supreme Court, asserting that the law was barred under freedom of contract principles. While the Court had accepted this argument in *Lochner*, holding that a state could not justify employment restrictions by reference to its police power, it flatly rejected the argument here. *Muller* was distinguished solely because the subjects of the regulation were women and not men.[8] According to the Court, women needed special protection in the workplace because they were more vulnerable to workplace hazards and incapable of protecting themselves against these hazards, largely because they had no access to the political process.

The *Muller* Court accepted the nineteenth-century view of women as being the mental, physical, and emotional inferiors of men. In the view of the Court:

> That women's physical structure and the performance of maternal functions place her at a disadvantage in the struggle for subsistence is obvious. This is especially true when the burdens of motherhood are upon her.[9]

The Court contended that women, unlike men, were highly vulnerable to workplace-induced injury. In *Lochner*, the Court was quite eager to dismiss all evidence indicating that being a baker imposed certain health risks; however, in *Muller*, the Court willingly agreed that the "scientific data" demonstrated serious health risks.[10]

More significantly, it appears that the Court distinguished *Muller* from *Lochner* in large part because it viewed the restriction as being necessary to safeguard child health. In what is perhaps the most often cited passage of the decision, the Court held that

> [woman's] physical structure and a proper discharge of her maternal functions—having in view not merely her own health, but the well-being of the race—justify legislation to protect her from the greed as well as the passion of man. The limitations which this statute places upon her contractual powers, upon her right to agree with her employer as to the time she shall labor, are not imposed solely for her benefit, but also largely for the benefit of all.[11]

Thus, the restrictions were intended for the benefit of both women and their potential children. Moreover, since these restrictions promoted child health, they benefitted the "race." According to the Court, concern about the welfare of future generations justified state regulation of women's working conditions.[12]

Many individuals and groups, even women's rights groups, were initially pleased by the *Muller* decision. Groups concerned about poor working conditions and disheartened by the Court's decision in *Lochner* were encouraged by the decision, believing that the proverbial half a loaf was better than none. It is apparent, however, that *Muller* and *Lochner* were not inconsistent decisions. Because much of the *Lochner* decision was grounded on the Court's conception of male workers and employers as functional equals, the Court's decisions in these two cases may be viewed as consistent.

In *Lochner,* the Court disallowed the state regulation because the risks associated with the occupation of baker were not seen as serious. The baker was also viewed as capable of assessing workplace hazards and deciding for himself to how much harm he would expose himself. The Court in *Muller* utilized the *Lochner* framework. In this case, however, it found that the scientific data demonstrated that working in excess of a certain number of hours threatened the health of the woman and of her offspring. Although the *Lochner* and *Muller* cases have different outcomes, in that the Court barred employment legislation in one while allowing it in the other, the cases are clearly consistent if one believes that women are more vulnerable to workplace hazards and that this vulnerability exposes their progeny to a greater risk of harm.

While the Court's decision in *Muller* was premised upon its belief that time limitations would benefit women, it ultimately served to thwart women's attempts to achieve economic equality. For more than 60 years, the *Muller* decision was used as the precedent for upholding nearly all gender-based classifications.[13] Moreover, as Wendy Kaminer has stated, "*Muller* established the state's power to regulate the behavior of women and restrict their freedom of choice in the interests of their children."[14] After *Muller,* states were less hesitant about enacting legislation that treated men and women differently on the basis of their different reproductive functions.

In the years immediately following the Supreme Court's decision in *Muller,* many states formulated protective laws. By the mid-1920s, the use of legislation restricting the hours and occupations of women was firmly in place in 47 of the 48 states.[15] Not all women who worked outside the home were protected by these laws, however; female domestic and agricultural workers were generally outside the jurisdiction of these laws.[16] In addition, the laws tended to be applied in an inconsistent manner, and women working for the same businesses were often treated differently. For example, in New York, female restaurant employees were barred from working between 10 p.m. and 6 a.m. Where women worked as performers, however, the law provided an exemption. In justifying this obvious inconsistency, a New York State official stated that, in the case of performers, "the places [these female performers fill] would obviously not be filled by men at night as can the places of regular employees."[17] This inconsistency suggests that the laws were used only in cases where the women *could* be replaced by men; women were "protected" only where they were readily replaceable. For this reason, the hours of women in some largely female occupations, like domestic service, were not restricted.

Moreover, in the years following *Muller*, legislatures and courts continued to treat male and female workers differently with regard to statutes regulating hours, wages, and working conditions. Throughout the 1920s and 1930s, the courts vacillated on the issue of protective legislation, and, in particular, with regard to minimum wage laws; however, by the late 1930s, they seemed willing to allow such legislation for women. Furthermore, in adjudicating cases involving protective legislation, the courts willingly accepted the conception that was at the heart of *Muller*, that men and women were fundamentally different. For example, in its 1937 case, *West Coast Hotel v. Parrish*, the Supreme Court upheld a minimum wage statute for women and implicitly overruled its 1924 decision in *Adkins v. Children's Hospital*. In *Adkins*, the Court had justified striking down a Washington, D.C., minimum wage law for women on the basis of freedom of contract principles like those used to invalidate the law at issue in *Lochner*.[18]

In *West Coast Hotel*, the Court used much of the reasoning of the *Muller* Court to validate a state minimum wage law.[19] As in *Muller*, the *West Coast Hotel* Court catalogued a number of reasons that female employees should be treated differently than men. The Court contended that female workers were more likely to be exploited by employers and were more susceptible to workplace harm because of their physical frailties. The *West Coast Hotel* Court reiterated the *Muller* decision, contending that women could be subject to more stringent labor legislation because their good health was necessary for the well-being of their future children.[20] Female workers were distinguished from their male counterparts not only because they occupied jobs with the lowest pay, but because of their inferior physical structure and responsibility for future generations. Thus, the minimum wage statute protected women's health and, in so doing, served the public interest.[21]

The Court was also willing to extend *Muller* beyond the issues of maximum hours and minimum wage restrictions. In its 1924 decision in *Radice v. New York*, the Court upheld a New York State law prohibiting night work for women.[22] In this case, the Supreme Court held that New York State did not violate the liberty of contract of women whose employment was restricted by a no-night law statute. The Court cited the *Muller* decision for the principle that women are more frail and subject to certain physical limitations.

Furthermore, the Court contended that the existence of physical differences between men and women served to distinguish its decision in this case from that reached in the *Adkins* case one year earlier.[23] Unlike the *Adkins* decision, which regulated wages, the Court in *Radice* found that a statute regulating the hours or working conditions of women did not infringe the worker's freedom of contract and did not violate the due process clause of the Fourteenth Amendment. The Court also rejected the plaintiff's contention that this statute violated the equal protection clause by making a distinction between restaurant employees and other female employees.

Judith Baer has contended that the Court's decisions in the line of cases from *Muller* to *Radice* were interpreted by later courts as "establishing the principle that permanent, rather than situation-bound distinctions between the sexes justified any sex-based employment discrimination."[24] By 1937, the Court had evinced a willingness to allow labor legislation for women, even where it struck down similar statutes for men. Moreover, the Court's holdings during the 1920s and 1930s indicated that the Court had accepted the conception of physical differences embodied in the *Muller* decision.

Even though women won the right to vote in 1920, the Court continued to believe that immutable biological characteristics prevented women from achieving economic equality. Since women had not reached parity with men, and would not be able to do so in the future, the Court allowed states to implement laws aimed at "protecting" women from further exploitation by employers. While many of these laws initially benefitted women, by reducing their hours of employment and setting a minimum wage level, these laws diminished women's economic opportunities in the long run. Moreover, the justification used by the Court in allowing these statutes, namely, that women were unable to achieve economic parity with men because of certain physical characteristics, continued to be used by the Court for many years after. As a result, the Court treated sex-based differences as creating inherent disabilities for women workers.

After its *West Coast Hotel* decision in 1937, the Supreme Court did not hear another case involving state protective laws until 1948, when it decided *Goesart v. Cleary*.[25] This case, which involved a state law barring women from working as bartenders unless they were the wives or daughters of a male owner, squarely raised the question of whether laws intended to "protect" women from certain workplace hazards were constitutional. In its holding, the Court held that a Michigan statute that denied women the right to work as bartenders did not run afoul of the Fourteenth Amendment's due process and equal protection guarantees. While recognizing that there had been "vast changes in the social and legal position of women,"[26] the Court nonetheless held that a state could bar women from working as bartenders because of the "moral and social problems" that might arise from employing them.[27]

The Court never defined the social or moral problems attendant to women tending bar. Instead, it relied upon a common-sensical conception of how the presence of a female barmaid might prompt customers, who might be compromised by their inebriated state, to behave in an improper fashion.[28] It appears that the Court believed that the mere presence of a woman in a bar increased the likelihood that men would commit crimes. Thus, the Michigan statute protected not only the women who sought to become bartenders, but the male customers who might be tempted to commit crime.[29]

In addition, the Court rejected the plaintiff's equal protection claims. The plaintiffs argued that Michigan violated the equal protection guarantee by prohibiting women from tending bar while allowing them to work as waitresses in the bar.[30] The Court did not explain why this distinction was valid, and instead, held that the equal protection issue was adequately dealt with by the District Court.[31]

In allowing this differential treatment of men and women working in the same environment, the Court implicitly relied upon its decision in *Radice v. New York*. As in *Radice*, the Court provided no real rationale for treating bartenders and waitresses differently; in fact, its decision in *Radice* to allow a statute barring night work for waitresses but not for performers would appear to contradict this decision. This inconsistency is resolved, however, when one discerns that the Court tended to permit statutes that bar women from jobs in which they are readily replaced by men. Clearly, in *Goesart,* as in *Radice,* there was an adequate supply of men available to fill the jobs from which the women had been barred.[32]

Thus, throughout the first half of the twentieth century, the federal and state legislatures and courts evinced a willingness, and at times, an eagerness, to allow gender-based distinctions. These protective laws, which regulated the hours, wages and working conditions of women, initially benefitted women. As a result of the laws, women's hours were reduced, their working conditions improved, and their pay increased.[33] This was critically important even after the Fair Labor Standards Act was passed in 1938, since, for the most part, women occupied positions that were not within the jurisdiction of the statute.[34] In the long run, however, these laws reinforced the subordinate position of women in the workplace.[35] The stated bases of these laws, that women were physically inferior to men, and that women had to be protected, not only for their own good but for the welfare of the race, undermined women's efforts to achieve economic equality. These restrictive laws remained in place until the late 1960s, when courts held that they violated Title VII of the 1964 Civil Rights Act.

Protective labor legislation has had a monumental impact upon the nature of work undertaken by women in the nineteenth and twentieth centuries. Moreover, the use of protective legislation to justify differential treatment of female workers has had a continuing impact upon women's attempt to achieve equality in the workplace. In fact, employer fetal protection policies, which derive from the belief that women are more susceptible to workplace hazards, and which are justified by concerns about fetal health, appear to be philosophically grounded in earlier state protective legislation.

There are a number of interesting parallels between the state protective laws of the late 1800s and early 1900s and the employer fetal protection policies of the 1980s. Both protective legislation and fetal protection policies are based upon a conception of women as potentially pregnant, marginal workers, whose primary concerns are, or should be, the health and well-being of their families and offspring. Both perceive of women's participation in the work force as potentially harmful to the health of their children. In addition, both fetal protection policies and earlier state protective legislation utilized scientific data that have been increasingly viewed as questionable. Both required courts to grapple with the difficulties inherent in analyzing scientific data.

The courts adjudicating both fetal protection policies and state protective legislation appear to have subscribed to similar viewpoints about the role of women in industrial society. For the most part, courts adjudicating protective legislation accepted the argument that men and women were fundamentally different, and that these differences justified disparate treatment in the workplace. Moreover, most courts accepted the contention that women's primary role was that of mother and wife, and that work-force participation was simply a secondary activity. Clearly, courts during this era were quite willing to accept state laws that treated men and women differently on the basis of their reproductive capacity, especially where employment was involved. Courts adjudicating both fetal protection policies and claims arising from gender-based legislation in the 1970s and 1980s have adopted a similar view about the differences between the sexes.

Clearly, the sexes are not identical; most obviously, they differ with regard to reproductive function. One's definition of equality largely determines his or her conception of the importance of sex-based differences. At the turn of the century, our governmental institutions subscribed to a view of the sexes as fundamentally different. The state and federal governments promulgated and upheld laws that treated male and female workers differently solely on the basis of their sex. These laws were based upon distinctions that were derived from characteristics engendered by both biology and culture. The next section examines governmental response to contemporary gender-based legislation, in particular, the Equal Rights Amendment and laws exempting women from registration for the military draft. Perhaps not surprisingly, throughout the 1970s and 1980s, our government continued to treat all distinctions between the sexes as if they were biologically based.

ERA and the Draft: Contemporary Governmental Responses to Gender-based Distinctions

To justify their approval of protective legislation in the late nineteenth and early twentieth centuries, state legislators and federal and state courts contended that women's work-force participation should be limited so as to protect the health of their offspring. In more recent times, governmental decision-makers also permitted gender-based classifications that were rooted in concerns about women's reproductive health and their role in the family. While the differential treatment of men and women was more subtle in the 1970s and 1980s than it had been during the earlier period, governmental action during these years also served to reinforce traditional gender roles. The response of legislators and judges to two proposed laws, one of which would have made sex a suspect classification under the 14th amendment, the other which would have invalidated the male-only military draft, reveals the extent to which our government remains unwilling, and perhaps unable, to change its approach to sex-related issues.

The Equal Rights Amendment, which some believe would have ensured gender equality by barring distinctions based upon sex, was defeated in the state legislatures, largely because its opponents were successful in convincing the public, and state legislators, that the amendment would usher in significant changes in sex roles. Opponents focused on the amendment's impact on cultural norms, rather than on its effect on biological distinctions between the sexes. Specifically, the ERA's opponents were successful in manipulating powerful cultural images of motherhood, marriage, homosexuality, and morality.

Courts, like legislatures, have also shown themselves to be unwilling to separate out cultural and social conceptions of sex roles in evaluating gender-based distinctions. Throughout the 1970s and 1980s, courts and, in particular, the Supreme Court, heard a number of cases involving such distinctions. The most significant of these was the Court's decision in *Rostker v. Goldberg*, which upheld the all-male registration for the draft. At the core of the Court's handling of all these cases, and especially of *Rostker*, is the belief that sex is somehow different from other protected classifications, like race, lineage, and religion, and that sex-based distinctions are acceptable. Underlying this differential treatment of sex is a belief that there are "real" differences between the sexes that may militate in favor of disparate treatment.

Legislators and the Equal Rights Amendment

The Equal Rights Amendment has had a long history, going back to the 1870s when the term "equal rights amendment" was attached to a bill introduced in Congress proposing to give women the right to vote. In fact, throughout the latter part of the nineteenth century, the Equal Rights Amendment was closely identified with the women's suffrage movement. It was not until after women won the vote that the Equal Rights Amendment was introduced as a separate amendment to the U.S. Constitution. In 1923, the ERA was introduced in Congress but failed to pass. The amendment was not reintroduced for nearly fifty years.

Section 1 of the Equal Rights Amendment introduced into Congress in 1972 read: "Equality of rights under the law shall not be denied or abridged by the U.S. or by any State on account of sex." As one commentator has noted, the language of section 1 encouraged the perception of the amendment as having a "broad, universal, inescapable impact on all women."[36] The amendment easily garnered the two-thirds vote necessary to pass in the House and Senate.

Once an amendment is passed in Congress, it must be ratified by three-quarters of the state legislatures. While the Constitution does not impose a time limit on the ratification process, Congress imposed such a limit in the case of the ERA: it required that ratification be accomplished by March 1979. At first, it appeared that the amendment would be easily approved. Within one year, 30 states had ratified it. In the remaining five years, however, only five more states ratified the amendment.[37] The ERA thus fell three votes short of the ratification requirement. The House and Senate allowed a 39-month extension, but ERA supporters were unable to win over the remaining three states, and the ERA was defeated in June 1982.[38] The debate over the ERA was remarkable for its ferocity, with supporters and opponents vigorously promoting their positions and attacking those of their adversaries.

ERA supporters contended that the amendment was necessary for the attainment of equality. Congresswoman Margaret Heckler, a staunch supporter of the ERA, claimed, "If we really believe in the inscription engraved on the Supreme Court building, equal justice under the law, the ERA is the only way to achieve it."[39] Supporters claimed that the ERA would eradicate gender discrimination by making sex classifications suspect under the Fifth and Fourteenth Amendments. With sex as a suspect classification, gender-based statutes would be permitted only if gender distinctions were necessitated by compelling reasons. This standard is much more rigorous than the existing requirement that sex classifications be substantially related to some important governmental interest.

Public support for the ERA was strongest in the first year after it was passed by Congress. Even in 1978, however, public opinion polls showed that a majority of Americans favored the amendment.[40] In addition, there appears to have been a wide spectrum of support for the ERA: conservatives like Senator Strom Thurmond, President Richard Nixon, and Governor George Wallace expressed their support for the amendment, as did moderates, libertarians, and liberals.[41] In the years following its passage, however, public support for the ERA did not increase.[42] Ultimately, the state legislators in the remaining fifteen states chose not to ratify the amendment, in large part because of the concerns raised by ERA opponents.

Those who opposed the ERA contended not only that the amendment was unnecessary to achieve equality for women, but that it would have harmful effects.[43] The anti-ERA counter movement that emerged in the mid-1970s was headed by Republican Phyllis Schlafly and composed of a number of conservative organizations. This opposition was concentrated in the fundamentalist South, including southern Illinois, and in the Mormon states of Utah and Nevada. Opposition to the amendment was strongest in the least affluent states, in those with a conservative, Populist tradition, and in those that tend to oppose legislative innovation.[44] The anti-ERA coalition was well-financed and well-organized and constituted a significant challenge to the ERA.[45] The coalition used its resources to stall ratification by calling into question the effect the ERA would have upon social mores. The success of the anti-ERA movement derived in large part from its ability to tie the ERA to a number of key issues. Among these issues were the compulsory drafting of women into the military; the legalization of abortion; the legalization of homosexuality and homosexual marriages; the repeal of state protective laws; the expansion of federal power at the expense of the states; and the abolition of marriage, the economic support of wives by husbands, alimony, social security benefits, and sex-segregated bathrooms.[46] Of these issues, it appears that abortion and the draft were most harmful to the ERA.

Opponents of the ERA contended that the amendment would require that women be subject to the military draft. Despite attempts by ERA supporters to make this issue work in its favor, by emphasizing the positive aspects of a military draft that included women,[47] the draft was an effective "scare tactic" that operated to the benefit of Stop-ERA forces. Similarly, opponents were able to draw strength from segments within the population who opposed abortion rights. Opponents capitalized on the public's fear of unchecked judicial expansion by linking the ERA to the abortion controversy. A number of conservative southern legislators, angry that the Court's decision in *Roe v. Wade* barred states from prohibiting abortion, sought to turn the debate over the ERA into a referendum on the abortion issue.[48] Conservatives contended that the ERA would provide a more concrete constitutional basis for legalizing abortion than the "penumbra" of personal privacy found by the courts in the First, Fourth, Fifth, Ninth and Fourteenth Amendments.[49]

Furthermore, fears about the effect of the amendment on the availability of abortion services and on the legalization of homosexuality drew upon growing concerns about the immorality of young Americans. Conservatives seized upon these concerns, contending that passage of the ERA would further contribute to what it called the ongoing moral decay of the American populace.

State legislators were particularly fearful that the amendment would be interpreted by the courts in ways that the legislators could not anticipate. Some commentators, Jane Mansbridge among them, have contended that the public's negative conception of the Supreme Court was ultimately was the cause of the ERA defeat.[50] After two decades of what many perceived as unwarranted judicial expansion, some feared that judicial interpretation of the ERA would have consequences far beyond those envisioned by supporters. Thus, the public and state legislators began to view the amendment with suspicion, fearful that it would impose other unwanted changes in American society. Stop-ERA forces capitalized on legislators' concerns about the ambiguity of the ERA, terming the amendment a "Pandora's Box." They were able to capitalize on the public's fear of unchecked judicial expansion, particularly in the areas of abortion rights and gay and lesbian civil rights. By emphasizing that the ERA could have a potentially enormous impact upon the culture and social mores of American society, ERA opponents were able to convince state legislators not to ratify the amendment.

Thus, the anti-ERA campaign succeeded because it shifted the debate from one that focused upon equality and equal rights to one that emphasized the substantive changes the amendment would have upon women's roles and behavior.[51] The debate over the ERA did not center upon the sexual differences between men and women; rather, the debate was focused upon the impact the amendment would have upon cultural norms. The promise of the ERA was that sex-based distinctions would be presumed to be unconstitutional. ERA opponents, however, expanded these distinctions to include not only physical, but social and cultural differences between men and women. In fact, the ERA failed in large part *because* of fear about its potential impact on sex roles.

It is impossible to know what the ERA's impact on gender equality would have been had the amendment been ratified. The ERA was premised upon the principle that sex should not be a factor in determining one's legal rights. Advocates of the ERA did not assert that the sexes were identical; instead, they contended that state and federal statutes and regulations should not treat individuals differently solely because of their sex. The ERA would have taken precedence over all other federal, state, and local laws, but it would not have affected any policies or practices outside the public realm.[52] For example, employment discrimination claims against private employers would have continued to be litigated under Title VII of the Civil Rights Act.

Some analysts have asserted that the ERA's greatest impact would have been symbolic, not substantive. These individuals contend that passage of the ERA was important because it would have demonstrated the nation's firm commitment to gender equality. Some have claimed that the ERA would have had no immediate effect upon women's employment, since Title VII and the 1963 Equal Pay Act would have continued to govern employment discrimination. These commentators dismiss concerns about judicial expansion of the amendment, contending that the Supreme Court would not have used it to bring about major changes in gender roles. Mansbridge, for example, contends that the Court probably would have sidestepped the issue of the draft by invoking the "war powers" clauses of the Constitution.[53]

While one can only speculate as to what the potential impact of the ERA would have been, the significance of the controversy over the amendment is apparent. Like the earlier state protective laws, debate over the ERA was framed not in terms of the impact of the amendment upon laws that were based exclusively upon the sex characteristics of men and women, but in terms of the effect of the amendment on widespread social and cultural norms. While supporters of the ERA attempted to present the amendment as one that would have a clearly defined impact upon gender-based legislation, its opponents effectively shifted the debate to encompass not only these distinctions, but other, more amorphous concerns about the relationship between men and women in society.

Perhaps it is unwise to interpret the demise of the ERA as evidence of the public's hostility toward legislation that eradicates sex-based distinctions. It is quite possible that the amendment would have succeeded if it had been presented as one that intended to minimize the impact of distinctions based on biological characteristics. Because it was framed in a way that heightened already existing public concern about altered sex roles, it was doomed to failure.

Courts, Strict Scrutiny, and the Draft

As the era of protective legislation and the failure of the ERA make clear, state legislators have been unable to separate out the biological differences between men and women from those differences based on social and cultural mores. Similarly, courts called upon to adjudicate gender-based claims have also been unable to distinguish between laws that derive from a consideration of physical characteristics and those that are based on a socially constructed view of gender. In a number of constitutional cases decided over the last twenty years, the courts have treated sex-based claims as implicating both biological and social distinctions between men and women. During this period, the Supreme Court has been hesitant to invoke the strict scrutiny approach in its analysis of these cases.

The manner in which the judiciary has dealt with cases involving sex discrimination reveals the judiciary's conception of sexual equality. In a number of cases, the courts have interpreted equal protection, which may be thought of as the constitutional mandate for equality, as allowing the state and federal governments to make sex-based distinctions. Although fetal protection policies were utilized by private employers and not by states, the judicial conception of equality encompassed in earlier equal protection cases has likely affected the disposition of fetal protection claims in the federal and state courts.

For much of the twentieth century, the courts permitted statutes and regulations that called for disparate treatment of the sexes. Until the early 1970s, the 1908 *Muller* decision was interpreted as allowing such gender-based distinctions. In its 1971 decision in *Reed v. Reed,* the Supreme Court changed its approach to such legislation and struck down an Idaho law that gave men preferential status as estate administrators where there were competing male and female applicants.[54]

The Court found that the Idaho statute violated the Fourteenth Amendment's equal protection guarantee because it did not bear a rational relationship to a legitimate state objective. To withstand scrutiny under the equal protection guarantee, the Court held that the state classification "must be reasonable, not arbitrary, and must rest upon some ground of difference having a fair and substantial relationship to the object of the legislation, so that all persons similarly circumstanced shall be treated alike."[55] Thus, the Court found that sex classifications were to be evaluated under the rational relationship test, rather than under the more rigorous strict scrutiny approach. While the Court found that the statute violated equal protection, it did not hold that sex was inherently a suspect classification, as is race.[56]

In 1971, the same year that the U.S. Supreme Court held that sex was not a suspect classification under the U.S. Constitution, the California State Supreme Court found that sex was indeed a suspect classification under the California Constitution, and as such required the application of the strict scrutiny test. In this case, *Sail'er Inn, Inc. v. Kirby,* the California Supreme Court struck down a state statute barring women from tending bar, finding that "[s]ex, like race and lineage, is an immutable trait, a status into which the class members are locked by an accident of birth."[57] The California court held that sex-based distinctions were to be evaluated under the strict scrutiny approach. Under this test, the state was required to prove that sex-based classifications were required by some compelling state interest, and that the classifications were necessary to further this interest.[58] Using this new, more rigorous standard, the court held that the statute could not be justified.

The state court's decision in *Sail'er Inn* is significant because it treated sex in much the same way as it treated race, lineage, color, and religion. In dicta that has often been cited, the California court held the following:

> Laws which disable women from full participation in the political, business, and economic areas are often characterized as "protective" or beneficial . . . These laws applied to racial or ethnic minorities would be recognized as invidious or impermissible.[59]

Thus, the state court contended that sex classifications were to be analyzed in much the same way as were other protected categories.

In 1973, a plurality of the U.S. Supreme Court appeared to follow the lead of the *Sail'er Inn* court when it decided another sex discrimination case. This case, *Frontiero v. Richardson,* involved a federal statute that mandated different housing and medical benefits for the spouses of male and female members of the armed services.[60] Spousal eligibility for benefits varied significantly under this statute: for the spouse of a service-woman to receive benefits, he had to prove that he was dependent upon his wife for at least one-half of his support. The spouse of a serviceman, on the other hand, received these benefits automatically, and did not have to prove dependence.

In its decision, the Court held that this federal statute violated the due process clause of the Fifth Amendment. The plurality in this case held that sex-based classifications are inherently suspect and must be subjected to strict scrutiny. In so doing, however, the plurality utilized the rational relationship standard rather than the compelling state inter-est test required by the strict scrutiny approach. In its decision, the plurality invalidated the statute, finding that it was "patently arbitrary" and bore no rational relationship to a legitimate governmental interest.[61]

The question of which standard the Supreme Court would use in adjudicating sex claims under the Constitution was finally resolved in 1976, when the Court decided *Craig v. Boren.*[62] At issue in *Craig* was an Oklahoma statute that prohibited the sale of "nonintoxicating" 3.2 per-cent beer to males under the age of 21 and to females under the age of 18. The issue raised was whether this sex-based age differential violated the equal protection clause. In resolving this question, the Court utilized a new standard, which has come to be known as the "intermediate" approach. To survive judicial scrutiny under this standard, a gender-based statute must serve important governmental objectives and be substantially related to achievement of those objectives.[63] In invoking this new intermediate standard, the Court attempted to place sex-based classifications under greater scrutiny than what the rational relationship test would require. Under this intermediate standard, the Court pre-sumes that gender classifications are unwarranted, thus placing the bur-den of proving the constitutionality of the statute or regulation upon the state. By shifting the burden of proof to the entity defending the classi-fication, the Court expressed its understanding that men and women are more likely than not to be similarly situated for the purposes of equal protection.[64]

On the other hand, by creating a separate proof framework for sex cases, and refusing to regard sex as a suspect class, the Court implied that sex classifications may be more often justifiable than classifications based upon race, lineage, color, or religion.[65] Underlying this distinction is the belief that there are real differences between the sexes that may militate in favor of differential treatment.[66]

In sum, during the twentieth century, the Court has been most likely to allow gender-based classifications where they appear to implicate biological or physical differences.[67] However, the Court's decisions in a number of cases, including those involving pregnancy and maternity benefits and the application of the bona fide occupational qualification exception to Title VII, strongly suggest that the Court frequently permits those gender-based distinctions that it views as based upon the "real differences" between the sexes. What is troubling is that the Court has interpreted these "real differences" as encompassing not only biological but social and cultural characteristics as well. One commentator has termed this approach "physiological naturalism," and contends that the Court treats reproductive differences as if they are dictated by physiological processes alone, and does not consider these differences as arising within particular social contexts.[68] The Court's decision in *Rostker v. Goldberg*, a case involving the eligibility of women for the military draft, is illustrative of this point.

The Military Selective Service Act authorizes the President to require the registration of men, but not women, for the military draft. In 1980, President Jimmy Carter reactivated registration and recommended to Congress that women, as well as men, be eligible for the draft. Congress ignored this request and refused to either amend the act to allow registration of women or to provide funding for such registration. In 1980, several men of draft age brought a case against the federal government, alleging that the Military Selective Service Act violated the Fifth Amendment due process clause.[69] This case, *Rostker v. Goldberg*, was heard by the Supreme Court in the following year.[70]

The district court that decided *Rostker* in 1980 enjoined registration of men, finding that the act violated the Fifth Amendment due process clause. The Supreme Court reversed this decision, holding that the registration provisions of the act did not violate the Fifth Amendment. In its decision, the Supreme Court emphasized that Congress should be granted deference in the area of military defense. In addition, the Court stressed that the judiciary lacked competence in this area, and for this reason, should be hesitant in substituting its judgment for that of Congress.[71]

In making its decision, the Court utilized the *Craig* standard, finding that the government's interest in raising and supporting armies is an important governmental interest and that barring women from registration was closely related to this interest. The Court explained that Congress exempted women from registration because it intended to bar women from combat positions, and since women are restricted from combat, men and women are not similarly situated for purposes of a draft or registration for a draft.[72]

The Court sidestepped the issue of whether this restriction from combat positions was itself constitutional. The Court cited a 1980 Senate report on women in combat, stating that

> [t]he principle that women should not intentionally and routinely engage in combat is fundamental, and enjoys wide support among our people . . . It is universally supported by military leaders who have testified before the Committee.[73]

Disturbingly, the Court's holding that combat restrictions are constitutional is based, in large part, upon its belief that these restrictions are palatable to the public and to the military leadership.

One section of this Senate report that was cited by the dissent in *Rostker* explained the public's reticence about placing women in combat positions. In this section, the Senate report stated that:

> [T]he Committee finds that any attempt to assign women to combat positions could affect the national resolve at the time of mobilization, a time of great strain on all aspects of the Nation's resources.[74]

While the Court stressed that there was significant public support for these restrictions, there is no discussion about whether these restrictions are acceptable under due process analysis. The Court ignored the due process issue, focusing instead upon assumptions about the desirability of women in combat.

In his dissent, Justice Marshall criticized the majority for its lack of insight:

> The Court today places its imprimatur on one of the most potent remaining public expressions of "ancient canards about the proper role of women . . ." It upholds a statute that requires males but not females to register for the draft, and which thereby excludes women from a fundamental civic obligation.[75]

Marshall contended that the majority's opinion had its basis in cultural and social norms, rather than constitutional principles.[76]

Women are barred from combat positions for a number of reasons. According to the 1980 Senate report, foremost among these reasons is the perception that placing women into combat positions will undermine public support for a military campaign. This understanding is in part rooted in the public's perception of women as weaker and less able to defend themselves than men. The lack of support for women in combat is also based upon the view that women have a primary responsibility for the propagation of the race, and should not be placed at risk on the battlefield.

As a result of the combat restrictions, women in the armed services are barred from at least 73 percent of the military jobs. The jobs from which women are excluded are typically those that are the highest-paying and have the best opportunities for advancement. The combat restrictions effectively bar women from positions of leadership in the military, and relegate women to the least-desirable jobs.[77] The long-term impact of the combat restriction on women's quest for equality may even be more significant than is the immediate impact on the jobs available to women. Because these restrictions are based upon assumptions about women's maternal responsibilities and physical incapacities, they reinforce traditional gender roles. As the Senate report suggests, the combat restriction derives not from a belief that women are less physically capable of waging war, but from the view that women's societal role precludes them from doing so.[78] Furthermore, societal norms are not only based on this exclusion, they are also shaped by it. As Deborah Rhode has stated, "[I]t is difficult for women to attain equal respect and equal treatment as citizens while exempt from one of citizenship's central obligations."[79] Women are not fully integrated in our society in part because of the conception of women that the combat restriction helps to foster. If women are viewed as frail creatures who need to be protected not only because of their physical shortcomings but because they bear children, then it is unlikely that they will be perceived as the functional equals of men.

The adjudication of gender-based claims during the 1970s and 1980s reveals that the Supreme Court has difficulty reconciling the existence of physical differences between the sexes with the constitutional and statutory mandate of equal protection. In large part, this difficulty stems from its inability to distinguish between biology and the social consequences attendant to it. Like the legislators who were faced with protective laws and those called upon to ratify the ERA, the judiciary has tended to treat gender as if it were the same as sex. Sex is determined by one's biological characteristics; gender, on the other hand, encompasses a much wider range of characteristics, many of which are not based on physical features. In responding to gender-based statutes and regulations, governmental decision-makers have treated gender differences as if they were sex differences: that is, as if they were immutable characteristics rather than cultural constructions.[80] Assumptions and stereotypes about the roles of the sexes are firmly rooted in our society. Decision-makers have shown themselves to be unable to move beyond these traditional gender roles, even when given the opportunity to draft new laws or engage in judicial policymaking.

Like state protective laws and contemporary gender-based classifications, fetal protection policies derived from cultural perceptions of gender roles, rather than scientific evidence about women's greater susceptibility to occupational harm. In fact, employers chose to utilize these policies, which required women to be surgically sterilized to gain access to more lucrative positions, because they had certain preconceptions about women's inability to control their reproduction. Moreover, in formulating these policies, employers were concluding that women's childbearing role should be granted primacy over other functions. Thus, the employer's conception of equality was interpreted in such a way that cultural expectations were permitted to determine women's work force participation at least as much as, if not *more* than, reproductive capacity.

Unlike earlier gender-based classifications like the ERA and protective laws, fetal protection policies were drafted by private individuals, not governmental bodies. Governmental decision-makers had the opportunity, and in fact, the statutory responsibility, however, of regulating these policies. The laxity of their response should not have been surprising, given our government's ambivalence about how "equality" should be interpreted. In fact, a government such as ours, which is itself uncertain about the proper role of social and cultural expectations in determining the importance of gender, should not have been expected to respond aggressively to these policies, since the policies themselves were based upon a social construction of gender roles.

2

Governmental Response to Fetal Protection Policies

Some political scientists speak of governmental decision-makers as "rational" beings. Rational policymakers are not arbitrary; they make their decisions after consideration of key facets of the policy issue at hand. A rational decision-maker called upon to assess the legality of a fetal protection policy likely would have focused on the "scientific evidence" upon which employers claimed that these policies were based. Extraneous considerations would not have entered into the decision-making calculus. The policymaker would not have based his or her decision on their conception of women's proper role in society or upon whether they believe that women can control their reproduction. A rational decision-maker would have singlemindedly ignored these societal mores and would have focused entirely on whether women are differentially susceptible to workplace hazards, and upon whether existing statutory and regulatory law bars employers from excluding women.

Ideal conditions did not exist for rational decision-making in the fetal protection debate. Most significantly, policymakers did not have perfect information, especially with regard to the sufficiency of scientific data. For example, while scientists believe that many substances may cause reproductive harm, relatively few chemicals that are used in American industry have been tested for their reproductive effects.[1] It has been estimated that 20 million workers are exposed to workplace toxins, and many of these toxins may adversely affect reproductive and fetal health.[2] Despite the large number of workers potentially affected by agents that impair their procreative capability and/or the development of their offspring, only a small number of chemicals used in American industry have been tested for their reproductive effects.[3] An even smaller number have actually been determined to be reproductive or developmental toxicants in humans.[4]

The lack of evidence about the reproductive effects of chemicals used in industry stems not only from the paucity of research in this area, but from the difficulty of detecting these effects and of establishing causation.[5] Scientists investigating reproductive hazards often rely upon the discovery of "clusters" of certain disorders of reproduction, like spontaneous abortions, stillbirths, or birth defects, as a sign that a reproductive toxicant may be present in the workplace. Even where an etiologic agent is suspected, definitive evidence is often difficult to obtain.[6]

At present, only thirty to forty chemical, physical, and biological substances are generally accepted as having potential reproductive and developmental effects.[7] Of these substances, only a handful—arsenic, carbon disulfide, chloroprene, DBCP, EtO, non-ionizing radiation, and lead—are regulated in part because of their danger to reproductive capacity.[8] Of this handful, reproductive concerns have been critically important in the regulation of only DBCP, EtO, and lead. A recent report by the General Accounting Office found that of the 117 regulatory actions taken by the Consumer Products Safety Commission, the Environmental Protection Agency, the Food and Drug Administration, and the Occupational Safety and Health Administration to deal with 30 substances, 61 percent were not based on reproductive or developmental risk.[9] Thus, nearly two-thirds of these substances were not regulated on the basis of concerns about reproductive or developmental toxicity. Of those agents that are regulated on the basis of these concerns, only dibrormochloropropane, a pesticide found to cause decreased sperm counts and infertility in male workers who used it, has been banned. In an interesting twist, it was the Environmental Protection Agency, not the Occupational Health and Safety Administration, that barred use of this chemical.[10]

There is also a lack of data about how toxins may be transmitted to a fetus. Until recently, nearly all research focused on maternal transmission[11] and ignored the effects of paternal exposure.[12] This concentration on the maternal contribution and the corresponding lack of research on the paternal factor seem to have been based on the antiquated notion that it is the woman, not the man, whose health determines that of her offspring. The health of the male germ cell was not questioned; it was assumed that any problems in fetal development were the result of maternally transmitted defects.

Scientists have begun to explore the possible link between birth defects and paternal exposure to environmental and occupational toxicants only recently.[13] There appear to have been two reasons that earlier research on the paternal contribution was not undertaken, or, where it was undertaken, was not accepted. First, scientists investigating the paternal contribution to birth defects had difficulty identifying the biological mechanism by which the toxicant was transmitted.[14] Second, scientists held what has been referred to as a "macho sperm theory of conception," which is the belief that only the fittest sperm would be capable of fertilizing an egg.[15]

Recent data suggest that a number of physical, chemical, and biological agents may produce spontaneous abortion or birth defects in children fathered by exposed males.[16] Moreover, recent epidemiological studies have found a strong association between paternal exposure to occupational toxins and birth defects.[17] Thus, paternal exposure to occupational toxins may be as problematic as maternal exposure.[18] For this reason, many scientists have concluded that permissible exposure levels for men and women should be the same.[19] Many believe that the lead and ethylene oxide standards, which do not distinguish between male and female workers in setting permissible exposure levels, should be the model for dealing with reproductive toxicants. These new data on the paternal contribution to birth defects appear to undermine the validity of fetal protection policies, which exclude women from jobs where reproductive toxicants are present while allowing men to continue to be exposed to these agents.[20] The data strongly suggest that there is insufficient evidence to support differential treatment.

Given that a fetus or child may be harmed by workplace toxins through the exposure of either the mother or father to these toxins, employers' willingness to exclude women but not men is puzzling. In attempting to understand why employers chose to exclude only women from jobs that might involve exposure to reproductive toxins, one might view the employer's motive from either a pessimistic or an optimistic stance. If one adopted a more optimistic view, he or she might believe that employers were compelled to adopt fetal protection policies out of concern about existing data on maternal transmission. If one adopted a more pessimistic view, however, he or she would likely focus on other factors which indicate that employers used these policies solely to bar women from traditionally male workplaces, and that, among these, concern about the costs of medical and liability insurance was a significant consideration.

Even if policymakers are rational, they had imperfect information with which to assess fetal protection policies. These policymakers did not have all the scientific data necessary to determine definitively whether reproductive hazards exist in the workplace and if such hazards harm men and women equally. In addition, the rational decision-maker could not establish employers' motives for adopting these policies with absolute certainty. This motive became increasingly important as the 1980s wore on and decision-makers demonstrated a willingness to consider the "benevolence" of employer motives when assessing the legality of these policies.

However, while there were gaps in decision-makers' knowledge of scientific data and employer motives, decision-makers would still have had sufficient information to evaluate the policies if, indeed, they were acting rationally. Nearly all fetal protection policies examined by governmental agencies or courts aimed at limiting fetal exposure to lead. Most scientists agree that the permissible exposure level to lead is the same for men and women. While there continues to be disagreement about whether the level should be lower for women, all scientists agree that men and their offspring are at risk of harm from some level of lead exposure. In sum, the scientific literature did not support the use of single sex exclusionary policies, especially for lead-exposed workers.

Thus, even with the imperfect information at hand, a rational decision-maker could have responded effectively to the use of fetal protection policies. Whether the decision-maker was a member of Congress, a judge, or a staff member of an administrative agency, he or she would have to have concluded that these policies violated both equal employment opportunity statutes and occupational safety and health regulations. These policies could not have been legitimated by their questionable beneficial impact on women and their offspring because the scientific evidence demonstrated that men were also placed at risk from toxic exposure.

The failure of decision-makers to behave "rationally" is indeed troubling. Throughout the 1980s and early 1990s, Congress, the regulatory agencies, and the courts were unable to respond effectively to these policies. This inability was not the result of some flaw in the scientific data. Instead, governmental actors charged with ensuring equal employment and occupational safety and health moved beyond the question of whether the policies violated existing caselaw and statutory law. Even though the policies clearly contravened this law, decision-makers attempted to legitimize them by focusing on how they benefitted women and, even more significant, fetuses. Policymakers were reluctant to strike down these policies, in many cases because they believed the underlying premise of these policies, that women's employment opportunities can, and in many cases should, be limited to protect the health of their potential fetuses.

4. Congress, Title VII, and Fetal Protection Policies

If government decision-makers had been eager to prevent gender discrimination in employment, and if they had been surefooted about the manner in which discrimination should be eradicated, they would have had the tools to accomplish their goals. Several federal regulations and statutes governing discrimination in employment were already established: among these were Title VII of the 1964 Civil Rights Act, the 1978 Pregnancy Discrimination Act (PDA), and Executive Order 11246, which was promulgated in 1965 and amended in 1967 and 1978. A government willing to respond effectively to the proliferation of fetal protection policies in the 1980s could have used any or all of these statutes.

Nearly all challenges to fetal protection policies in the 1980s were based on Title VII and, ultimately, the Supreme Court used the Title VII framework to strike down those policies. It took more than a decade of litigation, however, for the judiciary to issue such a holding. In fact, throughout the 1980s, Title VII was interpreted as permitting fetal protection policies, despite the fact that these policies explicitly discriminated on the basis of sex. The courts and administrative agencies can certainly be faulted for their misinterpretation of Title VII, but part of the problem also lay in the statute.

Title VII purports to protect women, among other groups, from discrimination in employment. There are serious flaws in Title VII itself, however, and these problems have been aggravated by judicial and administrative interpretations of the Civil Rights Act. Perhaps the most significant of these shortcomings is the fact that Congress never formulated the analytical frameworks for establishing discrimination. Instead, the courts were left to determine what these frameworks would be. As a result, the frameworks are ambiguous and have been the subject of frequent reinterpretations by the courts and the administrative agencies. Moreover, throughout its 30-year history, Title VII's legislative history and analytic framework and, in particular, its bona fide occupational qualification (bfoq) exception have been used repeatedly to justify gender-based discrimination.

From the beginning, Congress was ambivalent about the extent to which it was opposed to sex discrimination. This ambivalence is apparent in the legislative histories of Title VII and the Pregnancy Discrimination Act, and in Congress's response to judicial and administrative interpretation of both the PDA and the Civil Rights Act. On the rare occasion, Congress has taken action to strengthen Title VII protections against sex discrimination. In 1978, it added "pregnancy" to the list of categories protected under Title VII. Unfortunately, this legislation appears to have been a "blip" on an otherwise downward curve toward limiting employment rights. Moreover, even the PDA, which expanded protections for pregnant workers, was based upon cultural assumptions about motherhood and the roles of the sexes. These assumptions and stereotypes were later invoked to justify gender-based policies like fetal protection policies.

Fetal protection policies, unlike any other discriminatory employment practice or policy in the history of Title VII, brought the assumptions and stereotypes that underlay employment discrimination statutes into stark relief. The policies squarely raised the question of whether women's work-force participation should be limited to protect their reproductive function. The ambiguity of decision-makers about gender and biological differences confounded attempts to respond swiftly and effectively to these policies. Moreover, opponents of fetal protection policies found that Title VII, which had been formulated to ensure women's full integration in the workplace, could be interpreted by the courts and regulatory agencies to have the opposite result.

Title VII's Legislative History
and Analytic Frameworks

Title VII of the 1964 Civil Rights Act bars discrimination in employment on the basis of race, color, national origin, religion, and sex. Section 703 of the act mandates that:

(a) It shall be an unlawful employment practice for an employer—
    (1) to fail or refuse to hire or to discharge any individual . . . because of such individual's race, color, religion, sex, or national origin; or
    (2) to limit, segregate, or classify his employees or applicants for employment in any way which would deprive or tend to deprive any individual of employment opportunities or otherwise adversely affect his status as an employee, because of such individual's race, color, religion, sex, or national origin.

Thus, under Title VII, an employer is prohibited from differentiating among employees or potential employees on the basis of sex.[1]

The legislative history of the act indicates that there was little foresight given to making sex a protected classification. In fact, anecdotal evidence suggests that conservative southern representatives added the sex category in a last-ditch effort to defeat the bill.[2] In any case, it is questionable whether the Congress that enacted Title VII had a firm commitment to the principle of sexual equality.[3] This lack of commitment may have explained the poor enforcement of Title VII in the 1960s. During these years, the Equal Employment Opportunity Commission, which was created under the Civil Rights Act to oversee Title VII, did little to implement the legislation.[4] In part, this lack of activity may be attributed to the fact that the sparse legislative record gave the EEOC little guidance as to how to enforce the statute.

Most significant, Congress was silent about the proof framework to be utilized in Title VII cases. As a result, it has been left to the federal courts to determine how the statute should be enforced. In their adjudication of sex discrimination claims, the courts have evaluated employment discrimination charges under either the per se, disparate treatment, or disparate impact frameworks. The facts of the case dictate which of the frameworks are to be utilized.

Some scholars contended that fetal protection policies, which barred "fertile" women from workplaces simply because they could bear children, constituted per se discrimination. Until the Supreme Court's 1991 decision, however, the EEOC and nearly all the courts charged with evaluating these policies utilized the less rigorous disparate impact framework. Per se discrimination occurs when an employer acknowledges that he or she has discriminated against a group on the basis of race, color, religion, sex, or national origin. Employers charged with per se violations usually try to defend their discriminatory policy by demonstrating that the policy constitutes a bona fide occupational qualification for the job in question. Under section 703(e), this bfoq must be reasonably necessary to the normal operation of the business.[5] An employer who can establish that a policy constitutes a bfoq will not be found guilty of discrimination, even where his or her policy explicitly discriminates against a protected class.

The bfoq exception has been the subject of intense debate almost since Title VII's creation. The first controversy over the exception centered upon whether it could be used to validate state protective laws. In 1965, the EEOC issued interpretive guidelines stating that the bfoq exception could not be used where

> (i) the refusal to hire a woman because of sex [is] based on assumptions of the comparative employment characteristics of women in general; [or]
> (ii) [where] the refusal to hire an individual [is] based on stereotypical characterizations of the sexes.[6]

In its first application of the new guidelines, however, the agency held that "reasonable" state protective laws would be permissible. To utilize the bfoq defense, the state only had to demonstrate that it was acting in good faith and that the primary purpose of the state law was to protect, rather than to discriminate against women.[7]

The EEOC continued to permit state protective laws under the bfoq exception until 1972, when it established that the laws violated Title VII.[8] In its new interpretive guidelines, the EEOC stated that "the principle of nondiscrimination requires that individuals be considered on the basis of individual capacities and not on the basis of any characteristics generally attributed to the group."[9] This principle has been utilized in many Title VII cases, and was at the core of the most significant bfoq case to date, that of *Dothard v. Rawlinson*.[10] *Dothard* directly raised the question of whether the bfoq exception could be used to validate a policy that expressly barred one sex on the basis of certain assumptions about the ability of that group to perform certain jobs. The Supreme Court's decision in this case may be seen, at least doctrinally, as the embodiment of the view that men and women differ not only in their reproductive function, but in their role in the larger society as well.

Dothard v. Rawlinson, which was decided by the Supreme Court in 1977, involved the use of a state regulation that established gender criteria for assigning correctional officers for contact positions in Alabama state penitentiaries.[11] In this case, the plaintiffs, who were women, sought appointment as correctional officers at a male maximum security penitentiary. The Alabama Board of Corrections stated that women could not be employed in these jobs because correctional officers in these penitentiaries were required to maintain close supervision over potentially violent prisoners. The Board asserted that its regulation did not violate Title VII because it fell within the bfoq exception.

The Supreme Court agreed with the Board of Corrections that being male was a valid bfoq for the job of corrections officer. The Court gave a passing nod to the principle that the bfoq should be extremely narrow, but then proceeded to validate the Alabama policy by stating that the particular conditions of the Alabama penitentiary necessitated the gender classification. According to the Court,

> The environment of Alabama's penitentiaries is a peculiarly inhospitable one for human beings of whatever sex . . . The conditions of confinement . . . are characterized by "rampant violence" and a "jungle atmosphere."[12]

The Court stated that the prisons were not typical, and that the singular brutality of these penitentiaries constituted the basis for the bfoq.[13]

The Justices, apparently wary of using language that could be termed paternalistic, stated that the bfoq was instituted not out of a desire to protect female correctional officers, but by the need to maintain prison security.[14] The Court maintained that the essence of the job of correctional officer was to maintain prison security, and that women, as a class, were probably unable to do so in these Alabama penitentiaries. According to the Court,

> The likelihood that inmates would assault a woman because she was a woman would pose a real threat not only to the victim of the assault but also to the basic control of the penitentiary and protection of its inmates and other security personnel. *The employee's very womanhood*

would thus directly undermine her capacity to provide the security that is the essence of a correctional officer's responsibility.[15] (emphasis added)

Female corrections officers were considered at increased risk not only because one-fifth of the prison population were convicted sex offenders but also because other inmates, "deprived of a normal heterosexual environment," would assault a woman if they had access to her.[16] Thus, the increased likelihood of sexual assault on a female guard necessitated the use of the gender classification. The Court agreed that the exclusion of female guards stemmed not from a desire to protect the women from this assault but out of the need to control the inmates and ensure the security of the facility.[17]

While stating that women should have the right to choose their employment, even where jobs posed a risk of harm, the Court distinguished the jobs at issue in *Dothard.* According to the Court, "[M]ore [was] at stake in this case than an individual woman's decision to weigh and accept the risks of employment in a 'contact' position in a maximum-security male prison."[18] Concern about inmate safety justified the exclusion of women. This line of reasoning, which in essence justified discrimination where it was necessary to protect some third party, was later used to validate the use of fetal protection policies.

The *Dothard* decision threatened to expand the narrow bfoq defense by permitting employers to justify discriminatory practices by demonstrating that the practices were derived from some widely held belief about women's abilities or roles. In *Dothard,* the Alabama Correctional Board needed only to discuss the "barbaric" conditions in its prisons and the viciousness of its prisoners to convince the Court to allow it to exclude women. Women were not excluded because of their individual inability to perform the job of correctional officer: they were excluded because of certain preconceptions about the ability of women as a class to effectively control inmates.

Courts that later considered cases involving a bfoq for sex for the job of correctional officer almost always rejected the *Dothard* reasoning. In fact, most lower federal and state courts seem to have taken a cue from Justice Marshall's dissent in *Dothard.* In his dissent, Marshall attempted to limit the impact of the majority opinion by emphasizing that it should be read in light of the highly unusual and dangerous characteristics of the Alabama state penitentiaries.[19] An examination of cases similar to

Dothard reveals that the majority of federal and state courts have disallowed such a bfoq, contending that the conditions of the penal system in question did not justify the exclusion of either men or women.[20]

Even given the weakening of the bfoq exception under *Dothard*, the per se/bfoq framework imposes the strictest requirements on employers seeking to justify the differential treatment of men and women. This rigorous framework is used where the employer acknowledges that he or she is treating some group of employees in a disparate manner. Where the employer has adopted a policy that treats some class of individuals less favorably because of race, color, religion, sex, or national origin but the employer does not acknowledge such treatment, the per se/bfoq framework cannot be used. In such cases, a claimant may attempt to utilize the disparate treatment approach. Under the disparate treatment framework, the plaintiff bears the initial burden of establishing a prima facie case of discrimination.[21] If the plaintiff meets this initial burden, the employer is required to articulate some legitimate, nondiscriminatory explanation for his conduct. After articulating such a reason, the plaintiff is given the opportunity to establish that the rationale given by the employer is merely a pretext for discrimination. In disparate treatment cases, the plaintiff is required to prove that the employer acted out of an unlawful discriminatory motive; the courts, however, have been willing to infer such a motive from the circumstances of the particular case.

While discriminatory intent is a requisite factor in proving a disparate treatment case, under the disparate impact framework a plaintiff need not show that the employer intended to discriminate against him/her to prove a violation. In a disparate impact claim, the plaintiff contends that facially neutral employment policies weigh more heavily upon one group than another.[22] According to the Supreme Court, an employer practice or policy has a disparate impact where it creates "built-in head winds" against the economic advancement of this group.[23]

Where a plaintiff is able to prove that a policy has a disparate impact, the burden of proof shifts to the employer to show that the policy constitutes a business necessity that is related to job performance. To meet his or her burden of proof, the employer must show that the policy has a "manifest relationship to the employment in question," i.e., that the requirement is related to actual job performance.[24] If the employer is able to prove that the policy constitutes a business necessity that is related to job performance, the plaintiff has the opportunity to demonstrate that an alternative was available to the employer that had less adverse impact upon the group in question. If the plaintiff shows that such an alternative was available, the court will hold that the employer has violated Title VII.[25]

While a disparate treatment case hinges upon the inferential show-ing of discriminatory intent, the lack of such intent is not determinative in disparate impact cases. Thus, an employment practice that has a disparate impact upon a protected group, and that does not constitute a business necessity, violates Title VII, regardless of the "benevolence" of an employer's motives in formulating the policy. This aspect of the dispa-rate impact framework is extremely important in any discussion about fetal protection policies. Until the Supreme Court's 1991 decision, courts permitted these policies in large part because they believed that em-ployers adopted the policies for benevolent reasons. Under the disparate impact test, however, employer intent is not considered relevant.

The disparate impact framework was in jeopardy in the late 1980s, as the Supreme Court issued holdings that seriously weakened it by allow-ing employers significant latitude in demonstrating "business necessity."[26] In 1991, Congress implicitly invalidated these court decisions by passing the Civil Rights Act, which codified the original disparate impact/business necessity test, and placed the burden of persuasion on defendant employ-ers to establish the business necessity defense.[27]

While Congress did not create the analytical frameworks for estab-lishing discrimination, it can be faulted for its failure to respond swiftly and effectively to administrative and judicial interpretation that have made it more difficult to prove discrimination. For example, throughout the 1960s Congress allowed the EEOC and the courts to interpret the bfoq exception as permitting state protective legislation. It was not until the EEOC reversed this policy that these protective laws were found to be violative of Title VII.

In addition, Congress allowed the courts, and, in particular, the Supreme Court, to broaden the scope of the bfoq defense to encompass not only physical differences between the sexes but also stereotypical notions about men's and women's intellectual and emotional makeup. The Supreme Court's decision in Dothard suggests that it is willing to find sex a bfoq in certain circumstances: namely, where the safety of either the woman or some third party is at stake. This decision is grounded in the perception that women are less capable of protecting themselves than are men. In this case, the Court viewed women's very "womanliness" as being so provocative as to incite men to become violent. The failure of Congress to act to reverse this decision is indeed troubling. Had the lower federal and state courts not limited this holding, *Dothard* probably could have been interpreted as allowing significant restrictions on the employment of women on the basis not only of physical characteristics but also of stereotypical notions about the capacities of men and women.

Thus, it appears that Congress has exercised little control over the activities of the regulatory agencies and courts evaluating Title VII claims. There were virtually no checks placed on the EEOC's interpretation of key Title VII provisions, particularly the scope of the bfoq defense. Similarly, judicial interpretation of Title VII, especially in the *Dothard* case, was not countered by the legislature, despite the fact that this decision clearly limited the impact of Title VII.

Congress has attempted to address certain judicial decisions through legislation, but, in most cases, it has encountered significant difficulties. Congress's passage of the Pregnancy Discrimination Act, which amended Title VII to include pregnancy within the protected classifications, was one of its victories. While Congress was successful in formulating the PDA, disagreement about the role of women and the importance of childbearing, which was apparent in the statute's legislative history, re-erupts in debates like the one over fetal protection policies.

The Legislative History and Judicial Interpretation of the Pregnancy Discrimination Act

In the early to mid-1970s, there was much disagreement about the definition of the sex prohibition, particularly with regard to pregnancy discrimination. By the early 1970s, women who had been discriminated against on the basis of pregnancy began to file suit under Title VII. In large part, the 1978 Pregnancy Discrimination Act was an outgrowth of Congress's disapproval of two earlier Supreme Court decisions holding that pregnancy discrimination was not barred under Title VII. In 1974, the U.S. Supreme Court found that a California statute that created a state disability fund to cover all work disabilities except pregnancy did not violate the Fourteenth Amendment equal protection guarantee.

This state fund provided temporary wage replacement to employees in the private sector who were unable to work due to some disability. All work disabilities, including disabilities resulting from cosmetic surgery, hair transplants, skiing accidents, and prostatectomies, were covered by the fund. In this case, *Geduldig v. Aiello,* the Court found that the state had not run afoul of the Fourteenth Amendment in excluding from coverage those disabilities that resulted from pregnancy.[28] According to the Court, pregnancy was a unique physical characteristic, and, for this reason, exclusion of pregnancy did not constitute gender discrimination.[29] The Court held that:

> The lack of identity between the excluded disability [pregnancy] and gender as such becomes clear upon the most cursory analysis. The program divides potential recipients into two groups—pregnant women and nonpregnant persons. While the first group is exclusively female, the second includes members of both sexes.[30]

Thus, the Court seems to have contended that since women could belong to both groups, pregnancy discrimination did not necessarily constitute gender discrimination.[31]

This somewhat convoluted distinction between pregnant women and nonpregnant "persons" was utilized by the Court two years later in *General Electric Co. v. Gilbert,* a Title VII case that involved a company-sponsored disability insurance plan that did not include coverage for pregnancy.[32] As in *Geduldig,* the plan at issue covered almost all possible disabilities, including those arising from medical procedures that only men would undergo, like vasectomies, prostatectomies, and circumcisions.

Writing for the majority, Justice Rehnquist held that "gender-based discrimination does not result simply because an employer's disability benefits program is less than all-inclusive."[33] Despite the fact that pregnancy was excluded, the Supreme Court held that the plan did not constitute gender discrimination since the Court viewed pregnancy as "significantly different from the typical covered disease or disability."[34] The Court again cited its decision in *Geduldig* for the principle that pregnancy discrimination was not gender discrimination, since the exclusion of pregnancy from the disability plan did not impose a hardship upon nonpregnant women.[35]

The response to the Court's decision in *Gilbert* was immediate and intense.[36] A large number of groups lobbied Congress to draft legislation aimed at overturning the decision through legislation. In 1978, the Congress passed the Pregnancy Discrimination Act, which amended Title VII to make pregnancy discrimination unlawful. In effect, the PDA made pregnancy another protected classification under Title VII. The text of the act stated the following:

> The section 701 of the Civil Rights Act of 1964 is amended by adding at the end thereof the following new subsection:
> (k) The terms "because of sex" or "on the basis of sex" include, but are not limited to, because of or on the basis of pregnancy, childbirth, or related medical conditions; and women affected by pregnancy, child-birth, or related medical conditions shall be treated the same for all employment-related purposes.

Under the PDA, pregnant women are to be treated the same way as are other "similarly situated" workers. While pregnancy is, in a sense, unique, the act mandates that it be analogized to other temporary disabilities that affect the ability of employees to continue working.

The PDA established the principle that a policy which categorizes workers on the basis of pregnancy is never neutral. Under the PDA, classifications on the basis of pregnancy constitute per se discrimination, requiring that the employer justify his or her use of the classification through a rigorous proof framework. To defend against a claim of pregnancy discrimination, an employer must show that his or her discriminatory policy constituted a bfoq for the job in question. As one commentator has noted, after the PDA even a facially neutral rule, such as one governing employee health or reproductive health, "[could] be shown to be a pretext for discrimination on the basis of pregnancy and hence gender."[37]

Throughout the 1980s and early 1990s, opponents of fetal protection policies claimed that the policies violated the PDA because employers were distinguishing between workers on the basis of their capacity for pregnancy. They contended that while Congress did not explicitly bar the use of these policies when it enacted the PDA, the legislative history of the act revealed Congress's opposition to any policies that classified employees on the basis of pregnancy. An examination of the legislative history of the act helps to shed light upon congressional intent in defining the amendment.

The legislative history of the PDA is replete with criticism of the Supreme Court's decision in *Gilbert*.[38] Many individuals giving testimony indicated that an amendment to Title VII was needed to overturn this decision.[39] A number of individuals attested to the need for an amendment that would add pregnancy to the list of classifications protected under Title VII. In the House, Representative Carl C. Perkins (Dem.-KY) emphasized that "the assumption that women will become pregnant and leave the labor force leads to the view of women as marginal workers, and is at the root of the discriminatory practices which keep women in low-paying and dead-end jobs."[40] Many other proponents of the bill asserted that the capacity to become pregnant, and not just the fact of pregnancy itself, contributed to women being viewed as temporary workers who have little commitment to full-time employment.[41]

Throughout the 1980s and early 1990s, opponents of fetal protection policies emphasized that "pregnancy" as defined by the PDA, encompassed not only pregnancy, but "childbirth, and related medical conditions." These individuals contended that the inclusion of these other medical conditions necessitated a broad reading of the PDA. The legislative history apparently supports the view that Congress intended for such a broad reading. In particular, in his testimony to the House, Representative Perkins stated that the phrase was intended to apply to the whole range of reproductive processes.[42] More pointedly, Perkins stated that "until a woman passes the childbearing age, she is viewed by employers as potentially pregnant."[43] For this reason, Perkins contended, the eradication of discrimination based on pregnancy would help to ensure equal employment opportunity for women.

Representative Augustus F. Hawkins (Dem.-CA) echoed this concern about discrimination on the basis of one's potential to become pregnant. Hawkins acknowledged that "because many of the disadvantages imposed on women are predicated upon their capacity to become pregnant, genuine equality in the American labor force is no more than an illusion as long as employers remain free to make pregnancy the basis of unfavorable treatment of working women."[44] For this reason, legislation barring discrimination on the basis of pregnancy had to encompass not only pregnancy, but childbearing capability as well.

Similarly, there is testimony in the Senate that suggests that legislators intended that the PDA be interpreted broadly. A Senate report supporting the bill stated that "the assumption that women will become pregnant and leave the labor market is at the core of the sex stereotyping resulting in unfavorable disparate treatment of women in the workplace."[45] Another report stated unequivocally that the bill defined sex discrimination as "includ[ing] those physiological occurrences peculiar to women."[46] Thus, there was significant testimony that seems to indicate that Congress intended the prohibition against pregnancy discrimination to be interpreted as encompassing discrimination based on the capacity or potential to become pregnant.

In a number of cases challenging the use of fetal protection policies, employees and interest groups have contended that Congress intended to prohibit employer policies that barred women from certain jobs on the basis of concerns about fetal or child health. One interest group, the Equal Rights Advocates, which filed an amicus curiae brief with the Supreme Court in the *U.A.W. v. Johnson Controls* litigation, contended that an interchange between a representative of the Chamber of Commerce and Chairman Hawkins of the House Committee on Education and Labor put Congress on notice that the PDA might bar fetal protection policies. In this dialogue, the Chamber of Commerce representative told Hawkins that the bill "would prevent an employer from refusing certain work to a pregnant employee where such work posed a threat to either the mother-to-be or her unborn child."[47] Since Congress enacted the PDA without amendment, the Equal Rights Advocates contended that Congress intended for the bill to bar employer policies that limited the employment of women on the basis of fetal health hazards.[48]

During the 1980s and 1990s, supporters of fetal protection policies rejected the contention that Congress considered the effects of the bill upon such employer policies.[49] Instead, these individuals and groups claimed that Congress intended the PDA to protect fetal health. These individuals alleged that the PDA was enacted to ensure that women were not fired from their jobs or were not denied disability leave because of their pregnancies. Where women lost their jobs and their health benefits or were denied maternity leave, they argued, fetal health might be endangered.[50] As the U.S. Chamber of Commerce stated in its amicus curiae brief in the *Johnson Controls* litigation,

> [A] primary purpose of the legislation was to protect fetal health . . . [For this reason], it would be anomalous in the extreme to construe such legislation to require employers to employ women in hazardous occupations that unquestionably jeopardized such health. There is not the slightest indication that Congress intended the PDA to have that effect.[51]

Many advocates of fetal protection policies alleged that the legislative history of the bill indicated that Congress intended to promote and safeguard fetal health.

Opponents of fetal protection policies looked at the same legislative history and made quite different conclusions. These groups and individuals contended that testimony about the effects of pregnancy discrimination on the health of fetuses and children demonstrated Congress's understanding that the exclusion of women from better-paying jobs could pose a greater risk of harm to fetal health than would continued employment in a potentially hazardous job.[52] The legislative history of the PDA does not definitively establish whether it was intended to bar policies predicated upon one's capacity to become pregnant. While Congress did hear testimony about the effects of the bill upon employer policies barring pregnant women from certain hazardous jobs, it is not clear that Congress intended the act to bar these policies. As has been noted, only one individual raised this possibility in his testimony, and the failure of Congress to amend the act to reflect these concerns should not be viewed as an indication of Congress's intention to bar these policies. Moreover, Congress did not hear testimony about policies that barred women who might become pregnant, as opposed to those already pregnant, so the effect of the act upon these policies is even less clear.

While the PDA does appear to define pregnancy discrimination as encompassing distinctions made upon the capacity to become pregnant, Congress did not fully consider those policies that barred fertile women from jobs that might pose fetal health hazards. This lack of clarity about congressional intent may explain the inconsistency of lower court decisions in cases involving fetal protection policies.

It bears noting that the willingness of legislators to tie the PDA to wider notions about motherhood and the roles of the sexes may be the source of much of the ambiguity that exists regarding the legislative history of the act. In fact, both opponents and advocates of the PDA used assumptions and stereotypes about women, childbearing, and childrearing to bolster their arguments. By manipulating these cultural images, legislators clouded the issue of whether the PDA could be used to bar fetal protection policies. The institutional paralysis of Congress with regard to this issue may indeed have stemmed from this lack of clarity as to what the PDA demanded.

The 1991 Civil Rights Act and the 1990 Employee Protection Bill

In the wake of the decision by the Court of Appeals for the Seventh Circuit in *U.A.W. v. Johnson Controls* and prior to the Supreme Court's decision in this case, some members of Congress introduced legislation aimed at directly regulating the use of fetal protection policies. This activity was extremely limited, but it involved congressional activity at both the legislative and administrative levels. Moreover, this activity suggests that Congress may have been willing to undertake a more vigilant stance with regard to employment discrimination.

In 1991, Congress passed the Civil Rights Act. By clarifying the disparate impact framework, the act appears to have regulated the use of fetal protection policies, albeit indirectly. Much of the debate over fetal protection policies centered upon whether these constitute disparate impact or disparate treatment of a particular class. Throughout the 1980s, courts blurred the lines between these two frameworks by utilizing a disparate impact approach to evaluate the policies. Then, in 1991, Supreme Court's decision in *Johnson Controls* established that the more rigorous disparate treatment test was to be used in evaluating these policies. Even if the Supreme Court had decided *Johnson Controls* differently, the stricter disparate impact test that was imposed by the Civil Rights Act would likely have made it more difficult for employers to legitimate fetal protection policies.

By establishing the analytic frameworks for evaluating disparate impact claims, the 1991 Civil Rights Act makes it easier to challenge fetal protection policies under the Title VII framework. More direct attempts to regulate these policies by specific legislation, however, have failed. In March 1990, Representative Pat Williams (Dem.-MT) introduced the Employee Protection Act in the House. In a letter sent to other members of the House, Representative Williams stated that "this legislation is in response to the [Seventh Circuit's] *Johnson Controls* decision . . . [I]t is sex neutral and would effectively reverse the effect of this decision by creating new remedies for all workers who are threatened with loss of employment rights because they want to preserve the right to have children."[53]

The bill that Williams introduced prohibited employers from requiring that their employees be sterilized, submit to a fertility test, or refrain from procreating as a condition of employment, promotion, or transfer. This bill provided immediate remedies to employees whose rights were violated and imposed damages against employers beyond those imposed by Title VII. Representative Williams and the House Committee on Education and Labor chose to wait until the Supreme Court issued its holding in *U.A.W. v. Johnson Controls* before introducing the bill to the floor, and, given the Supreme Court's holding in *Johnson Controls,* it is unlikely that further legislation will be introduced.[54]

In addition to passing the 1991 Civil Rights Act and introducing the 1990 Employee Protection Act, members of the House and Senate have undertaken a number of other activities that bear on fetal protection policies.[55] These activities are relevant to the oversight of those administrative agencies having responsibility for responding to employment discrimination or to occupational safety and health hazards. In 1990, the Senate Committee on Governmental Affairs requested that the General Accounting Office undertake a survey of those agencies with responsibility for regulating reproductive and developmental toxicants.[56] This survey was intended to "describe or give descriptive information about the extent of federal regulation of environmental chemicals of concern to the expert community because of adverse reproductive or developmental potential."[57] The General Accounting Office's report, which was issued in late 1990, concluded that the four agencies with responsibility for regulating reproductive and developmental toxins, the Consumer Products Safety Commission, the Food and Drug Administration, the Environmental Protection Agency, and the Occupational Safety and Health Administration, have been slow to regulate these toxins. In fact, the report found that less than one third of the regulatory actions taken by these agencies with regard to suspected reproductive and fetal toxins was based upon concerns about reproductive or fetal health.[58] On the basis of these findings, the GAO called on Congress to increase its efforts to regulate known or suspected reproductive and developmental toxins.

In 1990, Congress also completed its study of the response by the EEOC to the use of fetal protection policies. This report constituted a scathing indictment of the Commission's lack of initiative in dealing with these policies. The House Committee on Education and Labor has responsibility for the oversight of the EEOC, and the study was undertaken out of a concern that the EEOC was not complying with its Title VII obligations with regard to fetal protection policies.[59] After completing this study, the committee made a number of recommendations to the EEOC for the disposition of fetal protection cases in the future. In addition, the committee hinted that they would continue to oversee the disposition of future cases of this kind.

Thus, by early 1991, Congress had begun to take interest in the issue of fetal protection policies. The extent of this interest has yet to be determined; moreover, while Congress has instituted a number of studies, among them the GAO study and the House study on EEOC activities, it is unclear what actions Congress will undertake to follow up these studies. Furthermore, now that the Supreme Court has held that fetal protection policies violate Title VII, it is unclear whether Congress will follow up on the actions it took during the 91st session.

Summary of Congressional Activities

Despite this recent, somewhat half-hearted attempt to regulate fetal protection policies, Congress has a demonstrated pattern of failure to respond effectively to judicial and administrative actions that undermine Title VII. For example, Congress failed to respond to the Supreme Court's decision in *Dothard,* which expanded the bfoq defense to encompass not only biological differences but cultural perceptions of the abilities of men and women. As noted above, the impact of this potentially wide-reaching decision has been limited by the adjudication of similar cases in the district courts and courts of appeals. Congress was also slow to pass the 1991 Civil Rights Act, which restored Title VII protections in disparate impact cases.

In addition to failing to respond to these administrative and judicial encroachments on Title VII, Congress has evinced a lack of clarity about the proper disposition of claims arising out of policies similar to those at issue in the fetal protection debate. The PDA barred discrimination based upon pregnancy; however, Congress was not clear about whether this statute also barred employer policies and practices restricting employment based upon childbearing capacity. This ambiguity contributed to the fetal protection debate, with each side finding support for its position in the legislative history of the PDA.

Thus, there have been two clearly defined trends in congressional response to policies that classify employees on the basis of sex. First, Congress has been largely ineffective in countering judicial interpretations of Title VII, even where those interpretations run counter to established caselaw.[60] Second, the legislative history of the PDA does not definitively establish how fetal protection policies should be dealt with—this despite the fact that classifications based solely upon childbearing capacity would seem to be barred under this statute. Given these two trends, it is perhaps not surprising that Congress was unable to formulate a response to fetal protection policies in the 1980s.

Executive Order 11246

A discussion of anti-discrimination statutes must include not only Title VII and the PDA but Executive Order 11246 as well. While Title VII and the PDA were most often invoked by those who challenged fetal protection policies, the potential impact of this order should not be overlooked. Executive Order 11246 was issued by President Lyndon B. Johnson in 1965. It prohibited federal contractors and subcontractors from discriminating against employees on the basis of race, color, religion, and national origin. The order was amended in 1967 by Executive Order 11375, which barred discrimination on the basis of sex.

Executive Order 11246, as amended, applies to businesses that act as contractors or subcontractors of government work.[61] The Office of Federal Contract Compliance Programs in the Department of Labor has responsibility for enforcing these Executive Orders. The potential reach of the orders is extremely broad; however, like Title VII and the PDA, the Executive Order was not utilized to regulate fetal protection policies in the 1980s.

In summary, there are several federal anti-discrimination statutes and regulations that could have been used to regulate fetal protection policies. Congress formulated a number of statutes barring discrimination in employment, including Title VII of the 1964 Civil Rights Act and the 1978 Pregnancy Discrimination Act. During the last 30 years, however, Congress has shown itself to be reluctant to take action to ensure that the sex provision is fully implemented. Congress has been ambiguous in its formulation of sex and gender provisions and has failed to respond to judicial and administrative actions that undercut Title VII.

Given this poor record, Congress's lackadaisical response to fetal protection policies is perhaps not surprising. The fetal protection issue did not reach Congress's agenda until 1990—more than a decade after these policies had begun to be adjudicated in the federal and state courts. While recent congressional initiatives revealed a willingness to begin to deal with these policies, and, more generally, to deal with the problem of reproductive hazards in the workplace, these efforts may prove to be "too little, too late."

A lack of clarity about how to handle cases involving sex-based differences appears to have impeded the ability of Congress to fully implement Title VII in a number of areas, including fetal protection policies. For example, from the outset, Congress allowed the EEOC to permit state protective laws under the bfog defense. Similarly, a preoccupation with gender roles, particularly, with childbearing, clouded the legislative history of the PDA, making it difficult to determine whether the Congress intended for this Act to bar fetal protection policies.

In addition, the heightened controversy over abortion, which was waged in both the state legislatures and Congress, likely discouraged legislators from taking aggressive action to deal with fetal protection policies. By the middle to the late 1980s, abortion had proven to be a political mine field, with pro-choice legislators being targeted for defeat by anti-abortion and New Right groups. Fetal protection policies appeared to involve many of the same issues that were being hotly debated in the abortion controversy, most significantly, the existence of independent rights for fetuses. It is likely that moderate and liberal legislators, who might otherwise have been strong opponents of these discriminatory policies, hesitated to take action to regulate the policies because they realized the symbolic connection between abortion and fetal protection.

As a result of congressional inactivity, the responsibility for responding to these policies shifted to the administrative agencies and the courts. Unfortunately, the regulatory agencies charged with enforcing Title VII, the PDA, the Executive Orders, and various occupational safety and health regulations were also slow to respond to the proliferation of fetal protection policies. The failure of the agencies charged with administering existing legislation and regulations to deal with these policies in a timely and effective manner made the courts the sole arbiters of these policies. This absolute reliance on the courts became increasingly troubling, as it began to be clear that judges were ignoring settled Title VII caselaw and formulating opinions that were based in large part upon their own conceptions of sex roles.

5. Equality in Employment: The EEOC, the OFCCP, and Fetal Protection Policies

While there are significant similarities between fetal protection policies and state protective laws, most notably their treatment of women as marginal workers, there is at least one important difference. State protective laws were passed in an era when government sanctioned the differential treatment of men and women, an era when women lacked the most fundamental of rights—the right to vote. In contrast, by the time fetal protection policies arrived on the scene, there were federal and state statutes aimed at ensuring equal employment opportunity. Title VII, passed in 1964, prohibited private employers from discriminating against employees or potential employees on the basis of sex. Executive Order 11246 was promulgated in 1965 and amended in 1967, and it placed a similar obligation upon independent contractors employed by the federal government. The Equal Employment Opportunity Commission (EEOC) is charged with enforcing Title VII, and responsibility for enforcing the executive order is lodged with the Office of Federal Contract Compliance Programs (OFCCP), an agency within the Department of Labor. Under the statutory mandates of Title VII and Executive Order 11246, these agencies had the authority and the obligation to regulate fetal protection policies, given the differential impact of the policies on female workers.

Despite the potentially far-reaching scope of these two federal statutes, however, an examination of the activities of these agencies during the 1980s and 1990s reveals that the agencies failed to ensure equal employment opportunity. The EEOC was reluctant to issue interpretative guidelines to assist in disposing of cases arising from fetal protection policies. Perhaps even more egregiously, the EEOC failed to enforce existing Title VII caselaw that should have governed the disposition of many of these cases. Similarly, the OFCCP's handling of fetal protection cases was ineffective. Both agencies lacked a uniform policy governing the disposition of these cases. Moreover, neither was willing to utilize existing caselaw or statutory authority to dispose of the cases.

Much of this analysis focuses upon the response of the EEOC to fetal protection policies, since the potential reach of Title VII is broader than is that of the Executive Order. An examination of the activities of both agencies is nonetheless important because it demonstrates the extent to which those agencies charged with enforcing federal anti-discrimination legislation failed to respond adequately to the proliferation of fetal protection policies in the 1980s. Moreover, this analysis reveals that these administrative agencies operated according to certain assumptions about the roles of the sexes and about women's employment rights.

Equality in Employment: the EEOC and Fetal Protection

The Equal Employment Opportunity Commission was created under section 705 of the 1964 Civil Rights Act. This section granted the EEOC "responsibility for the conduct of litigation" brought under Title VII and outlined in detail the procedural aspects of this responsibility. In 1972, Congress gave the EEOC authority to proceed in the investigation and filing of a charge of unlawful discrimination without the initiation of a suit by an individual plaintiff claiming to be aggrieved. Under this amendment, the scope of the EEOC's authority was significantly broadened.

In the years following, the EEOC has been criticized by both opponents and supporters for its interpretation and lax enforcement of Title VII. Opponents of Title VII have argued that the EEOC has been too creative in its interpretation of Title VII, and that it has broadened the scope of the statute to apply to situations that its drafters had not intended. Conversely, especially during the 1980s and early 1990s, supporters of equal employment opportunity have contended that the agency has failed to enforce the statute effectively and that administrative back-logs thwarted the statute's purposes.[1] As a result of this criticism, a number of congressional investigations were undertaken to examine the EEOC's enforcement activities. In fact, in the late 1980s, the House Committee on Education and Labor undertook an extensive study aimed at determining how the EEOC had been responding to claims arising out of fetal protection policies.

The EEOC is the primary agency responsible for the enforcement of Title VII. It enforces Title VII through both legislative rules, which are those standards established through formal rule-making procedures, and by interpretive rules, which are formulated internally and intended to provide guidance to agency personnel in the disposition of cases. The EEOC could have regulated fetal protection policies by enforcing exist-ing Title VII caselaw or by issuing interpretive rules intended to deal specifically with these policies. Unfortunately, however, it did not utilize either opportunity: it not only failed to implement guidelines to assist in the disposition of these cases, it also ignored settled Title VII caselaw that should have applied to these policies.

Administrative agencies frequently engage in rule-making, and agen-cies like the EEOC often utilize interpretive guidelines to assist in the disposition of certain kinds of cases.[2] In promulgating these guidelines, the agency is not required to fulfill extensive notice and comment re-quirements. Instead, the agency must meet only three procedural re-quirements: it must give prior notice of the interpretive rule, which is often done by publishing the rule in the *Federal Register;* it must provide interested persons with the opportunity to participate in the rule-making through the submission of written comments; and, after having consid-ered these public comments, it must issue a general statement regarding the basis and purposes of the final rules.[3]

The EEOC did attempt to adopt guidelines to assist it in disposing of claims arising from fetal protection policies, but these agency guidelines were often inconsistent with established Title VII caselaw. Moreover, for much of the 1980s, the EEOC functioned without having any interpre-tive guidelines in place with regard to these policies. It was still reluc-tant, even during these years, to utilize settled Title VII caselaw to dispose of these cases, and even later, when it did develop interpretive guidelines, it often disregarded them. As a result, the agency's commitment to Title VII and its ability to deal with novel areas of the law were frequently called into question.

On four occasions, the EEOC formulated interpretive guidelines for its handling of claims arising from fetal protection policies. In 1980, it issued its Interpretive Guidelines on Employment Discrimination and Reproductive Hazards, only to withdraw them quickly in the wake of fierce criticism by employers, civil rights groups, and unions. In 1981, the EEOC amended the section of its Compliance Manual on Charge Investigations that dealt with the bfoq defense to deal with fetal protection policies, but this draft section was also withdrawn. From 1981 through 1988, no guidelines were in place to assist the agency in dealing with claims arising from fetal protection policies. In 1988, the EEOC issued a policy guidance that became part of its Compliance Manual. This section remained in force until 1990, when it issued new policy guidance rules to deal with fetal protection claims.

The various sets of interpretive guidelines reveal that, throughout the period 1981–90, the EEOC believed that claims arising from fetal protection policies should be handled differently than other sex discrimination claims. The guidelines, often in conflict with commission precedent in other areas of employment discrimination law, were adopted specifically to deal with fetal protection policies; they had the effect of carving out a special area for cases involving fetal protection policies. The claims brought to the EEOC were, however, most often left unresolved.

In 1980, the EEOC adopted its Interpretive Guidelines on Employment Discrimination and Reproductive Hazards. According to the preamble, the guidelines were intended to quell "widespread confusion among employers, contractors and the public" as to the applicability of Title VII to fetal protection policies.[4] The guidelines barred employers from adopting policies excluding only one sex from jobs that exposed workers of both sexes to reproductive or fetal hazards. Where a job posed a hazard to the fetus through only maternal or paternal exposure, however, an employer was permitted to adopt a fetal protection policy, provided that the policy was based upon "reputable objective evidence of an essentially scientific nature."[5] These single-sex exclusionary policies were to be considered to constitute per se discrimination. According to the guidelines, the EEOC had to consider a number of factors when assessing the legitimacy of these policies under Title VII. Among these factors were the employer's past record of compliance with applicable occupational safety and health laws, the extent to which the employer had examined other reproductive hazards in the workplace, the employer's past record of employment discrimination, the extent to which the policy was narrowly tailored to affect the least number of workers possible, the effects of the reproductive hazard in question upon other organ systems, and the possibility of utilizing alternatives to the exclusionary policies.[6] Thus, while the EEOC stopped short of prohibiting all fetal protection policies, it did require that employers meet certain standards in adopting these policies.

Under the 1980 guidelines, the Occupational Safety and Health Administration was to play a significant role in evaluating the legitimacy of fetal protection policies. The guidelines required employers to consider engineering controls and protective equipment as alternatives to excluding workers. In addition, the EEOC was required to consider whether the employer in question had been complying with applicable occupational safety and health regulations. The presumption here was that an employer who was not in compliance with the provisions regulating the substance at issue had not considered all available alternatives.[7]

The 1980 guidelines also required the EEOC to defer to OSHA's expertise when the reliability or legitimacy or scientific data was called into question or when it was difficult to draw conclusions about the data.[8] Thus, the guidelines projected a significant role for OSHA in determining the legitimacy of fetal protection policies.[9] By requiring that the EEOC consider employer compliance with occupational safety and health, and by giving OSHA the responsibility for assessing scientific data, the guidelines attempted to create a comprehensive scheme for assessing the legitimacy of exclusionary policies.

In sum, while these guidelines did not bar fetal protection policies, they did place serious constraints upon the adoption of these policies. The guidelines did not, however, treat fetal protection policies as other facially discriminatory policies were treated. While the commission acknowledged that the policies constituted facial discrimination, it contended that the bfoq defense was not the only defense available to the employer. In fact, the guidelines held that the bfoq defense was not applicable to an analysis of fetal protection policies because an employer seeking to defend its policy could never meet the rigorous requirements of the bfoq defense.

The 1980 guidelines were fiercely criticized by employers, civil rights groups, and unions. For this reason, the guidelines were withdrawn just before the Carter Administration left office. In its statement of withdrawal, the EEOC stated that on the basis of the extensive comments it had received in response to the guidelines, it had concluded that claims arising out of fetal protection policies should be resolved on a case-by-case basis.[10] It asserted that this was more appropriate than relying upon interpretive guidelines.

After it withdrew its guidelines, the EEOC drafted a supplement to its 1981 Compliance Manual which provided the field offices with instructions for investigating charges involving fetal protection policies. This draft provided information on known or suspected fetal health hazards and types of fetal protection policies. In addition, the draft section outlined those factors that were relevant to the disposition of claims involving these policies. As in the 1980 guidelines, the commission stated that the bfoq defense was inapplicable to fetal protection cases and suggested that the business necessity defense might be of greater utility in evaluating the policies.[11]

In addition, the supplement suggested that the EEOC obtain assistance from other agencies, namely OSHA, in evaluating the scientific data relevant to a claim. This draft section was withdrawn after OSHA indicated that budget and personnel cuts rendered it unable to assist the EEOC in evaluating data.[12] From 1981 through 1988, there were no interpretive guidelines in place for assisting agency personnel in disposing of fetal protection cases. During these years, the EEOC instructed its field offices to forward all claims arising out of fetal protection cases to the Guidance Division of the Office of Legal Counsel. Unfortunately, however, claims forwarded to the Office of Legal Counsel remained stagnant, with the EEOC resolving very few of them.

In 1988, the EEOC issued its Policy Statement on Reproductive and Fetal Hazards Under Title VII. This statement was intended to provide guidance to agency staff in the disposition of fetal protection cases. In evaluating the legality of a fetal protection policy, the commission was required to apply the following test: first, it was to determine whether exposure to workplace toxins subjected the offspring of workers to a substantial risk of harm; second, it was to assess whether this harm was transmitted to employees of only one sex; and third, it was to determine whether the fetal protection policy effectively eliminated this risk of harm.[13] In addition, a number of other factors were to be considered in assessing whether a policy violated Title VII. Among these were the nature of the hazard, the conclusiveness of the scientific evidence relied upon by the employer, possible alternative measures, the over- or under-inclusiveness of the policy, the employer's history of compliance with federal, state, and local occupational safety and health laws, the applicability of existing collective bargaining agreements, and the extent to which the employees were informed of workplace hazards.[14]

Like the 1980 guidelines, the 1988 Policy Statement established that the business necessity defense, rather than the bfoq exception, should be used in fetal protection cases. Business necessity is a much less rigorous proof framework than is the bfoq exception. Employers seeking to justify a fetal protection policy on the basis of business necessity would have a much easier time than if they were required to establish a bfoq.

The 1988 Policy Statement implicitly recognized that these policies were facially discriminatory; however, it contended that the bfoq defense was inapplicable. In its Statement, the EEOC asserted that:

> [The] bfoq is not generally applicable in fetal protection cases bescause it is a narrow exception which applies only in a situation where all or substantially all members of a protected class are actually unable to perform the duties of the job in question . . . *These cases do not fit neatly into the traditional Title VII analytical framework and, therefore, must be regarded as a class unto themselves.*[15] (emphasis added)

As it had in the 1980 guidelines, the EEOC distinguished fetal protection cases from other cases of overt discrimination. In doing this, it not only endorsed the holdings of the appellate courts in *Hayes v. Shelby Memorial Hospital*[16] and *Wright v. Olin Corporation*,[17] it also contended that this approach should be utilized throughout the country.

This aspect of the guidelines was troubling to many advocates of equal employment opportunity. Perhaps even more disturbing, however, was the EEOC's treatment of risk evaluation and scientific data. Under the new guidelines, in cases where there was inconclusive evidence about the effects of workplace hazards upon male workers, the commission was to proceed as if the occupational hazard was "substantially confined to female employees."[18] This conclusion was to be made even where the inconclusive evidence was due to a paucity of research about male-mediated effects. As one commentator has noted, the new guidelines permitted an employer "to exclude women from the workplace where there was some evidence of fetal health risk through maternal exposure, but no research as to risk through paternal exposure."[19] As a result, the 1988 Policy Statement operated as a significant disincentive to employer-sponsored research on paternally transmitted risks.[20]

Worker and civil rights groups also criticized the statement's definition of less discriminatory alternatives. Under the new guidelines, the reasonableness of an alternative was to be determined "on a case-by-case basis, considering such factors as efficiency and cost in relation to the size and profitability of the business."[21] Many analysts believed that this definition allowed the employer far too much flexibility and, in effect, enabled the employer to ignore the requirement. Moreover, these analysts contended that the definition conflicted with Title VII caselaw on less discriminatory alternatives. In prior cases, the employer had not been permitted to justify its discriminatory practice simply because alternative measures were more expensive. In fact, the legislative history of the Pregnancy Discrimination Act suggests that Congress intended that sex discrimination was to be eliminated regardless of the "very high" costs that would be imposed upon employers.

Like the 1980 guidelines, the 1988 Policy Statement envisioned that OSHA would play a role in the evaluation of fetal protection policies. This role, however, was far less extensive than it had been under the earlier guidelines. While the 1980 guidelines anticipated that OSHA and the EEOC would work closely in assessing scientific data, the 1988 guidelines stated that the EEOC would rely upon the expertise of OSHA "whenever possible."[22] Similarly, the guidelines stated that the EEOC would defer to OSHA's determinations as to occupational hazards "where possible."[23] In spite of OSHA's greater expertise in this area, the EEOC was not to be bound by OSHA determinations about workplace hazards.

Worker and civil rights groups sharply denounced the 1988 Policy Statement. These groups argued that by evaluating fetal protection policies under the less rigorous disparate impact/business necessity framework, the new guidelines contradicted settled Title VII caselaw. In addition, opponents contended that the guidelines were too deferential to employers: they allowed employers to adopt exclusionary policies even where the evidence was inconclusive as to male-transmitted hazards, and they effectively exempted employers from having to demonstrate that less discriminatory alternatives could not be used.

While the EEOC stated that excluding all women of childbearing capacity was "probably overinclusive,"[24] it allowed employers to adopt policies where they could be justified "by reputable objective evidence of an essentially scientific nature."[25] In reality, however, the guidelines undercut existing risk assessment criteria by allowing employers to evade responsibility for researching paternally transmitted fetal hazards, and, in so doing, encouraged employers to exclude women as a means of cleaning up the workplace. Thus, these guidelines undermined not only equal employment opportunity but occupational safety and health as well.

The 1988 guidelines were short lived. In 1990, soon after the Seventh Circuit's decision in *U.A.W. v. Johnson Controls*,[26] the EEOC issued another policy guidance advising its field offices about how to dispose of fetal protection cases. The statement extensively reviewed, and at times openly criticized, the *Johnson Controls* decision. In the new policy guidance, the EEOC for the first time rejected the use of the business necessity framework in fetal protection cases. It also formulated a new legal framework for analyzing these cases.

In explaining the shift in its approach to fetal protection policies, the EEOC contended that at the time it formulated the 1988 Policy Guidance, which endorsed the use of the business necessity approach, it had not anticipated the Supreme Court's 1989 decision in *Wards Cove Packing Co., Inc. v. Atonio*.[27] *Wards Cove* placed the burden of disproving the business necessity defense on the plaintiff. As a result of this decision, the EEOC contended that it had become "convinced that the hybrid approach to fetal protection cases [was] problematic."[28] The commission contended that the bfoq approach was more appropriate for assessing fetal protection cases.

After establishing that the bfoq defense was to be utilized in fetal protection cases, the policy guidance went on at length to describe the framework to be utilized in these cases. To prove that a fetal protection policy fell within the bfoq exception, an employer had to meet four criteria: first, s/he had to prove that there was a substantial risk of harm to the offspring of his or her workers through the workplace exposure of one sex; second, s/he had to show that only one sex was susceptible to these risks; third, s/he had to demonstrate that the policy minimized the risk of fetal harm while excluding the smallest possible group of employees; and fourth, s/he had to prove that there were no equally effective alternatives that would impose a less onerous burden upon the excluded group.[29]

The 1990 Policy Guidance rejected the business necessity approach, but it did not bar fetal protection policies. It simply stated that the proof framework to be employed in these cases was to be more rigorous. Moreover, the commission stated that, in adopting a fetal protection policy, an employer could appropriately consider the potential harm to third parties from workplace exposure.[30] Thus, in establishing a bfoq, an employer was permitted to consider what effect maternal exposure to occupational toxins would have upon fetal health.

In criticizing the Seventh Circuit's opinion, the EEOC focused upon the court's treatment of scientific data and on the court's disregard for previous findings by OSHA. The Policy Guidance asserted that in assessing fetal protection policies, agencies like the EEOC should defer to those agencies with appropriate expertise in this area, such as OSHA or the Environmental Protection Agency.[31] The EEOC contended that the Seventh Circuit did not accord sufficient deference to OSHA determinations about the effects of lead upon both male and female workers.[32]

For these reasons, the Policy Guidance instructed the field offices to disregard the Seventh Circuit's opinion in *Johnson Controls*.[33] Field offices were told to view fetal protection policies as facially discriminatory and to impose the more rigorous bfoq requirement. Strangely, field offices were also instructed to continue to use the 1988 Policy Guidance in disposing of fetal protection claims. In fact, the EEOC stated that the new guidelines modified only two aspects of the 1988 Policy Guidance. First, the disparate treatment/bfoq approach was to be used in evaluating fetal protection cases. To prove a bfoq, the employer had to establish the following criteria: (a) the exclusion is necessary to the normal operation of the business; (b) there is evidence that the continued exposure of the effected group will create substantial risk to third parties; and (c) there are no less discriminatory alternatives that would serve the employer's purpose.[34]

The second aspect of the 1988 Policy Guidance that was modified by the new guidelines related to the sufficiency of scientific data. One element of the 1988 Guidance that had prompted substantial criticism was the EEOC's determination that in cases where there was inconclusive evidence of male transmission, it was to be assumed that the harm to a fetus was solely through maternal exposure. In an extensive footnote, the 1990 Guidance appears to have rejected this prior conclusion. In this instance, the EEOC contended that the provision was intended to refer to "situations in which evidence of risk to men was speculative and meager."[35] Moreover, the commission asserted that "where there was reliable—albeit inconclusive—evidence of harm [to the fetus] mediated through the male, [it would] conclude that the exclusion of women [was] not justified."[36] Thus, the EEOC attempted to modify its approach to dealing with issues involving scientific data.

In spite of the fact that the EEOC advised its field offices to continue to follow the 1988 Policy Guidance, as modified by the 1990 Guidance, there are significant differences in the two sets of guidelines. In its 1990 Guidance, the EEOC adopted the reasoning of Circuit Judge Easterbrook, who dissented in the *Johnson Controls* case. Citing Easterbrook's opinion, the Guidance instructed the commission to weigh the extent of the risk to fetal health against the breadth of the exclusion in fetal protection cases. The commission concluded:

> [W]here the risk is slight, in terms of the numbers and the nature of the harm, any exclusion will be hard to justify; conversely, severe harm to a high percentage of those excluded may warrant a broader exclusion.[37]

For an employer to justify its exclusionary policy it had to demonstrate that maternal exposure to workplace hazards posed a substantial risk of harm to a fetus.

Moreover, even where the risk of harm is through maternal transmission and not paternal transmission, an exclusionary policy like that adopted by Johnson Controls could seldom be justified. According to the EEOC, a policy that excluded all women of childbearing capacity "is not necessary to protect the offspring—rather it is a matter of convenience."[38] The Guidance pointed out that the exclusionary policy at issue in *Johnson Controls* was not necessary to protect fetal health, since the employer could have utilized blood tests to determine whether women in high-risk areas had unsafe blood-lead levels.[39]

Although the EEOC intended the 1990 Policy Guidance to modify, rather than replace, the 1988 Guidance, the new guidelines invalidated the earlier ones. While most commentators admit that the 1990 Guidance constituted a significant improvement in the commission's approach to fetal protection claims, many continued to be dissatisfied with the guidelines. Critics of the 1990 guidelines asserted that the new guidelines had not been sufficiently thought out and that the EEOC had failed to make a comprehensive assessment of the relationship between Title VII and fetal protection policies. In addition, they contended that the Guidance was analytically incomplete, since it did not discuss the relationship between the Pregnancy Discrimination Act and the bfoq requirement. Moreover, critics of the guidelines claimed that the Guidance was at odds with existing Title VII caselaw governing the bfoq exception. These individuals argued that the EEOC's application of the "safety" exception had substantially broadened the bfoq provision beyond what had been mandated by courts interpreting Title VII.

Thus, even though the 1990 Policy Guidance was seen by many worker and civil rights groups as a sign that the commission was beginning to move in the right direction in handling fetal protection cases, many remained dissatisfied with its approach. Moreover, the U.S. Supreme Court's 1991 decision in *U.A.W. v. Johnson Controls* effectively nullified the 1988 and 1990 Policy Guidances, since the Supreme Court's decision effectively barred the use of fetal protection policies. Thus, the 1988 and 1990 Guidances, which laid out the framework for evaluating fetal protection policies under Title VII, are not only superfluous, they are violative of Title VII.[40]

Thus, throughout the 1980s and early 1990s, the EEOC's policy guidelines provided little guidance to employers, workers, unions, or other governmental agencies evaluating the legality of fetal protection policies under Title VII. From 1981 through 1988, no guidelines were in place to evaluate these policies, and field offices were simply instructed to forward all fetal protection claims to the Office of Legal Counsel. When guidelines were issued, they often contradicted settled employment discrimination law and granted undue deference to employers. As a result, the commission's policy on fetal protection cases remained unclear through most of this period.

This lack of clarity about how the EEOC should handle fetal protection cases carried over into its enforcement activities. In early 1990, the majority staff of the House Committee on Education and Labor conducted an extensive study of the EEOC's disposition of fetal protection claims during the 1980s. The study, titled "A Report on the Equal Employment Opportunity Commission, Title VII and Workplace Fetal Protection Policies in the 1980s," examined the approximately 100 charges brought before the commission challenging employer fetal protection policies.[41] The report found that over half of these claims challenged an employer policy that was discriminatory on its face. Despite the fact that existing caselaw on disparate treatment governed the disposition of these claims, the field offices were instructed to forward the claims to the Office of Legal Counsel. According to the report, the Office then did little to resolve these claims.

According to the House report, the EEOC warehoused nearly all the fetal protection cases filed with it in the late 1970s and 1980s. During this time, it failed to take any action to resolve these cases. Even after the 1988 Policy Guidance was issued, which provided the field offices with a framework for evaluating fetal protection cases, most of the existing cases were "resolved" for procedural, rather than substantive, reasons. For example, a number of cases were dismissed because the commission was unable to locate the charging party. There is no record of any fetal protection cases having been decided on its merits.[42]

On the basis of these findings, the House report concluded that the EEOC's handling of fetal protection cases throughout the late 1970s and 1980s demonstrated "an alarming administrative paralysis."[43] Despite the fact that many of these cases could have been resolved in a timely manner on the basis of existing precedent, the EEOC separated the cases from other comparable claims, and failed to dispose of them in an appropriate manner. For example, in the early 1970s, the EEOC had decided a number of cases involving sex discrimination against pregnant X-ray technicians. In these cases, the employer had discharged the women upon being notified that they were pregnant. The employers contended that they had fired the women out of a concern about the effects of radiation exposure upon fetal health. As early as 1974, the EEOC rejected this defense, finding that the discharge had constituted unlawful sex discrimination.[44] Despite this precedent, however, it continued to treat fetal protection claims filed in the late 1970s and 1980s as "Non-Commission Precedent Decisions," stating that the issue presented a novel legal issue without commission precedent.[45]

The commission contended that it was unable to resolve these claims because there was no policy directive in place for most of the 1980s. In its report, the majority staff rejected this reasoning, arguing that even if the fetal protection claims filed in the 1980s had presented a novel legal issue, the commission was not absolved from its responsibility for dealing with this issue. Pointing out that the commission had withdrawn the 1980 Policy Guidance because it decided that fetal protection claims should be decided on a case-by-case basis, the report concluded that the EEOC's rationale for its failure to dispose of these claims throughout the 1980s was ironic.[46] According to the report, the EEOC "could not issue a policy because it preferred to resolve charges on a case-by-case basis, but it could not resolve any charges in the absence of such a policy."[47] The House report argued that this circular reasoning could not justify the commission's failure to adequately dispose of these claims.

In its written response to the House report, the EEOC attempted to justify its inaction by arguing that it did not have the scientific expertise to deal with the fetal protection claims brought before it in the late 1970s and 1980s. The commission argued that it lacked the funding and expertise to conduct research, and that it did not have the authority to require employers to conduct such research. The existence of serious questions about the reliability and validity of scientific data thus rendered it unable to dispose of the cases before it.[48] The commission argued that attempts to remedy this lack of scientific expertise through a cooperative arrangement with the Occupational Safety and Health Administration were thwarted by OSHA budgetary cuts.[49] Moreover, the commission pointed out that even those agencies with the expertise to assess the reliability of scientific data had been unable to formulate a comprehensive plan to deal with fetal protection policies.[50]

This rationale may seem to have some merit, but it is flawed at its core. At least forty of the claims involved maternal exposure to lead, for which OSHA had developed a standard by the late 1970s. In this standard, OSHA expressly stated that exposure to lead could harm a fetus through either maternal or paternal transmission. Thus, the EEOC's rationale for warehousing those cases involving lead exposure, i.e., that it lacked the expertise to assess whether the exclusion of only women was appropriate, was without basis. Since OSHA had already determined that excluding women, but not men, from high-exposure lead areas did not shield fetuses from harm, the EEOC had the scientific data necessary to find the employer guilty of sex discrimination.[51]

Even after the EEOC issued its 1988 Policy Guidance, which was intended to provide the framework for evaluating fetal protection policies, the commission was lax in disposing of these cases. Moreover, the Supreme Court's decision in *U.A.W. v. Johnson Controls* has not settled the issue of how the EEOC will deal with both pending and future fetal protection claims. Six months after *Johnson Controls,* there was still no record of any fetal protection claims having been filed. The individuals interviewed indicated that they were unsure as to how these cases would be resolved in the absence of some new policy guidance.[52] Even more troubling, it is unclear whether fetal protection claims will be disposed of in a more timely and effective manner in the future.

By the time *U.A.W. v. Johnson Controls* reached the Seventh Circuit in 1989, there were signs that the agency might be taking a more active role in the debate about fetal protection policies. The EEOC attempted to get the Department of Justice to file an amicus curiae brief in the appellate litigation, but Bradford Reynolds, head of the Civil Rights Division at the Department of Justice, steadfastly opposed such a filing. When the DOJ did consider filing a brief, it was on the side of the employer, and in April 1988, Assistant Attorney General Bradford Reynolds recommended that the Department of Justice file a brief in support of Johnson Controls in its litigation in the Seventh Circuit.[53] Ultimately, the DOJ did not file a brief in this litigation because of the split that was emerging between itself and the EEOC over the issue of fetal protection. The DOJ argued that fetal protection policies could be legitimated under the more rigorous bfoq defense while the EEOC contended that the policies could not be validated under bfoq.[54] While the EEOC was able to convince the DOJ not to file a brief in support of the employer in the appellate litigation, the EEOC itself did not file in this litigation.[55]

In spite of its inaction at the federal district and appellate levels, the EEOC did convince the Department of Justice to file an amicus brief with the Supreme Court in the *Johnson Controls* litigation. While it is impossible to be certain about why the EEOC filed in this case, and why the DOJ changed its mind and decided to file in support of the union, a number of key factors likely came into play in these decisions. First, many within the EEOC viewed the Seventh Circuit as having wrongly decided the *Johnson Controls* case. Moreover, the dissenting opinions by Judges Posner and Cudahy, both of whom were Reagan appointees, prompted many within the administration to reconsider the EEOC's stance on fetal protection policies.[56]

Second, it appears that personnel changes within both the EEOC and the DOJ made it possible for an agreement to be forged between the two agencies. It must be noted, however, that the original brief drafted by the EEOC was substantially different than that which was eventually adopted. In the original draft, the EEOC contended that an employer attempting to defend his fetal protection policy on the basis of a bfoq would be required to demonstrate that he had taken equally stringent measures to protect all workers. If he or she was unable to prove that such measures had been taken, it would be assumed that the fetal protection policy was merely a pretext for unlawful sex discrimination. The Department of Justice apparently did not perceive this to be the correct interpretation of the bfoq provision, and this aspect of the brief was deleted.[57]

A third reason that the EEOC and DOJ filed an amicus brief in the Supreme Court litigation stems from the fact that the brief itself was drafted in such a way that it encouraged the Court merely to remand the case to the appellate court. By remanding the case, it was believed that the Court would sidestep the larger substantive legal questions and focus instead upon procedural issues. It is likely that the DOJ believed that a remand of the case back to the Seventh Circuit would result in a decision for the employer.[58]

In addition to filing an amicus curiae brief with the Supreme Court in the *Johnson Controls* litigation, in late 1989 to early 1990, the EEOC appears to have begun to reevaluate its stance towards fetal protection policies. In *Johnson Controls v. State of California,* the EEOC found that the fetal protection policy in place in a Johnson Controls plant in Fullerton, California, violated Title VII. It was in this case that the EEOC first contended that employers needed to legitimate their fetal protection policies under the more rigorous bfoq framework, rather than under business necessity.[59]

In summary, during the late 1970s and 1980s, the EEOC was slow to issue guidelines for dealing with fetal protection policies and lax in its enforcement of existing Title VII caselaw on sex discrimination. Perhaps even more significant, the EEOC policy directives promulgated during these years instructed regional offices to treat fetal protection policies differently than other facially discriminatory policies or practices. The 1980 and 1988 Policy Guidances and the 1981 Policy Directive stated that fetal protection policies were not to be treated like other facially discriminatory policies, and that the business necessity defense, rather than the rigorous bfoq defense, could be used by employers in defending against sex discrimination claims. Even the 1990 Policy Guidance, issued in the wake of the Supreme Court's decision barring fetal protection policies under Title VII, allowed employers to utilize these policies in certain, limited situations. In formulating its policy, the 1990 Policy Guidance allowed employers to consider the effects that maternal exposure to occupational toxins would have upon fetal health.

By treating women differently than other protected classes, solely on the basis of their procreative capacity, these Policy Guidances sent a clear message about the EEOC's lack of commitment to gender equality. Moreover, by refusing to enforce existing caselaw and statutory law, the EEOC made clear its position that women's employment rights could be sacrificed wherever childbearing was at issue. The EEOC's policy during these years derived from the assumption that men and women were fundamentally different, solely because of their reproductive roles, and, for this reason, could be treated differently.

While the EEOC appears to have begun to take an more active role in the debate about fetal protection policies by filing an amicus curiae brief with the Supreme Court in the *Johnson Controls* litigation, and by utilizing its 1990 Policy Guidance in at least one case, it is unclear whether the commission will continue to be active in this area. Agency personnel indicated that the EEOC would take a more aggressive stance in disposing of fetal protection cases in the future. For example, one individual stated that the EEOC would seek to assume a leadership role in the formulation of a comprehensive policy to deal with reproductive hazards in the workplace.[60]

The continued uncertainty about the EEOC's stance on fetal protection policies is made worse by the fact that the agency has not taken any action, in either the policy formulation or enforcement areas, since the Supreme Court decided *Johnson Controls.* There are no agency guidelines in effect, since the Supreme Court's decision has nullified the 1988 and 1990 Policy Guidances. Similarly, it appears that the EEOC has not disposed of any fetal protection claims in the first 18 months since the case was decided. It remains to be seen whether it will become more active in either formulating new guidelines or implementing the Supreme Court's decision on fetal protection policies.

The OFCCP, Independent Contractors, and Sex Discrimination

Executive Order 11246 functions as a complement to Title VII: it specifically applies to private employers who contract or subcontract work for the federal government, providing a comprehensive enforcement network for eliminating employment discrimination in government contracting. The potential reach of the order is substantial: federal contractors and subcontractors employ more than 30 million workers, and the contracts themselves are valued at over $167 billion. Where the OFCCP finds that a contractor or subcontractor has violated the order, it may take a number of actions: the OFCCP may order the partial or total revocation or suspension of the federal contract; it may declare contractors ineligible for future government contract work; it may order the contracted to pay damages in back pay; or it may order the imposition of retroactive seniority.[61]

Invoking sanctions against an employer is often viewed as a last step in the agency's enforcement process. In fact, most cases are settled through conciliation, with the contractor agreeing to halt the discriminatory practices and pay damages in the form of back pay.[62] Where conciliation fails, the agency may invoke more severe penalties. In sex discrimination cases that are not settled through conciliation, those remedies that were most frequently proposed were the total cancellation of contracts and the declaration of a contractor's ineligibility for further government contract work.[63]

Executive Order 11246 has not been enforced as rigorously as it might have been, however. In part because of this, it is often overlooked in discussions about governmental activity in the area of equal employment opportunity. The order clearly could have been used to regulate fetal protection policies, throughout the 1980s and early 1990s, however, the OFCCP was extremely reluctant to take action against employers adopting these policies. In fact, throughout this period, the OFCCP contended that the EEOC was the lead agency in this area, and that it was obliged to follow Title VII principles in these cases.

Like the EEOC, the OFCCP had responsibility for responding to the state protective legislation of the early 1900s. Both agencies issued guidelines for the disposition of cases arising from protective laws, and, more significantly, both waffled on the question of whether the laws were permissible. The OFCCP's stance on state protective laws was unclear in the 1960s, but, by the middle to the late 1970s, it had moved to bar contractors and subcontractors from using these laws to justify their discrimination against women. Section 60-20.3 of the agency's guidelines holds that:

> An employer must not deny a female employee the right to any job that she is qualified to perform in reliance upon a State "protective" law . . . Such legislation was intended to be beneficial, but, instead, has been found to result in restricting employment opportunities for men and/or women. Accordingly, it cannot be used as a basis for denying employment or establishing sex as a bfoq for the job.

The OFCCP has vigorously enforced this order: it does not permit contractors to justify their discriminatory policies by relying on state protective laws. One agency employee stated that there have been many cases in which "contractors were found to have excluded women from jobs in reliance upon protective laws."[64] These cases have most often been resolved through conciliation, with the contractor agreeing to open the jobs to women.[65]

The agency's policy on state protective legislation has been quite effective. By the late 1970s, no contractor or subcontractor attempted to justify its exclusion of women on the basis of its reliance upon a state protective law. Since this time, the OFCCP's attention has shifted to cases "involving independent employer practices, rather than state sanctioned ones."[66] The first wave of cases involved contractors who explicitly excluded women from certain job categories. For example, in the late 1970s, the OFCCP revoked the government's contract with Uniroyal, Inc., which explicitly classified blue-collar jobs as either "male" or "female."

Unlike this earlier group of cases, which involved relatively clear-cut cases of sex segregation, most of the claims adjudicated by the OFCCP in the middle to the late 1980s have involved informal employer practices. One OFCCP official related the outcome of a recent case that the agency settled against Precision Cast Parts of Portland, Oregon. In this case, the employer had steered women into traditionally "female" blue collar departments that paid less and provided little opportunity for transfer into traditionally "male" jobs.[67] In its settlement, the OFCCP levied a $3.1 million penalty against the employer in damages for back pay.

Despite the spectacular awards sometimes granted to plaintiffs, it appears that the number of administrative complaints issued by the OFCCP against employers for unlawful sex discrimination is relatively small.[68] Again, an administrative complaint is the last step in the OFCCP's enforcement process. One OFCCP staffer indicated that many cases are resolved before reaching this point, with a full remedy, i.e., back pay and a new job offer.[69] OFCCP officials would not provide any other information on the disposition of claims disposed of prior to issuance of an administrative complaint. For this reason, it is impossible to assess the effectiveness of the agency's enforcement efforts in sex discrimination cases.

Similarly, interviews with agency personnel failed to reveal the extent to which the agency has attempted to deal with fetal protection policies. In a letter from the OFCCP, the director of the Policy, Planning, and Program Development Division wrote the following:

> While the OFCCP views the burden of proof to be on an employer to show that sex is a bona fide occupational qualification for any job from which it excludes women—for any reason, including a fetal protection policy—the applicability of a BFOQ standard to such policies and what it takes to meet that standard for such policies are among the matters at issue in the *Johnson Controls* case.[70]

Thus, the agency admitted that it had not taken action on this issue and, perhaps more significantly, that it would not take action until after the Supreme Court issued its holding in *Johnson Controls*. Moreover, the scope of the OFCCP's bona fide occupational qualification provision mirrors that of the EEOC, since the OFCCP Compliance Manual states that "the OFCCP follows Title VII principles when determining whether a policy excluding women from a job because of a concern about reproductive hazards is discriminatory."[71]

Prior to May 1990, the OFCCP did not distinguish fetal protection policies from other sex segregation cases. As a result, no record was kept of how these cases had been handled. In May 1990, the OFCCP designated these cases as raising "novel issues," and directed that they be sent to the OFCCP National Office for referral to the National Solicitor's Office.[72] Since 1990, there have apparently been no cases brought before the agency involving fetal protection policies. Since the Supreme Court decided *Johnson Controls* in March 1991, there has been little activity in the OFCCP aimed at amending the Compliance Manual to reflect the Court's ruling. As a result, the agency is operating without any internal guidance as to how to dispose of cases involving fetal protection policies. It appears that agency officials intend to deal with any cases that might arise on a purely ad hoc basis.

The lack of available data on the OFCCP's enforcement activities makes it impossible to assess the agency's response to these policies. As has been noted, even in the larger category of sex discrimination, the agency contends that it does not keep a record of how many cases are handled through the grievance and conciliation procedures. Given the small number of cases for which the OFCCP issues an administrative complaint, however, this number is also likely to be small. There is no record that the OFCCP has handled any fetal protection cases, either before or after the Supreme Court's decision in *Johnson Controls*. Similarly, the OFCCP has failed to formulate guidelines for dealing with employers who have adopted fetal protection policies. Like the EEOC, the OFCCP appears to have adopted a "wait and see" attitude about disposing of these cases.

Conclusions

An examination of the response of the EEOC and the OFCCP to employer fetal protection policies reveals a troubling lethargy in both agencies. The EEOC, the lead agency charged with enforcing Title VII, failed to adopt a coherent strategy for disposing of fetal protection cases that came before it in the late 1970s and throughout the 1980s. The agency's stance on these policies flip-flopped throughout these years, as it adopted policy guidances that conflicted with established sex discrimination caselaw. Similarly, the OFCCP failed to establish a policy for dealing with federal contractors and subcontractors who adopted fetal protection policies. The OFCCP Compliance Manual stated only that it was following EEOC precedent in this area. The difficulty, once again, was that EEOC's stance on these policies was unclear.

Furthermore, in disposing of these cases, neither agency fulfilled its mandate of ensuring equal employment opportunity. Even where case-law existed that should have determined the outcome of many cases, the agencies failed to enforce this law. Instead, claims brought before the agencies were largely ignored. The EEOC warehoused over one hundred fetal protection claims brought before it in the late 1970s and 1980s, and many of these cases remain unresolved today. Moreover, recent attempts to close these cases have focused upon the procedural, rather than the substantive, aspects of the cases.

While the EEOC warehoused fetal protection cases, separating them from other sex discrimination cases that raised similar issues, the OFCCP failed to distinguish these cases in any way. As a result, it is impossible to determine how many fetal protection cases were brought before the OFCCP in the 1980s, or how these cases were handled. The effectiveness of the OFCCP in combatting gender discrimination is also uncertain because the agency prefers to process grievances through informal rather than formal channels. There does not appear to be any public accounting of these informal grievance and conciliation procedures.

The evidence strongly suggests that neither the EEOC nor the OFCCP vigorously responded to the proliferation of fetal protection policies in the 1980s. In fact, the EEOC was openly hostile to claims challenging these policies. The agency separated these from other cases involving facial discrimination, preferring to treat fetal protection cases as if these raised some novel issue of law. Similarly, the OFCCP failed to adopt its own strategy for handling these cases and instead relied upon the EEOC's non-policy. In the wake of the Supreme Court's decision in *Johnson Controls,* it is as yet unclear whether the EEOC and the OFCCP will develop a comprehensive plan for handling fetal protection policies. Personnel from both agencies contend that, since the Supreme Court's decision, there have been no claims filed challenging any of these policies. In the absence of new policy guidances, it is impossible to predict how the agencies will deal with fetal protection claims in the future.

The inaction of the EEOC and the OFCCP may be explained in a number of ways. Perhaps most significantly, these agencies, particularly the EEOC, are extremely sensitive to changes in the political climate of the nation. The policy orientation of agencies like the EEOC is often dependent upon that conception of civil rights and civil liberties embraced by the administration in office. When the Carter Administration was in office, the EEOC, like many government agencies, took a more active stance in dealing with discrimination. During these years, the agency attempted to utilize more innovative means for eliminating employment discrimination. For example, the chairperson of the EEOC during most of these years, Eleanor Holmes Norton, publicly embraced the concept of comparable worth as a means of eradicating pay disparity. After Ronald Reagan took office, the EEOC abandoned its attempts to construct a system of comparable worth. The new chairperson of the EEOC, Clarence Thomas, publicly derided the concept of comparable worth, and, in 1985, the EEOC explicitly rejected the concept of comparable worth as the basis for a claim of employment discrimination.[73]

Clarence Thomas, who served as chairperson of the EEOC through much of the 1980s, showed himself to be ambivalent, if not downright hostile, to gender discrimination claims like those that came to the commission as a result of employer fetal protection policies. In part, this hostility may have been an outgrowth of Thomas's own experiences. From 1977 to 1979, Clarence Thomas served as an attorney for Monsanto Corporation, one of the Fortune 500 companies that adopted a fetal protection policy, and as a result of this experience, he may have been sympathetic to employer rationales about these policies.[74]

Thomas's overall approach to employment discrimination also likely had an impact on his approach to fetal protection policies. Under his stewardship, the EEOC's backlog of cases increased significantly, in large part because the agency undertook full investigation of individual cases. In addition, the agency shifted its focus from pattern and practice cases, which typically involved systemic claims like those at issue in the fetal protection debate, to individual cases.[75]

Even more alarmingly, Thomas stated publicly that "[t]here are limits to the usefulness of litigation, and in my view strict reliance on litigation in civil rights enforcement is neither good policy nor permitted by statute."[76] Furthermore, Thomas asserted that "discrimination does not explain *all* the problems of minorities, women, or anyone else."[77] Thomas also contended that the EEOC had "no interest in unfairly attacking employers," but was responsible instead for "defending the rights of all individuals in this society."[78]

As a judge on the Circuit Court for the District of Columbia, Thomas demonstrated the same thinly veiled hostility to women's rights as he had shown as Chair of the EEOC. In a case involving the Federal Communication Commission's "enhancement" of a woman's application for a radio station license, Thomas strongly suggested that the FCC's policy of promoting diversity would not be met by expanding the number of female license holders.[79] Given Thomas's approach to systemic claims and gender discrimination, perhaps it should not have been expected that the EEOC would vigorously attack employer fetal protection policies.

While the OFCCP, a division of the Department of Labor, is usually regarded as less susceptible to policy shifts than is the EEOC, it, too, was influenced by changes in executive leadership. Most significant, the agency's approach to affirmative action shifted abruptly after Ronald Reagan became president. Prior to 1982, the OFCCP had vigorously implemented affirmative action regulations. In fact, prior to the Reagan Administration, affirmative action traditionally enjoyed the nonpartisan support of the executive branch.[80] In 1983, however, the OFCCP issued a proposal that would have made affirmative action requirements much less stringent.[81] This proposal was withdrawn after fierce criticism by Democrats, unions, and civil rights and worker rights groups; however, the agency's commitment to affirmative action goals remains clearly in question. Throughout the 1980s, the OFCCP shelved many affirmative action cases, and administrative delay appears to have accomplished what the agency was unable to achieve through legislative changes.[82]

Thus, neither the EEOC nor the OFCCP demonstrated a firm commitment to equal employment opportunity during the 1980s.[83] An examination of the response of these two agencies to the proliferation of fetal protection policies reveals that they were indifferent and, at times, hostile to worker rights during this period. The hostility of the Reagan and Bush Administrations to claims challenging fetal protection policies may be explained in a number of ways. The most innocuous explanation is that the administrations, concerned with reducing governmental spending, simply did not comprehend the repercussions of agency cutbacks that made it impossible for personnel to dispose of these cases effectively. The more sinister explanation is that the administrations were hostile to the principle of gender equality in employment and saw these policies as a means of limiting women's work-force participation. As has been seen, the EEOC's Policy Guidances and enforcement record indicate that the agency intended to treat women differently where their procreative capacity was at issue. While this more sinister explanation does explain much of the EEOC's inactivity in this area, it likely overestimates the ability of the Executive to conceive of, and carry out, such a comprehensive plan aimed at undermining women's rights.

A more likely cause of this inactivity is that neither the Reagan nor the Bush Administrations had a firm commitment to equal employment opportunity and, as a result, did not provide the EEOC or the OFCCP with the resources or the incentive to develop a comprehensive policy for dealing with fetal protection cases. Moreover, the ability of proponents of these policies to manipulate cultural images of motherhood and pregnancy likely had an impact on the Executive's desire to correct this agency inactivity. The obvious connection between fetal protection policies and the abortion debate may have made the Reagan and Bush Administrations even more ambivalent about pressuring the agencies to develop such a plan. The open hostility of both administrations to the *Roe v. Wade* decision makes plausible the suggestion that these administrations may have supported fetal protection policies as a means of safeguarding fetal health.

In fact, the subtle balancing of fetal rights and women's rights that was so apparent in the abortion debate throughout the 1980s and early 1990s was also employed in the agency response to fetal protection policies during this period. The four sets of EEOC guidelines that were formulated during this period did not bar fetal protection policies, even though the policies clearly constituted disparate treatment of women. Instead, the guidelines allowed employers to use these policies to protect fetal health, provided there was documentation of the potential for fetal harm from maternal exposure to occupational toxins. Similarly, the lax enforcement of employment discrimination statutes by both the EEOC and the OFCCP suggests that these agencies were reluctant to regulate fetal protection policies, preferring instead to "wait and see" how the judiciary would respond to them. The shared language of fetal rights likely alerted officials to the linkage between fetal protection policies and abortion, and, as the abortion controversy heated up in the late 1980s, these officials probably became even more reluctant to take action to respond decisively to the policies.

In sum, an examination of the response of the administrative agencies charged with enforcing federal anti-discrimination legislation reveals that these agencies were extremely lax in investigating and adjudicating claims arising from fetal protection policies. In part, the problem was that neither the OFCCP nor the EEOC had a coherent policy in place for dealing with these employer policies. It is also fair to say that agency inactivity in this area was compounded by the fact that those policy directives that were in place treated fetal protection policies as different than other facially discriminatory policies and practices. Employer claims that these policies protected "fetal rights" likely contributed to this view that fetal protection policies were different than other forms of discrimination.

The conception of equality utilized by these agencies during the 1980s was one that emphasized the differences between the sexes and minimized the similarities. Agency heads proceeded on the assumption that women and men differed, especially where procreation was at issue, and that these differences could form the basis for disparate treatment by employers. In spite of the fact that this conception of employment rights was clearly at odds with Title VII caselaw and statutory law, the EEOC and the OFCCP continued to utilize it throughout the 1980s and early 1990s. Moreover, even though the Supreme Court's decision in *Johnson Controls* effectively barred employers from utilizing fetal protection policies, it is unclear whether the agencies will more vigorously prosecute employers using these policies in the future.

6. Fetuses and Workplace Health and Safety

While most of the debate about fetal protection policies has focused on the application of anti-discrimination statutes like Title VII, occupational safety and health regulations provided what may have been an even more appropriate avenue for the regulation of these policies. Fetal protection policies clearly implicated worker health and safety, since fetuses were presumed to be at risk of harm from maternal or paternal exposure to occupational toxins. In the late 1970s, when employers began adopting these policies, employees and workers' rights groups turned first to occupational safety and health agencies, particularly the Occupational Safety and Health Administration (OSHA), believing that the policies violated health and safety regulations. During the course of the fetal protection controversy, however, aggrieved individuals and groups found little assistance from occupational safety and health agencies and, as a result, began to turn their attention to the EEOC and to the courts.

There are a number of federal and state occupational safety and health statutes that could have been used to regulate these policies. The Occupational Safety and Health Act was formulated to limit workplace exposure to toxins. The act also has a provision that enables states to adopt their own plans for occupational safety and health. Once approved, a state plan takes the place of OSHA in that particular state. In addition, the Environmental Protection Agency has limited jurisdiction in the area of workplace safety and health under the Toxic Substances Control Act.

OSHA has encountered significant difficulties in promoting workplace health and safety and, more particularly, in regulating reproductive and fetal hazards. Moreover, OSHA, which should have been the lead agency in regulating these policies, opted out early in the fetal protection debate. The state plan provision, an innovation intended to allow states to modify the OSH Act to provide additional protections to workers, has rarely been used to accomplish this goal. The EPA's Toxic Substances Control Act, which is by far the most far-reaching statute in terms of its requirements and penalties against recalcitrant employers, has not been utilized at all in the area of workplace health and safety.

OSHA, *American Cyanamid*, and Fetal Protection

In the late 1960s, there was significant pressure on the U.S. Congress to formulate a national law governing workplace safety and health. When OSHA was created in 1970, only a few states had laws dealing with occupational safety and health, and even fewer had effective enforcement programs in place. Proponents of the federal law criticized the lack of uniformity among state laws, claiming that this lack of uniformity "created competitive disadvantages and discouraged nationwide progress toward a safer workplace."[1] Congressional concern about the differences among the states was a significant impetus for a national law. It was believed that a federal law would create a uniform standard of occupational safety and health and would distribute the costs of such a standard more equally among employers.[2]

The OSH Act. In 1970, Congress passed the Occupational Safety and Health Act. In its preamble, the act stated that it was intended "[t]o assure safe and healthful working conditions for working men and women."[3] The coverage of the act was to be as wide as the Commerce Clause of the U.S. Constitution.[4] In its definitional section, the act stated that it was to apply to every person "engaged in a business affecting commerce who has employees."[5] Employees of the federal, state, and local governments were not covered by OSHA; however, most states and municipalities have adopted workplace safety and health rules that apply to governmental employees. The scope of the act's coverage is quite broad: it is estimated that the OSH Act covers 75 million workers, three-fourths of the nation's work force.[6]

The OSH Act charged both employers and employees with promoting workplace health, since each was "encouraged to decrease the number of occupational safety and health hazards at their places of employment."[7] The OSH Act imposed additional responsibilities upon employers, including the following:

> (1) [to] furnish to each of his employees employment and a place of employment which are free from recognized hazards that are causing or are likely to cause death or serious physical harm to his employees; and (2) [to] comply with occupational safety and health standards promulgated under this Act.[8]

Thus, the employer was obligated to provide a workplace that did not pose any danger to the health or well-being of his employees.

The first clause of this provision, which requires that the employer furnish employment that is free from recognized hazards, has become known as the general duty clause. This clause is one of the OSH Act's most controversial provisions. It was included because the framers believed that specific, detailed standards on all possible workplace hazards could not be developed, and, at first glance, this clause seems to be very broad. It does not, however, impose an absolute obligation upon the employer to guarantee workplace health and safety. One House report stated that:

> An employer's duty under [this section] is not an absolute one . . . It is the [House] Committee's intent that an employer exercise care to furnish a safe and healthful place to work and to provide safe tools and equipment. This is not a vague duty, but is the protection of the worker from preventable dangers.[9]

The general duty clause has been one of the most heavily litigated provisions of the act. The scope of the phrase "free from recognized hazards" has been strongly contested, and the absence of legislative history on the intended scope of the provision has compounded the difficulty inherent in interpreting it.

To prove a violation of the general duty clause, it must be demonstrated that the employer has failed to eliminate a workplace hazard that poses a substantial risk of death or serious bodily harm to his or her employees. The hazard must be such that a reasonably prudent employer would be aware of its existence. The courts have construed this requirement to mean that the employer should have a general knowledge of industry hazards, and should be aware of the hazardous conditions that exist in his or her own workplace.[10] To prove a violation of the general duty clause, it must also be demonstrated that it was feasible for the employer to eliminate this hazard.

In theory, the general duty clause applied to all occupational hazards, including those chronic health hazards caused by toxic substances. As such, the general duty clause would have obligated an employer to eliminate occupational toxins impairing reproductive or fetal health. The individuals and worker groups that challenged fetal protection policies relied on this interpretation of the general duty clause. The courts litigating these early fetal protection cases, however, were unwilling to allow plaintiffs to bring a cause of action based upon this clause. Instead, the courts interpreted the general duty clause in such a way that it did not encompass reproductive or fetal health hazards.

An employer can violate the OSH Act by failing to comply with the general duty clause or by violating a specific standard.[11] Under the OSH Act, the Secretary of Labor was given the authority to promulgate occupational safety and health standards.[12] In promulgating a standard, the Secretary was instructed to consider "the latest available scientific data in the field, the feasibility of the standards, and the experience gained under this and other health and safety laws."[13]

The Occupational Safety and Health Administration may promulgate either permanent health standards or emergency temporary standards. A permanent health standard may be issued for a single substance, for a group of substances, or for a class of substances. This standard contains detailed requirements for the monitoring, medical surveillance, engineering controls, and the training of employees working with a specific substance. An emergency temporary standard is issued if OSHA determines that employees are being exposed to "grave danger," and that exposure to the substance should be regulated immediately.[14] OSHA's record in setting permanent health standards is only slightly better than it is in promulgating temporary standards. To date, OSHA has succeeded in setting permanent standards for only twenty six substances.[15] These standards have typically taken more than one year to promulgate, and some standards have been pending promulgation for more than five years.[16]

State Plans.   As has been noted, the OSH Act was promulgated in large part out of a concern about the lack of uniformity among state occupational safety and health laws. However, despite its recognition of the inadequacy of state-initiated occupational health and safety programs, when Congress created the OSH Act, it provided for extensive state participation. It is likely that Congress included the state plan provision because it believed the provision would foster state participation, including enforcement efforts.[17]

The OSH Act included two key provisions that allowed states to assume responsibility for implementing occupational safety and health laws. First, the act allowed states to continue to regulate those occupational safety and health issues with which the act did not deal.[18] Under this provision, states were permitted to regulate any areas that were not preempted by the OSH Act. Second, even when the OSH Act did promulgate health and safety standards for a particular area, states could attempt to regain responsibility for this area by submitting and obtaining approval of a state plan.

The state plan provision is quite interesting: it establishes an extensive procedure for the approval of a state plan for occupational safety and health. Under this provision, the Secretary of Labor may approve a state plan if it meets a number of criteria. The plan must designate a state agency or set of agencies that will promulgate and enforce health and safety standards. More significantly, the plan must be "at least as effective in providing safe and healthful employment and places of employment as the standards promulgated [in the OSH Act]."[19] In addition, a state seeking to have its own plan approved must provide for inspections of the workplace that are at least as effective as those required under the federal OSH Act. A state may choose to adopt health and safety regulations that are more stringent than those provided in the federal OSH Act. Unless these additional protections unduly burden interstate commerce, they are deemed permissible. When a state plan is approved, that plan effectively preempts the federal OSH Act. In states with state plans in effect, the state occupational safety and health department has jurisdiction over employers, and the federal OSHA has virtually no role.[20]

A state may choose to adopt a state plan for a number reasons. First, states with these plans retain autonomy with regard to the regulation of occupational safety and health. This is a significant area of autonomy, and it appears that many states prefer to administer their own plans, even when those plans provide identical protections as those provided in the federal OSH Act. Second, states with state plans receive federal grants for the administration and enforcement of the plans. In fact, a significant portion of the budget for implementing a state plan may be provided by these federal grants. Thus, states may be less concerned about the costs attendant in administering their own plans.

States with state plans play a significant role in the enforcement of occupational safety and health law. At present, 25 states and territories, nearly half of those jurisdictions eligible to submit state plans, have plans in effect.[21] Over 40 percent of those workers covered by OSHA are already covered by state plans. In addition, more than 50 percent of the nation's health and safety compliance officers are employed by state agencies. Furthermore, states with state plans in effect also have provisions to protect state and local employees from occupational hazards. These workers would not be covered under the OSH Act.

The provisions of most of these state plans mirror those of the federal OSH Act. In fact, the majority of state plans have standards that are identical to the federal standards. While the state plan provision allows states to provide additional health and safety protections, few states actually do so. In the area of reproductive and fetal hazards specifically, only a few states have attempted to formulate their own standards.

OSHA's Effectiveness. Like the Equal Employment Opportunity Commission, the Occupational Safety and Health Administration (OSHA) has been fiercely criticized for its lackadaisical approach to enforcement. Critics have faulted the agency for its "failure to push for higher budgets and more manpower, for the inconsistent penalties it imposes against employers for safety violations, for not listening to its construction safety advisory committee, for its inexperienced inspectors, and for reporting rules that allow disastrous accidents to go unchecked."[22] Throughout the 1970s and 1980s, there were significant delays in workplace inspections and in litigation against employers.[23] The agency had difficulty establishing a policymaking agenda; and, perhaps more important, it was unable to promulgate new standards in an expeditious manner.

During the Reagan years, OSHA had extreme difficulty fulfilling its statutory mandate. Individuals appointed to key leadership positions were often hostile to the organizational goals of the agency, and, in some cases, these officials explicitly stated that occupational safety and health needed to be deregulated. As a result, during this period, OSHA was lax in enforcing existing standards. In fact, in the early years of the Reagan presidency, the Administration targeted nearly all the stringent standards for either revision or repeal. OSHA's inspections and enforcement efforts were also sharply curtailed. In the early 1980s, the agency adopted a targeting program whereby employers whose injury rates were below the national average were exempted from routine safety inspections. As a result, 45 percent fewer employers were subject to inspections. Many commentators believe that the possibility of being inspected has a deterrent value, and that employers who may be inspected are more likely to have cleaner workplaces.[24] While this targeting program was abandoned in early 1988, it appears that the effects of the program will continue to be felt in the future.[25] In spite of this targeting program, the number of OSHA compliance officers and hygienists remained inadequate throughout much of the 1980s and the early 1990s. This inadequate staffing compounded OSHA's enforcement and inspection problems.

Throughout the 1980s, OSHA was also slow in adopting new standards and in updating and supplementing existing standards. During these years, critics charged OSHA with having abandoned its policymaking responsibilities. They contended that OSHA had failed to take the initiative in promulgating new standards.[26] In the mid-1980s, many unions and worker rights and consumers groups began to utilize the courts to force OSHA to create new standards, and in a number of cases these groups were successful.[27] In fact, during the middle to the late 1980s, the most frequent source of rule-making initiatives was by petitions from interested groups, backed by the threat of a "bureaucracy-forcing lawsuit."[28]

While OSHA clearly suffers from poor management, inadequate funding, and a lack of agency direction, it also labors under significant institutional constraints. The regulatory framework itself places serious constraints upon the agency's ability to function effectively. One commentator has categorized these constraints as being substantive, managerial, legal, and political in nature.[29]

Among the substantive constraints is the agency's mandate to evaluate complex scientific, engineering, and policy decisions despite enormous scientific uncertainty. Since the data themselves do not resolve many occupational safety and health issues, the agency is required to make assessments that are often based upon data that are not definitive. Among the serious managerial constraints is the fact that decision-making authority is often divided between OSHA and the National Institutes for Occupational Safety and Health (NIOSH). The two organizations are located in different departments: OSHA is in the Department of Labor, and NIOSH is in the Department of Health and Human Services. As a rule, NIOSH has more scientific expertise than does OSHA, and coordination problems prevent OSHA from being able to utilize this expertise.[30]

Significant legal constraints also hinder OSHA's ability to function effectively. It is generally well-recognized that OSHA's rule-making procedures present a serious impediment to the promulgation of new standards. The requirement that OSHA adopt the health standard that is most protective while being "feasible" also impairs OSHA's ability to issue new rules. Moreover, before issuing a new standard, OSHA must demonstrate that a workplace hazard poses a significant risk to worker health. Other agencies, like the Environmental Protection Agency, are not required to meet this stringent test.

Most significant of all perhaps, OSHA operates under heavy political constraints. The unusually high degree of political controversy surrounding the agency is due to the fact that the decision-making process closely approximates a "zero-sum game," where gains for labor occasion corresponding losses for business. In addition, there are a number of political compromises built into the act itself that impair the functioning of the agency. Among these are the creation of NIOSH, the agency outside of OSHA that independently reviews scientific data; the creation of the Occupational Safety and Health Review Commission, which reviews OSHA fines; and the use of the "substantial evidence" test for judicial review, which is a much more stringent test than the "arbitrary and capricious" test used to evaluate the activities of other administrative agencies.[31]

The high degree of political controversy surrounding the agency has harmed it in other ways as well. The fact that OSHA is challenged on nearly every rule it attempts to promulgate means that the agency is always attempting to buttress its activities by supporting evidence. It also means that the agency is much less likely to innovate on health and safety issues. In addition, the intensity of the controversy has effectively forestalled any attempt to reform the OSH Act. Since both labor and business are apprehensive about the outcome of an all-out battle in Congress over such reforms, they shy away from attempting such reforms.[32]

Thus, OSHA's activities are significantly limited by serious institutional constraints. The effects of these constraints are perhaps most apparent in OSHA's inability to respond effectively to advances in scientific knowledge by promulgating more stringent health and safety standards.[33] Delay has long characterized OSHA's rule-making process; however, during the Reagan years, the agency was both unable to issue new standards and unwilling to enforce existing ones.

Many of the general problems that OSHA encountered throughout the 1980s in rule-making and enforcement were apparent in the agency's inability to deal with reproductive hazards in the workplace and with employer fetal protection policies. While OSHA was one of the first agencies to attempt to regulate reproductive hazards and fetal protection policies, the agency early on relinquished its jurisdiction over fetal protection policies. Throughout this same period, it was unable to formulate the guidelines needed to regulate both reproductive and fetal hazards in the workplace. Thus, by the middle to the late 1980s, OSHA, the lead agency for workplace health and safety issues, had a relatively minor role in the debate over fetal protection policies and reproductive and fetal health hazards.

OSHA and Fetal Protection Policies.   The first fetal protection policy to come to the public's attention was adopted by the American Cyanamid Company in 1978. This policy was instituted by Cyanamid in its Willow Island, West Virginia, plant, and it barred all fertile women from working in those areas that might involve exposure to toxic substances. The medical director of the plant contended that the exclusion was necessary to prevent birth defects in fetuses.

Women working in these areas were given a choice: they could either accept a transfer into other jobs, or they could submit to sterilization. If they chose to be transferred, they would retain their current rate of pay for 90 days; after this, their pay would be reduced to whatever the new job paid.[34] If the women chose sterilization, which would be covered by company medical insurance, and for which sick time could be used, they were permitted to retain their higher paying jobs.[35]

At the time the fetal protection policy was instituted, only 30 of the 560 employees at the Willow Island plant were women. After the policy was implemented, there were only seven jobs available for women who had not been sterilized. For those women who did not have these jobs, or were not able to transfer into them, they could either choose to undergo sterilization or lose their jobs. Of these women, five chose to be sterilized.[36] When the policy first came to public attention in late 1978, the U.S. Secretary of Labor ordered an investigation into the Willow Island Plant. After investigating the plant, the Secretary issued a citation against Cyanamid for violating the general duty clause of the Occupational Safety and Health Act.[37] In his citation, the Secretary of Labor stated that:

> The employer did not furnish employment and a place of employment which were free from recognized hazards . . . in that: the employer adopted and implemented a policy which required women employees to be sterilized in order to be eligible to work in the areas of the plant where they would be exposed to certain toxic substances.[38]

Moreover, the Secretary contended that "any condition of employment which can ultimately result in reduced functional capacity is a hazard within the meaning of the general duty clause."[39] Since exposure to certain toxins threatened reproductive and fetal health, the presence of these toxins in the workplace constituted a violation of the OSH Act. The f͏ ͏policy which attempted to safeguard fetal health by r ͏ ͏sterilization, violated the act, since s ͏

͏y of Labor to an ͏ny. The Secretary ͏th and Safety Re- ͏sion of the Admin- ͏policy was not the ͏te when it formu- ͏is neither a work ͏alter the physical ͏k or work-related ͏Act's "functional ͏ecretary of Labor. ͏ility did not affect a ͏ ͏nable under the O͏

O͏ ͏physical capacity, wi ͏ ͏ation did not fall tha͏ ͏ommission found ͏zation as a condi-

tion of employment, did not violate the OSH Act because the employee had a choice about whether she would submit to the procedure. OSHRC overlooked the fact that this "choice" was often illusory: the social and economic factors that were supposedly outside the scope of the act often pressured workers into taking the best-paying jobs, regardless of the health hazards. Moreover, OSHRC essentially ignored the existence of occupational toxins which threatened both fetal and reproductive health.

Thus, OSHRC contended that fetal protection policies did not violate the general duty clause for two reasons: first, sterilization did not impair the functional capacity of a worker; and second, even if it did impair this capacity, the worker had a choice as to whether to undergo the procedure. The commission focused on the fact that the employer did not force the worker to become sterilized; instead, the worker herself chose this option.[43]

The Secretary of Labor appealed the OSHRC decision to the Court of Appeals for the District of Columbia. In an interesting opinion by Circuit Court Judge Robert Bork, the court upheld the decision of the Occupational Safety and Health Review Commission.[44] In his decision, Judge Bork stated that the general duty clause did not apply to fetal protection policies because they were "policies," and not a part of the physical conditions of the workplace.[45] This manipulation of the term "working conditions" enabled the court to separate the employer's sterilization policy from other workplace policies and procedures.

Moreover, Judge Bork found that the policy did not constitute a hazard under the general duty clause.[46] In his opinion, Bork contended that "the sterilization exception was an attempt not to pass on the costs of unlawful conduct but to permit employees to mitigate the costs to them imposed by unavoidable physiological facts."[47] According to Bork, this was not an issue of occupational safety and health, since employees could choose whether or not to undergo sterilization. Like OSHRC, the Court of Appeals contended that since economic and social pressures were outside the control of the employer, the employer was not responsible for any worker decisions that were an outgrowth of them. Thus, a woman who chose to submit to sterilization in order to keep her job, or to avoid being transferred into a job that paid less, was acting on her own accord. The employer could not be faulted for providing her with this "choice."[48]

In language that can certainly be termed gratuitous, Judge Bork voiced his approval of the fetal protection policy at issue. Noting that the

OSHA lead standard was promulgated out of a concern about the effects of lead exposure upon fetal neurological development, Bork implied that the employer was justified in adopting the fetal protection policy because it was unable to reduce the women's exposure levels to a blood level that would be safe for fetuses.[49]

The appellate decision in *O.C.A.W. v. American Cyanamid Co.* effectively foreclosed all future litigation of fetal protection policies under the OSH Act's general duty clause. The opinion by the Court of Appeals has been fiercely criticized by unions and public interest groups. Many commentators have argued that the decision was at odds with the legislative history of the OSH Act and with established caselaw on occupational safety and health.[50] One analyst has noted that "[l]egislative history and judicial precedent indicate that the OSH Act is intended to prohibit employers from forcing workers to choose between their health and their jobs."[51]

The OSH Act's legislative history supports the view that *American Cyanamid* undermined the purpose for which the act was created. A House report on the OSH Act stated the following:

> Today's [1970 pre-OSH Act] law and practices allow workers to receive thousands of cases of occupational disease and illness without any effective protection . . . [The worker] should not be economically coerced into a hazardous job.[52]

Congress intended to prohibit employees from choosing to undertake work that was hazardous to their health, regardless of whether employees would be paid well for this work. By holding that employees could choose sterilization, and that the employer was not responsible for the consequences of this decision, the Court of Appeals contradicted the act. Moreover, by stating that sterilization arose from economic and social factors, rather than from workplace exposure to hazardous substances, the court attempted to place these policies outside the reach of the act.

The appellate court's decision in *O.C.A.W. v. Cyanamid Co.* precluded OSHA from attempting to regulate fetal protection policies under the general duty clause.[53] In addition, OSHA was lax in promulgating standards to regulate worker exposure to reproductive and fetal toxins. As mentioned above, a large number of substances are known or suspected to be reproductive and fetal health hazards.[54] Of these substances, however, only a handful are regulated on the basis of their impact upon reproductive health: these are arsenic, carbon disulfide, chloroprene, DBCP, EtO, non-ionizing radiation and lead. Moreover, concerns about reproductive health were critical in the regulation of only three substances—DBCP, EtO, and lead.

Standards for Reproductive and Fetal Hazards. The EPA has banned the use of DBCP, a pesticide suspected of causing testicular cancer among men who work in landscaping. OSHA has regulated only ethylene oxide and lead on the basis of concerns about reproductive health. Moreover, OSHA was extremely reluctant to regulate either of these substances. There were extensive hearings and negotiations prior to the lead standard being enacted, and the standard was issued in the face of fierce opposition by employer groups. Specifically, employer groups opposed two provisions: one establishing the permissible exposure limits for lead, another creating medical removal protections. The medical removal protection allows a worker who is planning to conceive to be removed to a job where he or she would not be exposed to lead, while retaining the higher rate of pay. The conflict between employer and worker groups over the lead standard was extremely intense, and it appears that OSHA adopted the standard only after Congress placed considerable pressure upon the agency to do so.

Similarly, OSHA was unwilling to issue a standard for ethylene oxide on its own initiative. It was only after unions and consumer rights groups brought an action against the Secretary of Labor to compel such regulation that the standard was issued. Furthermore, the standard on EtO that was eventually adopted was much less stringent than what worker and consumer advocacy groups had sought. Like the lead standard, the ethylene oxide standard required that workers be given education and training for dealing with the substance, and that there be medical surveillance of exposed workers. As part of this medical surveillance, company physicians were required to inquire about a worker's reproductive history. In addition, the doctor had to counsel a worker in the case where the worker wanted "medical advice concerning the effects of EtO exposure on his/her ability to produce a healthy child."[55] The standard also required that an employer do fertility testing for workers who requested this testing. The permissible exposure limit established by OSHA for both lead and ethylene oxide are substantially higher than the limit sought by worker and consumer rights groups; nevertheless, the standards do provide workers with a minimal level of protection.

Recent attempts to regulate substances on the basis of their effects on reproductive and fetal health have been unsuccessful. Despite the fact that OSHA recognizes that at least nine of the substances it regulates may be toxic to reproductive and fetal health, it only regulates lead and EtO on the basis of these concerns. The other substances are regulated, but, since they are not regulated on the basis of their effects on reproductive and fetal health, certain precautions that would minimize the effects of this exposure are not required. In 1990, the General Accounting Office surveyed four governmental agencies that have the authority to regulate reproductive and developmental toxicants: the Occupational Safety and Health Administration, the Environmental Protection Agency, the Food and Drug Administration, and the Consumer Products Safety Commission.[56] The survey was intended to be an accounting of the existing standards that regulate substances that are teratogenic or that cause infertility.

Table 6.1 is derived from OSHA's response to the survey. As the chart demonstrates, OSHA recognizes that a number of substances may endanger reproductive and fetal health. While the agency claims that it engages in enforcement activities for all nine substances listed, it requires labeling for only four substances. The agency has numeric standards for all nine substances; however, concerns about reproductive or developmental toxicity were only "partially" the basis for the regulations concerning seven of the substances, and they were "not at all" the basis for the regulation of the other two. Moreover, the agency has issued permissible exposure levels for only lead and ethylene oxide. Thus, as the chart demonstrates, there has been little activity by OSHA in the area of reproductive hazards. The agency has been inactive, despite the fact that it has examined the effects of the substances on reproduction and fetal development and has found toxicity in almost all instances. Moreover, the GAO study found that only 33 percent of OSHA's regulatory actions, which include the formulation of both standards and guidelines, are protective of reproductive health.[57]

The agency's hesitancy in issuing comprehensive guidelines to regulate the other substances may be explained by a number of factors. OSHA's unwillingness to regulate these substances on the basis of their reproductive or developmental effects appears to stem, at least in part, from the continuing debate about whether reproductive impairment is actionable under the OSH Act. While the lead standard held that "dam-

Table 6.1. OSHA regulation of fetal and reproductive toxicants

Toxicant	Action			Regulation based on reproductive fetal toxicity	Health outcome
	Enforcement	Labeling	Numeric standard		
Arsenic	X	X	X	partially	fetal toxicity; male and female reproductive toxicity
Carbon disulfide	X		X	partially	fetal toxicity; female reproductive toxicity
Carbon monoxide	X		X	not at all	n/a
Chloroprene	X		X	partially	fetal toxicity; male and female reproductive toxicity
DBCP	X	X	X	partially	male reproductive toxicity
Ethylene oxide	X	X	X	partially	female reproductive toxicity
Lead	X	X	X	partially	fetal toxicity; male and female toxicity
Mercury	X		X	partially	fetal toxicity
Toluene	X		X	not at all	n/a

Source: U.S. General Accounting Office (1990).

age to the fetus represents impairment of the reproductive capacity of the parent and must be considered material impairment of functional capacity under the OSH Act," the appellate court's decision in *O.C.A.W. v. American Cyanamid* holds that reproductive and developmental harm is not actionable under the act.

OSHA's reticence to regulate these substances also stems from the formidable task of identifying these effects and protecting workers from them. Despite the serious political obstacles that existed in the formulation of the lead standard, that standard was relatively easy for OSHA to promulgate, because there was extensive scientific data on the health effects of lead exposure, and many scientists were in agreement about these effects. Regarding the effects of most substances used in the workplace, however, there is a paucity of scientific data, and there is substantial uncertainty about how to interpret the data that do exist.[58] This uncertainty, coupled with the formidable institutional obstacles facing OSHA, makes it extremely difficult for OSHA to target those substances that should be regulated on the basis of their reproductive and developmental effects.

Thus, the Occupational Safety and Health Administration has promulgated standards to deal with reproductive and fetal hazards in only two instances. In 1978, OSHA issued its lead standard, and, in 1984, the agency issued its standard on ethylene oxide.[59] Since 1984, the agency has been at a standstill in dealing with reproductive hazards in the workplace. A 1983 report by the Department of Labor stated that:

> OSHA feels that a lack of information [about reproductive hazards in the workplace] makes it impossible for it to address workplace reproductive hazards as a generic issue. Thus, it considers and deals with reproductive hazards to human health *on a case by case basis.*[60] (emphasis added).

Recent interviews with OSHA officials suggest that the agency has shelved the problem of reproductive hazards in the workplace. Even though most recognize that the general duty clause might permit the agency to regulate these toxins, it is generally understood that the agency will not undertake such action without there being considerable external pressure on it to do so.[61]

Virtually the only attempt by the Department of Labor or by OSHA to deal with the issue of reproductive and developmental toxins has been the convocation of a series of meetings by the National Institute of Occupational Safety and Health. In February 1989, NIOSH held a meeting to review a project aimed at developing methods to determine evidence of mutation during spermatogenesis; in June 1989, NIOSH had a meeting to discuss "studies assessing reproductive indicators in workers, new methodologies for the analysis of reproductive effects, and the evaluation and regulation of reproductive toxicants"; and in October 1989, NIOSH held a meeting to assess a developmental study on methods for evaluating reproductive potential in women.[62]

It is unclear whether the meetings by NIOSH have had an impact on the development of a coherent strategy for dealing with reproductive and developmental toxicants. While OSHA has been lax in dealing with this issue in the past, it appears that it now recognizes its responsibilities in this area. In an August 1990 oversight hearing on OSHA activities, Representative Joseph M. Gaydos (Dem.-PA), chairperson of the House

Subcommittee on Health and Safety, asked about OSHA's official stance on private sector fetal protection policies. Gaydos concluded that fetal protection policies appear to violate the general duty clause of the OSH Act and asked whether the agency would consider the exclusion of certain workers for "high hazard" areas to be a violation of the OSH Act.[63] In a written response to Representative Gaydos, OSHA emphasized that while it did not have an occupational standard regarding fetal protection policies, it had adopted several standards to deal with reproductive hazards, among these the lead standard. In addition, the agency implied that reproductive and fetal hazards should be actionable under the general duty clause of the OSH Act:

> The intent of the OSH Act is to assure a safe and healthful workplace, to the extent feasible, for every worker . . . [T]he general duty clause requires employers to adopt feasible measures to render their workplace free of recognized hazards. This would include hazards to reproductive health. *OSHA's strong preference would be for employers to eliminate health hazards through engineering controls.*[64] (emphasis added)

OSHA suggested that fetal protection policies might be governed by the OSH Act. It also stated that reproductive hazards should be dealt with by reducing exposure levels, rather than by excluding those workers at risk of harm. It remains to be seen, however, whether the agency will be able to formulate an effective policy for protecting workers from these hazards.

Thus, much of the debate over OSHA's role in regulating workplace reproductive and developmental toxins has focused on the scope of the general duty clause of the OSH Act. While a common-sensical reading of the act would seem to dictate that the agency should have responsibility for regulating substances that are reproductive and developmental hazards, certain court decisions, most notably, the decision of the Circuit Court for the District of Columbia in *O.C.A.W. v. American Cyanamid Co.*, compel a much different interpretation. In *American Cyanamid*, the appellate court held that the employer's sterilization policy did not result in "material impairment of health," and that OSHA did not have the authority to regulate this policy. The court effectively precluded OSHA from regulating these policies, and sidestepped the issue of whether the act was violated by the very existence of potentially dangerous substances in the workplace.

Some commentators have argued that fetal protection policies are outside the scope of the OSH Act for another reason as well. While OSHA appears to have the authority to regulate certain substances on the basis of their effects upon the reproductive systems of workers, it is not clear that the agency has the authority to regulate substances on the basis of concerns about fetal harm. These individuals assert that, under the OSH Act, fetuses are not covered, and employers do not owe a duty of care to fetuses.

Regardless of whether one believes that OSHA has the responsibility for safeguarding fetal health, it appears to be clear that the agency has not fulfilled its statutory mandate of protecting workers from reproductive hazards in the workplace. At the same time, however, while OSHA's inactivity has often been commented on, the role of those states with state plans is often overlooked. Since OSHA provided a floor, not a ceiling, for occupational safety and health legislation, it is conceivable that a state with its own occupational safety and health plan would provide workers with more extensive protections.

State Plans and Reproductive Hazards

Twenty-five states and territories have adopted state plans for occupational safety and health. Of these 25, 24 were available for analysis.[65] Nearly all of these states had adopted occupational safety and health regulations that were identical to those adopted by the federal OSHA. Four states, however, had adopted specific regulations aimed at combating reproductive hazards in the workplace (see Table 6.2). Of these four, only two states, California and Washington, have been successful in formulating additional guidelines. Connecticut's 1981 law banning sterilization as a condition of employment was the most far-reaching statute passed by any state. This law, however, has not been enforced, and interviews with state officials suggest that while the law is still on the books, it will not likely be invoked. Washington's bills, which would have given the state the authority to regulate workplace hazards on the basis of concerns about fetal health, have been defeated. These bills were conditioned on the federal OSH Act being interpreted to include fetuses. While such an event is not unthinkable, it is unlikely that it will occur in the near future.

Thus, there have been relatively few successful attempts by states

Table 6.2. Reproductive hazard regulation in 1992 by 24 U.S. states and territories with active state plans for occupational safety and health

State or territory	State plan provision for dealing with reproductive hazards in the workplace	Citations for reproductive hazards
Alaska	Identical to federal OSHA standards	n/p
Arizona	Identical to federal OSHA standards	n/p
California	Additional funding for state Hazard Evaluation System and Information Service to conduct research and training programs on occupational reproductive hazards City of San Francisco: A 1991 ordinance to regulate use of video display terminals would set up commission to study effects of vdts on miscarriage	>1%
Connecticut	In 1981, passed legislation that prohibited sterilization as a condition of employment; however, no record of complaints being filed	n/p
Hawaii	Identical to federal OSHA standards	n/p
Indiana	Identical to federal OSHA standards	n/p
Iowa	Identical to federal OSHA standards	4–5%
Kentucky	Identical to federal OSHA standards	n/p
Maryland	Identical to federal OSHA standards	n/p
Michigan	Identical to federal OSHA standards	"very low"
Minnesota	Identical to federal OSHA standards	n/p
Nevada	Identical to federal OSHA standards	n/p
New Mexico	Identical to federal OSHA standards	n/p
New York	Public Employee Safety and Health (PESH) Act allows Commissioner of Labor to promulgate standards that are necessary to protect employees. No standards have been promulgated to date; however, reproductive hazards in the workplace would be under this provision of the PESH Act. In 1988, Suffolk County passed an ordinance that would have required employers to implement safeguards for employees working with video display terminals. This ordinance was struck down by the state supreme court for Suffolk County as being violative of the Municipal Home Rule Law.	n/p
North Carolina	Identical to federal OSHA standards	n/p
Oregon	Identical to federal OSHA standards	n/p
South Carolina	Identical to federal OSHA standards	n/p
Tennessee	Identical to federal OSHA standards	n/p

Table 6.2. Reproductive hazard regulation in 1992 by 24 U.S. states and territories with active state plans for occupational safety and health (*continued*)

State or territory	State plan provision for dealing with reproductive hazards in the workplace	Citations for reproductive hazards
Utah	Identical to federal OSHA standards	>2%
Vermont	Identical to federal OSHA standards	n/p
Virginia	Identical to federal OSHA standards	n/p
Virgin Islands	Identical to federal OSHA standards	n/p
Washington	Efforts are in their beginning stages to deal with the problem of reproductive hazards in the workplace. The compliance staff has been provided with training and a list of known or suspected reproductive hazards to heighten their awareness during workplace inspections. Also, the department is developing activity outlines for a reproductive hazards team. In addition, during the 1989 and 1990 legislative sessions, bills were introduced regarding workplace regulations for reproductive hazards. These bills would have given the state authority to restrict the use of materials that pose a risk to fetal health. Both bills were defeated. One Washington state official contended that the bills were defeated because the state "did not have authority over the fetus." This official claimed that the federal OSH Act would have to be amended to allow the department of occupational safety and health to regulate these hazards.	1–5%
Wyoming	Identical to federal OSHA standards	n/p

Note: Percentages refer to the percentage (of all citations issued) of citations issued against employers for reproductive hazards; "n/p" indicates state officials' non-response to questions on this point.

with state plans to regulate reproductive hazards in the workplace. At present, only California and Washington have implemented specific programs to educate workers about reproductive hazards. While New York State has a statute on the books that would appear to permit further regulation, it is unclear whether its Department of Labor will initiate this activity.[66] As a result, the federal OSHA standards, which are inadequate for dealing with the problem of reproductive hazards in the workplace, remain the criterion for nearly all the states, including those with state plans in effect. While limited activity has occurred at the state level, the debate over fetal protection policies and workplace reproductive and developmental hazards has remained at the national level. Given this lack of activity by the state occupational safety and health departments, OSHA's lackadaisical response to these problems is even more problematic.

Moreover, recent attempts by OSHA to "nationalize" right-to-know laws have further compounded these problems. In 1988, OSHA's Hazard Communication Standard became operative. This standard preempted the right-to-know laws in effect in many states. These state right-to-know laws placed stringent requirements upon employers to inform workers of the hazardous effects of all substances to which they were exposed. The national Hazard Communication Standard placed far less rigorous notification requirements upon employers.[67]

There is a striking irony in OSHA's adoption of this standard, especially as it applies to reproductive hazards in the workplace. According to a recent survey of Massachusetts businesses, workers need to receive more training and education for dealing with hazardous substances. This study found that 68 percent of surveyed workers received neither training nor education on the reproductive hazards they encounter in the workplace.[68] Given that the national Hazard Communication Standard places less rigorous notification requirements upon employers than those required by the state right-to-know laws, this national standard will likely undermine recent attempts to inform workers of the risks inherent in their jobs.

In summary, throughout the 1980s, OSHA appears to have been indifferent, and at times even hostile, to the rights of workers exposed to workplace reproductive hazards. Part of the blame for this inactivity clearly lay in the organization's inability to break free of certain institutional constraints, in particular, its difficulties in formulating standards for reproductive toxins. OSHA's lack of activity also stemmed from the fact that the courts had barred it from using the general duty clause of the OSH Act to prohibit employers from adopting fetal protection policies as a substitute for eliminating workplace hazards.

The inability of the federal OSHA to formulate a coherent strategy for dealing with reproductive and fetal hazards has been compounded by the fact that states with state plans, which may include occupational safety and health regulations that are more stringent than the federal standards, closely followed the lead of the federal OSHA on this issue.

Few states attempted to formulate their own policies for dealing with workplace hazards. Furthermore, the creation of the Hazard Communication Standard, which preempts state right-to-know laws, places more power in the hands of the federal OSHA for dealing with the issue of occupational hazards. This Hazard Communication Standard requires less extensive disclosure than that which had been required by a number of state right-to-know laws.

The lack of activity in states with state plans and the creation of the Hazard Communication Standard effectively delegate all responsibility for occupational health and safety law to the federal OSHA. Given this, OSHA's general failure is even more unfortunate. Throughout the 1980s, there was inadequate regulation of reproductive and fetal hazards under occupational safety and health law. Employers adopting fetal protection policies had virtually no responsibility for cleaning up their workplaces; they could simply exclude workers rather than providing what might have been costly engineering controls.

While OSHA is the primary agency responsible for ensuring workplace health and safety, there are other agencies that have enforcement responsibilities in this area. Most notably, the Environmental Protection Agency has the statutory mandate to enforce the 1976 Toxic Substances Control Act, which regulates the manufacture, importation, processing, distribution, use, and disposal of chemical substances. Unfortunately, the EPA, like OSHA, has had enforcement problems, and these difficulties are apparent in its treatment of workplace reproductive and fetal toxins.

The EPA and Toxic Substances

In 1976, Congress passed the Toxic Substances Control Act in an attempt to regulate the wide array of chemicals used in industry. Congress stated that the act was prompted by the need for effective regulation of substances that "may present an unreasonable risk of injury to health or to the environment."[69] The legislative history of the act strongly suggests that it was intended to fill the holes left by existing laws regulating toxic substances.[70] Congress meant for the TSCA to supplement the OSH Act by providing a regulatory mechanism for evaluating the safety of raw materials used in the workplace. Given that there are more than 1,000 new chemicals introduced in the United States each year, the

TSCA was viewed as necessary to ensure the health and safety of both workers and the public.[71]

The TSCA.   The Toxic Substances Control Act gave the Environmental Protection Agency broad authority to regulate the chemical industry. Under the act, the EPA was responsible for evaluating the risks attendant to the manufacture, importation, processing, distribution, use, and disposal of chemical substances. TSCA was intended to provide comprehensive coverage for both new and existing substances. Moreover, the EPA was given responsibility for evaluating substances at the earliest stages of their use.[72] By enabling the agency to examine substances at the manufacturing stage, the TSCA aimed at minimizing the risks to workers and the public. Some analysts have noted that in this sense it was quite different than its predecessors. According to one commentator, "[T]he TSCA required the EPA to begin its regulatory response by asking the question: should the toxin be used at all?"[73]

Under the TSCA, the EPA has a number of enforcement responsibilities. The agency is required to test all chemicals for their effects on health and the environment. Those that are found to be carcinogenic, mutagenic, or teratogenic, or to cause behavioral disorders, cumulative or synergistic effects, or "any other effect which may present an unreasonable risk of injury to health or to the environment," are to be closely regulated by the agency.[74] Where these risks are found to exist, the EPA is required to undertake an extensive monitoring procedure.[75]

This risk assessment is required for both new and existing chemicals. For existing chemicals, the EPA is given the authority to evaluate the health and environmental effects of the chemicals. Under section 6, the EPA has the authority to ban the production of any chemical that poses unreasonable risk to the public or to workers. For new chemicals, the manufacturer or processor is obligated to give the EPA pre-market notification that a new chemical was to be released at least 90 days before it is released.[76] Upon notification, the EPA has 90 days to conduct research on the substance and to decide whether or not to permit its release. Under the TSCA, the EPA can also require additional testing before the chemical is released.

Despite the fact that the TSCA was created because legislators perceived that existing regulations were not safeguarding the health and safety of workers and of the public, the act provides for the delegation of responsibility for certain toxins to other agencies. Under section 9 of the act, where the EPA determines that the risk of injury can be prevented by the action of another agency, the EPA has to delegate responsibility for regulating this chemical to the other agency.[77] The legislative history of the act suggests that this provision was intended to ensure that the TSCA would not preempt OSHA's authority to regulate workplace hazards. Since TSCA is broad enough to cover chemicals used in the workplace, Congress sought to ensure that the OSH Act would not be truncated.[78] In practice, the EPA has used the section 9 inter-agency referral to evade responsibility for regulating certain chemicals. In particular, the EPA has thrust responsibility for chemicals used in the workplace upon OSHA and thus has ignored its statutory mandate in this area.

In fact, despite its comprehensive framework for regulating harmful chemicals, the TSCA has been little used since its formulation in 1976. With the exception of the 1986 Asbestos Hazard Emergency Response Act, the TSCA has lain dormant since its inception. The EPA has essentially ignored its information-gathering responsibilities. It is estimated that more than 70 percent of the chemicals described in the TSCA inventory have not been evaluated for their health effects.[79] While some commentators claim that the EPA has begun to step up its enforcement efforts in the last few years, there is little evidence of this activity.[80]

The TSCA proved to be ineffective in regulating fetal protection policies for a number of reasons, some of which were also true of OSHA. First, like OSHA, the EPA is sensitive to changes in the political environment. During the 1980s, when the Reagan Administration actively pursued a policy of deregulation, the EPA was subject to serious budget cuts. In addition, the EPA, perhaps even more than other agencies, was headed by individuals who were hostile to its organizational goals. Nearly all of Reagan's appointees lacked expertise or experience in the field in which they were placed. In addition, most were selected on the basis of political ideology, rather than knowledge of a subject area.[81] Under the leadership of Anne Burford, the EPA's budgets for four major regulatory programs—air, water, hazardous wastes, and toxics—were slashed by 44 percent from 1981 through 1984. The enforcement staff was also reorganized every eleven weeks during Burford's first year in office. Moreover, the number of civil cases and administrative orders issued by the agency dropped more than 50 percent from 1981 to 1984.[82]

The EPA has had trouble enforcing the TSCA for other reasons as well. The TSCA requires a showing of "unreasonable risk" before the agency is permitted to regulate a chemical. It also requires that the agency utilize a balancing approach in determining unreasonable risk, taking into account the economic effects of regulation. The nature of the unreasonable risk requirement requires the agency to manage a great deal of scientific uncertainty. Moreover, the agency is clearly constrained in its data collection efforts: while companies are required to provide information on chemicals, they often do not provide information on all the health effects of these chemicals. Furthermore, since the testing rules themselves often do not evaluate the effects of a chemical on the reproductive and developmental systems, this information is also often incomplete.[83]

The requirement that the EPA take into account the economic effects of a proposed regulation also places serious constraints upon the agency's ability to enforce the TSCA. This requirement essentially codifies the risk assessment criterion. Even if the EPA is able to find that a chemical poses a serious risk of harm to a class of individuals, it may not be able to regulate this chemical if its regulation were to have an adverse economic impact.[84]

The EPA's enforcement of the TSCA has been lax for another reason as well. The inter-agency referral provision in section 9 enables the agency to evade responsibility for regulating a number of substances, particularly those used in the workplace. As has been discussed, this provision was intended to ensure coordination among agencies, and to eliminate "duplicative requirements."[85] The effects of this delegation provision have been felt most keenly by OSHA. Since 1982, the EPA has followed a "pro-referral" policy when dealing with any substances that are in any way associated with the workplace.[86] In these cases, the EPA delegates responsibility to OSHA for regulating the substance.

Thus, although the inter-agency referral provision was intended to increase organizational efficiency by preventing an overlap in administrative responsibilities, it has instead become what one analyst has termed "an escape hatch for the EPA to avoid regulatory responsibility that it should legitimately exercise."[87] This referral has had deleterious effects: since OSHA is clearly unable to discharge its responsibilities under the OSH Act, it is even less capable of handling inter-agency referrals under the TSCA.[88] Moreover, it appears that the EPA is better equipped to regulate toxic workplace chemicals than is OSHA. Since the TSCA was formulated to assess the risk of chemical exposure at every level of use, from manufacture to disposal, it is a more effective vehicle for regulating these chemicals than is OSHA.[89]

TSCA and Fetal Protection Policies. In retrospect, the TSCA would probably have been the best possible arena for evaluating both fetal protection policies and workplace reproductive and fetal hazards. This statute deals exclusively with hazardous chemicals and has extensive provisions for chemical testing and use. Moreover, the fact that the TSCA bars the use of any chemicals that pose an unreasonable risk to the health of workers and the public would seem to make this the perfect statute for regulating fetal protection policies. Under the TSCA, an employer must inform the EPA of any workplace toxins that pose a risk of harm to a worker.

Since fetal protection policies were enacted to shield women and their fetuses from exposure to hazardous materials, an employer adopting such a policy would have had to have been aware that workplace hazards exist. In such a circumstance, the TSCA would have required the employer to inform the EPA of the existence of these toxins. An employer who adopted a fetal protection policy without informing the EPA of the presence of hazardous materials would have violated the TSCA. A violation of the TSCA is punishable by up to $25,000 a day. In addition, an employer who willfully failed to comply with the act could be sentenced to up to one year in prison.[90]

Moreover, the problems encountered in interpreting the OSH Act to apply to fetal health do not exist in the case of the TSCA. Since the TSCA is written in such a way that it takes into account the mutagenic and teratogenic effects of chemicals, it is likely that this statute could have been interpreted to bar chemicals that would harm a fetus. In addition, the TSCA might have been even more protective of workers' rights than was Title VII. While Title VII only addressed the issue of whether women in traditionally male-dominated workplaces may be "protected," TSCA would have ensured that all women, including those in female-dominated jobs, were protected from exposure to teratogenic and mutagenic substances.[91] Thus, it appears that the TSCA would have been even better suited than either the OSH Act or Title VII for the regulation of workplace fetal and reproductive hazards.[92]

In practice, employers have not utilized the TSCA to protect either their workers or their workers' fetuses. In fact, it appears that employers who adopted fetal protection policies violated the TSCA by allowing chemicals in their workplaces that could pose a serious risk of harm to their workers. The TSCA has great potential for compelling employers to reduce the risk of occupational toxins that may harm the reproductive capacity of their workers and the health of their offspring. In the past, the EPA has virtually ignored this statute. It remains to be seen whether the EPA will enforce it in the future.

Conclusions

During the 1980s and early 1990s, the effectiveness of agencies like the EPA and OSHA was clearly on the wane. In early 1981, President Reagan announced that one of his highest domestic priorities was "relieving" businesses and state and local governments from the burdens placed upon them by administrative regulation. The Reagan Administration vigorously pursued this goal of deregulation, and environmental regulations were directly targeted for reversal. Both OSHA and the EPA were victims of this deregulatory policy: their budgets and operating staffs were drastically cut, and their ability to formulate policy and enforce existing regulations was significantly diminished. As a result, neither agency was able or willing to respond to the proliferation of fetal protection policies, or to the attendant disclosure that reproductive and fetal toxins were present in a large number of workplaces.

Neither OSHA nor the EPA attempted to fulfill their statutory mandate. OSHA was barred from utilizing its general duty clause to prohibit employers from conditioning employment on sterilization. Moreover, OSHA was lax in enforcing existing standards and in formulating new standards to regulate reproductive hazards in the workplace. Where OSHA did attempt to regulate these policies, its efforts were thwarted by the courts, which determined that fetal protection policies were not within the scope of the OSH Act.

The overwhelming majority of states with separate state plans followed the lead of OSHA and were extremely reluctant to formulate policies to deal with reproductive hazards in the workplace. Of the few that did attempt to deal with this problem, only two, Washington and California, appear to have been successful, and the extent of this success has yet to be determined.

The EPA, the other agency charged with regulating workplace exposure to potential toxins, was no more effective than either OSHA or the states with state plans in regulating workplace reproductive and fetal hazards. The EPA failed to enforce the Toxic Substances Control Act, a statute that directly governed the workplace use of hazardous chemicals. In fact, the EPA frequently attempted to "turf" its responsibility in this area to OSHA, which, as has been shown, was unable and unwilling to deal with the problem.

The response, or non-response, of OSHA and the EPA paralleled that of the EEOC and OFCCP. All of these agencies engaged in a balancing approach forced by political exigency. The EPA simply opted out of the debate about these policies, allowing OSHA to balance what were viewed as the competing interests of workers, employers, and fetuses. OSHA, charged with protecting employees from occupational hazards, chose to ignore the increased use of fetal protection policies. Where it did regulate workplace hazards, it adopted permissible exposure levels that were not protective of reproductive or developmental health. Medical removal protections were provided only to workers exposed to lead, and not to workers exposed to other suspected reproductive or developmental toxins. OSHA thus engaged in an approach that balanced the rights of employers, who opposed all medical removal protections and sought permissible exposure levels that were higher and therefore less protective of employee health, and workers, who sought more extensive removal protections and lower exposure levels.

In the vacuum created by the non-activity of OSHA and the EPA, a large number of employers adopted fetal protection policies, excluding many women from jobs that were potentially hazardous. These policies undermined the OSH Act, by allowing employers to exclude workers rather than clean up the workplace. Furthermore, the use of these policies appears to have violated the TSCA, which requires that employers notify the EPA wherever hazardous materials are being used in the workplace. In effect, fetal protection policies thwarted attempts to make the workplace safer by allowing employers to shirk their responsibilities for providing a workplace free of reproductive hazards. By allowing employers to avoid this responsibility, fetal protection policies were ultimately detrimental to both equal employment opportunity and occupational safety and health.

7. Courts, BFOQs, and Fetal Rights

When it became apparent that Congress and the regulatory agencies were opting out of the debate about fetal protection policies, opponents of the policies began shifting their attention to the courts, in hopes of convincing judges that the policies violated Title VII. Throughout the 1980s, federal and state trial courts and appellate courts heard a number of cases involving fetal protection policies, and, in the vacuum of inactivity by the other branches, these courts became the sole policymakers in the area of fetal protection. Unfortunately, the courts quickly demonstrated that they, like other governmental actors, could not break free of societal stereotypes about gender roles and capabilities of men and women. During the 1980s, five federal appeals courts heard challenges to fetal protection policies. While all of these courts recognized that the policies constituted facial discrimination, they nevertheless treated those policies differently than they treated other policies or practices that explicitly discriminated against a protected class. After nearly a decade of judicial policymaking, the Supreme Court rendered its 1991 decision in *United Auto Workers v. Johnson Controls.*[1] In this holding, the Court demonstrated its ambivalence about sex and gender, as well as its reluctance to place women's employment rights above their role as childbearers.

Certain patterns emerge in the adjudication of fetal protection cases in the 1980s and early 1990s. Most significantly, the federal appeals courts seemed willing, and in some cases even anxious, to allow these policies on the grounds of what were termed moral concerns or higher principles of public policy. The courts often referred to fetuses as "un-born children," and granted these fetuses rights separate from those of women. In their analyses, the courts frequently confused the Title VII frameworks for per se discrimination with those of disparate treatment, and so gave employers broad latitude in crafting these policies. The Supreme Court also hedged its bets in its adjudication of the *Johnson Controls* policy, issuing a holding that may leave the door open to certain exclusionary policies in the future.

Like Congress and the regulatory agencies, the courts were unable to evaluate these policies solely on the basis of the statutory provisions of Title VII. Instead, judges tended to rely on stereotypical notions of women's differential susceptibility to environmental toxins and on cultural expectations about women's role as childbearer and mother. As seen in the judiciary's handling of other sex-based statutes and policies like the all-male military draft and the use by state prisons of all-male guards, the courts are frequently unable to rise above cultural images of gender roles. Instead, judicial holdings serve to reflect and, more significant, to reinforce existing social mores of sex differences.

Litigation of Fetal Protection Policies in the Appellate Courts

A number of federal and state trial courts and appellate courts heard cases involving fetal protection policies prior to the Supreme Court's 1991 decision in *Johnson Controls*. There were five federal appellate cases involving these policies: *Zuniga v. Kleberg County Hospital* (Fifth Circuit, 1982)[2]; *Wright v. Olin Corporation* (Fourth Circuit, 1982)[3]; *Hayes v. Shelby Memorial Hospital* (Eleventh Circuit, 1984)[4]; and *Grant v. General Motors Corporation* (Sixth Circuit, 1990).[5] All of the cases involved the application of Title VII of the 1964 Civil Rights Act. Only one state appellate court issued a holding on a fetal protection policy, and this was a California court of appeals in *Johnson Controls v. California Fair Employment and Housing Commission*.[6] The California case involved the same policy at issue in the federal litigation, but in the state court it was brought under both Title VII and a state human rights statute.

Employer policies or practices may be evaluated under either the per se discrimination, disparate treatment, or disparate impact models.

As was discussed in Chapter 4, the courts created these frameworks to apply to different types of discriminatory policies: a per se violation occurred when an employer admitted that it was discriminating against a protected class but justified the discriminatory practice or policy by demonstrating that it fell within the bfoq exception to Title VII. A disparate treatment violation occurred when the employer did not admit that it was discriminating against a protected class but the claimant could prove that a policy or practice harmed the class and that the employer intended such harm. A violation based on disparate impact is found where a claimant demonstrates that a facially neutral policy weighs more heavily on a protected group and where the employer can not establish that the policy constituted a business necessity. Intent to discriminate is a necessary requisite for a finding of disparate treatment but not for disparate impact.

Prior caselaw and statutory law strongly suggests that fetal protection policies, which explicitly barred fertile women from certain jobs, constituted per se discrimination, and that these policies could only be validated by showing that the exclusion was a bfoq. Throughout the 1980s, however, courts hearing fetal protection cases frequently confused these proof frameworks, permitting employers to justify their policies under the far less rigorous disparate impact framework. The few courts that did use the per se model misconceived the requirements of the framework and contended that concerns about fetal safety could constitute a bfoq of sterility. In most cases this judicial reconstruction of the disparate impact and per se frameworks permitted employers to implement their exclusionary policies. Even more significant, however, the courts' holdings in all the federal cases were based upon cultural stereotypes about women's role in reproduction and their differential susceptibility to workplace hazards.

Disparate Impact. Four of the seven federal and state appellate courts to consider fetal protection policies in the 1980s and early 1990s analyzed the policies using the disparate impact framework. Three of these, *Zuniga v. Kleberg County Hospital, Wright v. Olin Corporation,* and *Hayes v. Shelby Memorial Hospital,* used only this framework; the fourth, *U.A.W. v. Johnson Controls,* held that the policies could be evaluated under either the disparate impact or the per se models.

The first case, *Zuniga,* which was decided in 1982, was actually the least damaging in terms of its impact on women's employment rights. In this case, the Fifth Circuit used the disparate impact test to find that the exclusion of a pregnant X-ray technician violated Title VII.[7] The Fifth Circuit held that the employer's exclusionary policy could not be justified under the business necessity defense because there were feasible alternatives that would have prevented pregnant women from being exposed to radiation. The court pointed out that the employer itself had issued guidelines establishing that employees could be transferred and temporary replacements employed where there were "family health" concerns.[8] The Fifth Circuit dodged the question of whether the hospital's concern about fetal health or potential liability constituted a business necessity. Instead, the court focused on the existence of feasible alternatives to the employer's policy.

The same year the Fifth Circuit issued its decision in *Zuniga*, the Fourth Circuit announced its holding in *Wright v. Olin Corporation*.[9] In this case, the Fourth Circuit also used the disparate impact framework, but, unlike the Fifth Circuit in *Zuniga*, it focused solely on the question of whether concerns about fetal health could constitute a business necessity. The fetal protection policy in this case barred fertile women from lead-exposed areas, but it permitted men, who are also at risk from lead exposure, to continue in their jobs.[10] The fetal protection policy at issue in *Wright* was part of a widespread discriminatory employment scheme that affected both women and people of color. The EEOC charged Olin Corporation with more than 50 race and sex discrimination charges, alleging that Olin had engaged in unlawful discrimination in recruitment, hiring, job assignments, promotions, terminations, and re-employment. The Fourth Circuit affirmed the district court's holdings on all of these charges except those involving Olin's "fetal vulnerability" policy. Most of the appellate decision dealt with the legitimacy of this policy.

In evaluating the fetal protection policy, the court rejected the more rigorous per se framework, finding that this framework did not apply because it "prevented the employer from asserting a defense that it should be able to use under Title VII caselaw."[11] This conclusion begged the question of whether fetal protection policies *could* be legitimated under the bfoq exception. In fact, the court recognized that the policies would not be permitted under bfoq and it was likely looking for a way to justify them under Title VII. This result-oriented behavior recurred throughout most of the later fetal protection cases.

In remanding the case back to the district court for disposition of the claim involving the employer's fetal protection policy, the Fourth Circuit advised that concerns about the safety of the "unborn" could constitute a business necessity under the disparate impact framework. The court analogized fetuses to other third parties, like customers or other individuals who were in the workplace but were not employed by the employer, and found that the employer's duty of care to third parties extended to fetuses. In essence, the court held that the "unborn" were the functional equivalents of workplace visitors and that the employer could bar its female employees from being exposed to lead as a means of protecting these fetuses. Moreover, the Fourth Circuit created a special category for these "unborn children" and placed in this category "all invitees and licensees legitimately on business premises and exposed to any of its associated hazards."[12]

Not surprisingly, on remand to the federal district court, the lower court found that the fetal protection policy was permissible under the disparate impact test.[13] The district court's holding is remarkable, however, for two reasons. First, it simply dismissed the possibility of less discriminatory alternatives, stating that no alternative could have been as effective in preventing fetal harm as was the exclusion of female employees. Second, the district court's holding was significant because of its unabashed praise for Olin Corporation. In its conclusion, the court held the following:

> An employer such as Olin can justifiably choose a policy of fetal protection as a moral obligation to protect the next generation from injury, and it is a social good that should be encouraged and not penalized. Women in general should applaud the effort and there is every indication that most of the women employees at the Olin plant appreciate and support the policy.[14]

It is ironic that the court lavished such praise on the Olin Corporation, a company that it had found to be guilty of widespread race and sex discrimination. It is also worth noting that the court believed that *women* should be grateful for employer efforts to reduce fetal hazards. That this court conceived of fetal health as being of special concern to women, as opposed to society in general, is an interesting sidelight.

Thus, the Fourth Circuit, in *Wright v. Olin*, carved out a special category for fetuses and accorded fetuses certain protections separate from those enjoyed by women. While the appellate court questioned

whether the employer's concern about fetal safety could properly constitute business necessity, it provided the district court with this proof
framework and, in so doing, allowed such an interpretation. It is perhaps
this aspect of the case that is so troubling: while the appellate court
claimed that it was simply interpreting congressional intent, its distortion
of the proof frameworks constituted a substantial deviation from settled
Title VII case law. By holding that an employer could legitimate its fetal
protection policy by proving that the policy constituted a business necessity, not a bfoq, the court allowed the employer to justify this facially
discriminatory policy with a far less rigorous defense.

Two years after the *Zuniga* and *Wright* holdings, the Eleventh Circuit issued its decision in *Hayes v. Shelby Memorial Hospital*.[15] In this
1984 decision, the Eleventh Circuit muddied its analysis of Title VII
caselaw, as had the two earlier courts. The Eleventh Circuit recognized
that the hospital's policy of firing pregnant X-ray technicians because of
concerns about the effects of radiation exposure on fetal health constituted per se, or facial, discrimination. But the court found that where a
policy equally protected the offspring of all employees, it should be
evaluated under the disparate impact test.

According to the Eleventh Circuit, an employer attempting to justify
its fetal protection policy under the facially neutral business necessity
test had to prove that maternal exposure to workplace hazards posed a
substantial risk of fetal harm and that these hazards did not apply to
men.[16] The court found that the employer's policy did not meet this test,
since it did not protect fetuses from radiation exposure.[17]

After concluding that the hospital in this case had not presented a
viable business necessity defense, the court discussed at length the mechanism by which a valid business necessity defense would survive Title
VII scrutiny. The court recognized that the traditional business necessity
defense did not ordinarily encompass fetal protection policies. The court
conceded that the business necessity defense could only be utilized
where an employer's policy related to job performance and admitted that
"fetal protection does not in a strict sense have anything to do with job
performance."[18]

In spite of the fact that fetal protection policies did not fall within the
traditional business necessity defense, the court contended that fetal
protection policies should be allowed under certain circumstances because they were based upon some "higher public policy."[19] The court's

conception of fetal protection as a foresighted, laudable public interest is an interesting twist to this opinion. While the court recognized that this employer was utilizing its fetal protection policy as a pretext for discriminating against women, it also acknowledged that certain policies might not only survive a Title VII challenge, but might promote the public interest.[20]

More important, the court advised the employer that it should frame its justification of the policy in terms of protecting fetal health, not in terms of avoiding tort liability. In emphatic terms, the court held that a desire to avoid tort litigation could not form the basis for the business necessity defense.[21] This aspect of the case became increasingly important in cases litigated in the late 1980s and early 1990s. Employers whose policies were challenged began to utilize the fetal health justification, either in conjunction with the litigation rationale or alone.

In 1989, the Seventh Circuit decided *United Auto Workers v. Johnson Controls.* Like the courts in *Zuniga, Wright,* and *Hayes,* the circuit court held that the disparate impact test could be used to evaluate a fetal protection policy. Unlike the earlier courts, however, the Seventh Circuit also held that these policies could be evaluated and legitimated under the more rigorous per se discrimination framework. In justifying the use of the business necessity defense, the court held that "neither the text of Title VII nor Supreme Court pronouncements mandate a holding that all forms of facial discrimination are justifiable only with a bfoq defense."[22] The Seventh Circuit adopted the test utilized by both the *Wright* court and the district court below. The court found that the first aspect of this standard, that the workplace hazard pose a substantial risk of harm to the fetus, was readily met. According to the court, both the employer and the union agreed that lead poses a substantial risk of harm to a fetus.[23] Much of the court's analysis dealt with the second requisite, that the risk of harm be borne only by the affected sex.

In a holding that has been cited for the court's lack of understanding of scientific data and research in general, the court rejected the use of studies based upon animal subjects. The court found that the union was unable to demonstrate that paternal exposure to lead may harm a developing fetus.[24] It contended that, unlike the substantial research compiled indicating the effects of maternal exposure to lead on fetal health, "the evidence of risk to the unborn child resulting from the exposure of the father to lead levels . . . is, at best, speculative and unconvincing."[25]

Thus, the paucity of data on the effects of paternal exposure rendered the union incapable of negating the second element of Johnson Controls' business necessity defense.

The court also held that Johnson Controls had met the third requisite of the business necessity defense, namely, that it demonstrate that there were no other acceptable alternatives available that would accomplish its aims while having a less differential impact upon the affected class.[26] Thus, the circuit court contended that the three requirements of the business necessity defense "balance[d] the interests of the employer, the employee, and the unborn child in a manner consistent with Title VII."[27] Furthermore, the majority asserted that, as a result of the Supreme Court's 1989 decision in *Wards Cove Packing Co., Inc. v. Antonio,* an employer who utilized the business necessity defense was not required to prove that the challenged policy was "essential or indispensable" to its business in order for it to be acceptable under Title VII case law.[28] As a result, the Seventh Circuit's decision expanded the business necessity defense and allowed fetal protection policies to stand, essentially because the policies are protective of fetal health.

Thus, the appellate courts that considered fetal protection policies from 1982 to 1989 refused to evaluate these policies under the rigorous per se or facial discrimination framework, despite the fact that the policies expressly barred women from the workplace. The decisions of the federal appeals courts in the *Zuniga, Wright, Hayes,* and *Johnson Controls* cases revealed the judiciary's willingness to bend the Title VII frameworks to permit certain facially discriminatory policies. Moreover, as the decade wore on, the appellate courts demonstrated that they were willing, indeed, anxious, to allow policies that barred women from the workplace solely out of a concern about fetal health. In the early 1980s, the *Zuniga* and *Hayes* courts had struck down the fetal protection policy at issue. In both cases, however, the appellate courts implied that concerns about fetal health were laudable, and, in *Hayes,* the court suggested that other policies, crafted to promote fetal health and not to limit tort liability, might be justifiable by some "higher public policy."

The *Wright* and *Johnson Controls* appeals courts expanded the reasoning of the earlier *Zuniga* and *Hayes* courts to permit fetal protection policies. In *Wright,* the court analogized the fetus to other third parties, thus granting the fetus rights separate from those of the women. The *Johnson Controls* court also gave the fetus rights independent of the woman. This court balanced the interests of the employer, employee, and "unborn child" and implied that these interests were to be given equal weight. The *Johnson Controls* court used both the disparate impact and per se frameworks to validate the fetal protection policy. In applying the disparate impact/business necessity test, the court ignored existing data on the effects of paternal exposure to lead. In addition, the court disregarded the OSHA lead standard, which sets identical permissible exposure levels for men and women.

Thus, the first four federal appeals courts to have considered fetal protection policies were increasingly willing to permit these policies under the disparate impact test. It is much easier for an employer to defend against a disparate impact claim than a claim based on per se discrimination or disparate treatment. While the first appeals court, the Eleventh Circuit, found in *Zuniga* that the fetal protection policy violated Title VII under disparate impact, by the time *Johnson Controls* was decided six years later, the Seventh Circuit strongly suggested that these policies would almost always pass scrutiny under this framework. Moreover, the appellate decision in *Johnson Controls* signaled a change in the framework to be used in evaluating fetal protection policies. Partly as a result of the Seventh Circuit's opinion, which permitted the policy under both disparate impact and the much more rigorous per se frameworks, later courts relied solely on the per se framework in evaluating fetal protection policies. From 1990 on, the federal and state appeals courts that considered these policies stated unequivocally that the policies constituted per se discrimination and had to be evaluated under the much more rigorous per se/bfoq framework.

Per Se Discrimination.   The Seventh Circuit's decision in *Johnson Controls* was a turning point in the discussion about fetal protection policies. Not only did the majority state that these policies expressly discriminated against women, it also contended that infertility could, and, in fact, should, be a bfoq for certain jobs. This holding and the dicta that accompanied it raised the debate about these policies to the national level. The appellate decision in *Johnson Controls* was openly criticized by the two federal and state appeals courts that followed it in evaluating fetal protection policies. Moreover, the Seventh Circuit's decision in *Johnson Controls* was the first fetal protection case for which the U.S. Supreme Court granted certiorari.

The Seventh Circuit's decision was handed down in 1989. In 1990, the Sixth Circuit decided *Grant v. General Motors*, and a California Court of Appeals decided *Johnson Controls v. California Fair Employment and Housing Commission.* In addition, the Supreme Court handed down its decision in *U.A.W. v. Johnson Controls* in early 1991. Thus, in less than two years, the nature of judicial policymaking on the fetal protection issue changed radically, with the Seventh Circuit stating that these policies should be evaluated under the per se framework and could be legitimated under this rigorous standard, and the later appellate courts and the Supreme Court stating that while this framework should be used, the policies would not likely pass muster under it.

It made sense for fetal protection policies to be evaluated under the per se framework: these policies explicitly barred individuals capable of bearing children, that is women, from the workplace in order to prevent fetal harm. To legitimate a practice or policy that constitutes per se discrimination, an employer must demonstrate that there exists some bfoq that justifies the exclusion. As discussed in Chapter 4, the bfoq exception was intended to be very narrow. The majority in the Seventh Circuit's *Johnson Controls* decision, however, expanded this exception far beyond what Congress had intended.

In validating the employer policy, the Seventh Circuit found that the bfoq had to be evaluated in such a way that it gave "meaningful and thoughtful consideration" to the interests of the employer, the employee, and the "unborn child."[29] Moreover, the bfoq could encompass employer concerns about pregnancy, including considerations about the health of the fetus. The court disregarded Title VII's legislative history and existing caselaw, which dictated that the bfoq center on an employee's ability to do the job in question. Instead, the Seventh Circuit expanded the definition of "ability" to include concerns about fetal health hazards.

In addition, the majority used prior holdings of the Seventh Circuit and the U.S. Supreme Court as support for its contention that "Congress intended the bfoq as recognition of the real differences between men and women."[30] According to the majority, the Supreme Court's decisions in *Dothard v. Rawlinson* and *Rostker v. Goldberg* and the Seventh Circuit's decision in *Torres v. Wisconsin Department of Health and Social Services* were evidence that courts were permitted to consider the innate physical differences between men and women when assessing a bfoq defense.[31] The court failed to recognize that the two Title VII cases, *Dothard* and *Torres,* were based on the court's belief that the job in question could not be safely performed by one sex or the other. While the courts in these cases recognized the existence of sex differences, these differences related more to physical or social characteristics, like strength or privacy concerns, than to reproductive differences.[32]

One of the most significant aspects of the Seventh Circuit's decision in *Johnson Controls* was the elevation of concerns about fetal health over the employment rights of women. Throughout its decision, the majority referred to the fetus as "the unborn child" and subtly criticized those women who placed at risk the safety of their fetuses. In language that incensed civil rights advocates, feminists, and pro-choice advocates, the court held the following:

> *More is at stake in this case . . . than an individual woman's decision to weigh and accept the risks of employment.* Since they have become a force in the workplace as well as in the home *because of their desire to better the family's station in life, it would not be improbable that a female employee might somehow rationally discount this clear risk* in her hope and belief that her infant would not be adversely affected from lead exposure. The unborn child has no opportunity to avoid this grave danger, but bears the definite risk of suffering permanent consequences.[33] (emphasis added)

By implying that women work outside the home for extra money, the court ignored the financial situation of many families that are headed by women or that rely upon the woman's income to provide the basic necessities of living. Moreover, the majority contended that women are not capable of assessing the risks inherent in their employment, and implied that employers are better able to weigh these risks. The circuit court insinuated that women's employment rights had to be sacrificed wherever there was some evidence of fetal health hazards.[34]

The majority also demonstrated that it was willing to treat fetuses as if they were independent individuals with rights analogous to those of children or adults.[35] For example, the majority attempted to bolster its decision by citing court decisions in other cases that have involved the rights of minors to receive blood transfusions even when the parents object to these transfusions on religious grounds.[36] This parallel is, in many ways, an outrageous one: the court seems to have implied that someone other than the mother should make decisions about whether a fetus should be exposed to workplace toxins. Moreover, the court suggested that if the woman did not make the "right" choice in this case, she might be guilty of child neglect.[37]

Johnson Controls was decided by a seven to four margin: seven judges signed on to Judge Coffey's majority opinion, while four other judges either wrote or concurred in three dissents. The dissenting opinions by Judges Posner and Easterbrook are most significant for the purposes of this study because other courts, including the Supreme Court, have drawn on them in evaluating fetal protection policies. Judge Posner struck down the fetal protection policy at issue in *Johnson Controls;* however, he suggested that these policies might be acceptable in certain situations. Judge Easterbrook, on the other hand, stated that these policies are never permissible under Title VII.

In his dissent, Judge Posner held that fetal protection policies had to be analyzed under the per se framework, since these policies explicitly discriminated against women.[38] Posner stated that the bfoq had to be read quite narrowly, since to do otherwise would essentially gut the statute.[39] Posner contended that these policies could not be adopted solely out of a desire to limit the employer's liabilities for workplace harm. Judge Posner did state, however, that tort liability might at some point become large enough to justify the bfoq exception. While Posner contended that the bfoq was not justified in the *Johnson Controls* case, he stated that it might be justified in other situations. In particular, the employer might be able to prove a bfoq for tort liability where this liability was "large enough to affect the company's normal method of operation."[40] As evidence of the potentially huge impact of tort litigation upon corporate solvency, Judge Posner cited the bankruptcy of the Manville Corporation.

Moreover, Posner stated that the normal operation of a business "encompasses ethical, legal, and business concerns about the effects of an employer's activities on third parties."[41] Among these ethical considerations may be the employer's "moral qualms about endangering children" or concerns about the effects of fetal exposure to workplace toxins upon public relations.[42] These practical and ethical concerns about fetal health might constitute a valid bfoq, and for this reason, Judge Posner contended that Title VII did not bar all fetal protection policies.[43]

Judge Easterbrook was less circumspect than was Judge Posner in assessing the legitimacy of fetal protection policies under Title VII. While Posner contended that these policies might, under certain circumstances, pass muster under Title VII, Easterbrook claimed that the policies were never permissible.[44] For Easterbrook, the *Johnson Controls* case was clear-cut: fetal protection policies constituted disparate treatment of women; this treatment was not justified as a bfoq; therefore, these policies violated Title VII.[45]

Easterbrook emphasized that Congress intended the bfoq exception to be extremely narrow and to apply only where an employee was unable to perform the job in question. Since one's ability to bear children did not directly affect her ability to make batteries, infertility could not be considered a bfoq. Unlike Judge Posner, Judge Easterbrook rejected the view that potential tort liability might constitute a bfoq, contending that "the prospect of tort judgments means only that female employees' average cost to Johnson exceeds that of male employees."[46] According to Easterbrook, Title VII required employers to deal with individual employees rather than group averages.

In addition, Easterbrook asserted that, while barring all women from lead-exposed jobs might eliminate fetal exposure to lead, "demanding zero risk [would] produce not progress but paralysis."[47] Easterbrook contended that Title VII imposed certain costs upon the society, and among these are prenatal injuries.[48] For this reason, society had to decide how much risk of fetal injury it was willing to tolerate. Easterbrook warned, however, that this risk assessment had to be completed by either Congress or by the Occupational Safety and Health Administration: employers were not permitted to restrict the employment of women out of a concern for fetal health.[49]

Thus, Judge Easterbrook held that fetal protection policies were not permissible under the bfoq exception and that these policies would always run afoul of Title VII. Moreover, Easterbrook suggested that it might be impossible to eliminate all workplace hazards and that Title VII requires that we, as a society, assume some of these risks of these hazards. As will be seen, many of the concerns voiced by Easterbrook were repeated by the Supreme Court in its decision in *Johnson Controls*.

The Seventh Circuit's decision in *Johnson Controls* was the most extreme of all the appellate cases involving fetal protection policies decided from 1982 through 1989. Like the courts in *Zuniga*, *Wright*, and *Hayes*, the Seventh Circuit asserted that employer concerns about fetal protection could justify the exclusion of women. While the earlier courts simply alluded to fetal rights and the welfare of the "unborn child," the

Seventh Circuit explicitly stated that concerns about the fetus could form the basis of a bfoq exception. The court held that fetuses were independent individuals and that employers were permitted, and, in fact, should be encouraged, to balance the "rights" of fetuses against those of female employees.

The Seventh Circuit's holding in *Johnson Controls* permitted employers a greater range of flexibility in formulating these policies than had been afforded by any of the courts that considered fetal protection policies in the 1980s. Of all the courts to have considered these policies, the Seventh Circuit provided the most unequivocal support to employers seeking to protect fetuses by excluding women from the workplace. The reaction was immediate and intense, and both appellate cases decided after *Johnson Controls* cited the Seventh Circuit's opinion as an example of how Title VII could be wrongly interpreted.

Grant v. General Motors Corporation was the first federal appeals case involving fetal protection policies to be decided after the Seventh Circuit's opinion in *Johnson Controls*. This case was decided by the Court of Appeals for the Sixth Circuit in early 1990. While the appellate court in *Johnson Controls* was the first to state that fetal protection policies should be evaluated under the per se framework, the *Grant* court was the first to hold that these policies violated Title VII. The court held that "[t]he PDA, its legislative history, and the Supreme Court's *Newport News* decision inexorably lead to the conclusion that fetal protection policies that disqualify fertile women from various employment opportunities must be characterized as facially discriminatory under Title VII."[50] The Sixth Circuit stated that the other courts of appeals that had decided fetal protection cases had been confused about which proof framework to utilize, and for this reason, had erroneously decided the cases.[51] According to the Sixth Circuit, the only appropriate framework that a court adjudicating a fetal protection policy could use was the per se approach, not a hybrid per se/disparate impact approach like that used by the *Johnson Controls* court.

The Sixth Circuit criticized these other courts, claiming that in deciding *Wright v. Olin*, the Fourth Circuit had "prevented this seemingly ineluctable conclusion [that the per se approach should be used] by essentially overlooking the PDA."[52] Similarly, the court claimed that the Eleventh Circuit had wrongly decided *Hayes v. Shelby Memorial Hospital* by following an "independent analytical course." According to the

Sixth Circuit, the *Hayes* court had attempted to adopt a new standard for adjudicating sex discrimination claims by holding that fetal protection policies were permissible where workplace toxins threatened the fetus through maternal, but not paternal transmission.[53] The Sixth Circuit reserved its strongest criticism for the Seventh Circuit's decision in *Johnson Controls*. It charged that the majority opinion in *Johnson Controls* had further confused the fetal protection issue by being unclear about the analytical framework to be employed in evaluating the policies.[54]

In addition to criticizing the majority opinions in these cases, the Sixth Circuit voiced its agreement with the dissenting opinions in *Johnson Controls,* stating "[w]e agree with the view of the dissenters in *Johnson Controls* that fetal protection policies perforce amount to overt sex discrimination, that cannot logically be recast as disparate impact and cannot be countenanced without proof that infertility is a bfoq."[55] In addition, the *Grant* court stated that the appropriate test for evaluating these policies had been set down by a dissent to the *Johnson Controls* decision. This test required that an employer defending a fetal protection policy "demonstrate its factual basis for believing that all or substantially all excluded women would be unable to efficiently perform the duties of a job without inordinate risk to a fetus."[56]

While the Sixth Circuit held that General Motors' policy did not constitute a bfoq, it contended that an employer's concerns about fetal health and safety might constitute a legitimate basis for a fetal protection policy. Even though the Sixth Circuit's opinion imposed the most stringent requirements upon an employer seeking to justify its fetal protection policies, it still allowed the employer to bar women from certain jobs that appear to pose a serious risk of harm to a fetus.

Thus, all of the federal appeals courts that considered fetal protection policies in the 1980s and early 1990s contended that employers might, under certain conditions, validate their policy under either the disparate impact or per se discrimination frameworks. Even the Sixth Circuit, which imposed the most rigorous standard for evaluating fetal protection policies, hinted that these policies might be legitimated by employer concerns about fetal health. The only court that balked at the suggestion that fetal safety might override women's employment rights was a California court of appeals. In February 1990, a California court of appeals decided *Johnson Controls v. California Fair Employment and Housing Commission*. This case was decided at the same time that *U.A.W.*

v. Johnson Controls was working its way through the federal district and appellate courts. Both cases involved essentially the same question: did a policy adopted by Johnson Controls that barred women from positions in its manufacturing plants that would have exposed them to lead violate existing anti-discrimination legislation?

The same fetal policy was in place in all of Johnson Controls' plants, and it was this policy that was at issue in both the federal and state cases. Unlike the federal cases, however, the California case implicated not only Title VII but a provision in the state human rights code. One section of this state code was identical to the bfoq provision in Title VII; another added an additional protection to employees. This second provision established that "[i]t is unlawful to refuse to hire a female because she is of childbearing age . . . [and] [i]t shall be an unlawful employment practice for an employer to require any employee to be sterilized as a condition of employment."[57] The appellate court held that the Johnson Controls' exclusionary policy violated both Title VII and the California Human Rights Code.[58]

According to the appellate court, a classification based upon one's capacity to become pregnant constituted gender-based discrimination. The PDA made this per se discrimination and required that an employer attempting to defend the classification prove that the policy falls within the bfoq exception.[59] The court found that the employer could not defend the policy on the basis of bfoq, because procreative capacity was not directly related to one's ability to perform lead-exposed jobs. The state court found that the California Fair Employment and Housing Administration (FEHA) had been correct in refusing to allow the bfoq exception, since the company had been unable to prove that "all, or substantially all fertile women are unable safely and efficiently to perform the job . . . and that the essence of the business operation would be undermined if the company were to employ fertile women."[60] Thus, this court rejected the approach of the federal courts that had considered this issue.

The state appellate court also addressed the relationship between state and federal anti-discrimination law and the role of a state court in interpreting Title VII case law. The state court distinguished its holding from those of the federal appellate courts by emphasizing that Title VII and the state FEHA were substantially different. As a result, the California state court was not required to utilize Title VII caselaw in construing a state law.[61] Regardless of whether Congress intended Title VII to bar these policies, the court stressed that the state legislature had intended the FEHA to prohibit this type of policy. For this reason, the state courts were not required to follow federal precedent in matters relating to state statutes.

The court also criticized the disposition of fetal protection cases by the federal bench. First, the state court pointed out that, even if it were to follow federal caselaw, it would not be clear *which* precedent it was required to follow. As has been said, the federal court holdings in fetal protection cases had not been uniform. Furthermore, the state court decided to "decline[] to follow the federal cases."[62] The court then criticized each of the federal courts for its failure to correctly address the Title VII issues raised by fetal protection policies.[63] Specifically, the court stated that it was "substantially at odds with the Seventh Circuit's decision in *Johnson Controls*," and it strongly criticized the federal court for its distortion of the bfoq exception.[64]

According to the state court, the Seventh Circuit wrongly disregarded OSHA's findings that both maternal and paternal exposure to lead could harm a developing fetus.[65] Moreover, the state court contended that employers bar fertile women not because they are *capable* of becoming pregnant, but because they *will* become pregnant. The court held that "this discrimination . . . is based on categorical, long discarded assumptions about the ability of women to govern their sexuality and about the comparative ability of women to make reasoned, informed choices."[66]

Moreover, the state court claimed that at the heart of these policies were a number of unfounded assumptions about women, among these: that all unmarried fertile women are actively involved in sexual relationships with men or will be; that these fertile women are involved with fertile men; that fertile women involved with fertile men cannot be trusted to use birth control; and that fertile women, even when informed of workplace hazards, are not capable of assessing reproductive and developmental hazards.[67] According to the court, employers adopted these policies because they believed that women were incapable of properly assessing workplace hazards to fetal health. Thus, the state court in *Johnson Controls* found that fetal protection policies violated both Title VII and the state FEHA. Its holding went far beyond that of any other state or federal court that had dealt with these policies.[68] Even *Grant v. G.M.* did not explicitly bar these policies; the only court that did was the state court in *Johnson Controls*.

Throughout the 1980s and early 1990s, state and federal appeals courts evaluating fetal protection policies used either the disparate impact or the per se discrimination framework. The first four courts, including the appellate court in *U.A.W. v. Johnson Controls,* utilized the disparate impact framework, despite the fact that the policies expressly excluded women from the workplace. For these courts, fetal health was a predominant concern, and while only two of these courts validated the fetal protection policy at issue, all four contended that these policies could be justified under the disparate impact/business necessity test. The remaining courts used the much more rigorous per se framework. What is perhaps most troubling is that even those courts using this stringent standard found that fetal protection policies might be permissible under Title VII of the 1964 Civil Rights Act. Only the state court found that these policies could not be validated under the per se/bfoq framework, and this court relied not only on federal statutory law and caselaw, but on state law as well.

By the time *U.A.W. v. Johnson Controls* found its way to the Supreme Court in 1991, there was widespread disagreement about whether fetal protection policies were permissible under Title VII. While the Court established the proof framework to be used in evaluating these policies, it left open the question of whether further fetal protection policies could be legitimated under the bfoq exception.

Litigation of Fetal Protection Policies in the U.S. Supreme Court

In March 1991, the Supreme Court handed down its decision in *U.A.W. v. Johnson Controls.* This decision had been anxiously awaited by both advocates and opponents of fetal protection policies. These groups and individuals believed that the decision would have a significant impact upon the use of these policies: a holding that allowed the fetal protection policy at issue might encourage employers to adopt similar policies, while a decision barring Johnson Controls' policy would preclude employers from utilizing these policies.

Many of the groups that filed amicus curiae ("friend of the court") briefs in this case believed that the Supreme Court would remand the case back to the federal district court for a trial on its merits, since the district and appellate courts had decided the case by summary judgment.[69] Many believed that, by remanding the case, the Court would effectively sidestep the contentious issue of whether fetal protection policies were barred under Title VII. In a move that surprised many, the Court decided to resolve the issue of whether the policies violated Title VII. In a holding that was unanimous in its judgment, the Supreme Court found that the fetal protection policy adopted by Johnson Controls did violate Title VII.

Most of the Supreme Court's decision in *Johnson Controls* was concerned with the scope of the bfoq exception; the majority opinion did not venture far from this issue. While the concurrences, especially that of Justice White, did briefly touch on the question of whether fetuses were independent parties for purposes of Title VII analysis, this decision was almost exclusively concerned with the narrow question of whether Johnson Controls' policy was barred under employment discrimination caselaw and statutory law. The focus on this aspect of the fetal protection policy at issue in *Johnson Controls,* however, may mean that this holding will not govern fetal protection policies adopted in the future. Thus, the fetal protection debate may not have been laid to rest by the Supreme Court's decision in *Johnson Controls.*

Before discussing the limitations of the Supreme Court's holding in *Johnson Controls,* it would be helpful to examine closely both the majority and concurring decisions. There were three opinions filed in this case: the majority opinion was written by Justice Blackmun and joined by Justices Marshall, Stevens, O'Connor, and Souter; another opinion was written by Justice White and joined by Chief Justice Rehnquist and Justice Kennedy; a third opinion was written by Justice Scalia. All three opinions are explored in this section because although the Justices agreed upon the judgment, there were substantial differences among them as to the proof framework to be utilized in assessing fetal protection policies and the scope of the bfoq exception.

A thorough reading of the transcript of the oral argument in this case reveals that the justices were troubled about a number of issues. First, the justices were concerned about the impact that this case might have on tort actions brought against employers for fetal exposure to occupational toxins. In one exchange, a justice questioned the attorney for the U.A.W. about the possibility of tort liability against employers who, while complying with Title VII, exposed the offspring of their workers to developmental toxicants. Second, the justices were concerned about how a court would decide whether occupational hazards necessitated a bfoq of sterility. At least one justice echoed Judge Easterbrook's observation that "zero risk" in the workplace was an impossibility. Justice Scalia pointed out that "zero risk" was not a plausible goal and questioned the attorney for the employer about how much fetal risk was necessary to justify the use of an exclusionary policy.[70] These concerns about tort liability and the scope of the fetal hazard are apparent in the court's decision.

Majority Opinion. The majority opinion was written by Justice Blackmun and joined by Justices Marshall, Stevens, O'Connor, and Souter. After reviewing the district court opinion and the majority and dissenting opinions by the Court of Appeals for the Seventh Circuit, the majority opinion held that fetal protection policies were not gender-neutral. The Supreme Court categorically rejected the use of disparate impact/business necessity, finding that fetal protection policies explicitly discriminated against women on the basis of sex.[71] The Court found that the policy at issue classified employees on the basis of gender and child-bearing capacity, and held that it was discriminatory because it required that female, but not male, employees prove that they are fertile. Moreover, the Court held that discrimination on the basis of capacity for pregnancy violated the Pregnancy Discrimination Act. The Court asserted that "[Johnson Controls] has chosen to treat all its female employees as potentially pregnant; that choice evinces discrimination on the basis of sex."[72] Thus, the fetal protection policy at issue was facially discriminatory.

In addition, the Court contended that the employer's motive had no bearing on whether these policies were lawful. As may be recalled, a number of courts validated these policies in part because they determined that the employers had enacted the policies out of the good faith belief that they protected fetal health. The Court held that the benevolence of an employer's motives did not determine the legitimacy of these policies under Title VII caselaw.[73] According to the Court, fetal protection policies constituted facial discrimination under Title VII. Policies that were facially discriminatory were permissible only where they fell within the bona fide occupational qualification exception.[74] If the policies did not constitute bfoq's, they were barred under Title VII.

The Court next turned its attention to the question of whether fetal protection policies were permissible under the bfoq exception. There was serious disagreement among the Justices about the scope of the bfoq exception. The majority held that the bfoq exception was extremely narrow, and only applied in certain situations. In particular, a bfoq had to relate to job-related skills and aptitudes.[75] The Court discussed *Dothard v. Rawlinson* and the airline cases, including *Western Airlines Inc. v. Criswell,* and stressed that a bfoq had to relate to the essence of the employer's business for it to be legitimate.[76]

The majority rejected the employer's argument that fetal safety was essential to the business of battery manufacturing. The majority stated that:

> The unconceived fetuses of Johnson Controls' female employees . . . are neither customers nor third parties whose safety is essential to the business of battery manufacturing. No one can disregard the possibility of injury to future children; *the BFOQ, however, is not so broad that it transforms this deep social concern into an essential aspect of battery-making.*[77] (emphasis added)

Moreover, the majority stated that the Pregnancy Discrimination Act qualified the bfoq exception by requiring that employers treat pregnant women the same as other employees "not so affected but similar in their ability or inability to work." The majority held that the legislative history of the PDA indicated that the act aimed at protecting women from being treated differently on the basis of their capacity for childbearing.[78]

After establishing that the scope of the bfoq was extremely narrow, the majority found that the fetal protection policy at issue did not constitute a bfoq. According to the Court, pregnant women were able to manufacture batteries as efficiently as other workers. Moreover, the employer's moral concerns about fetal safety did not establish a bfoq, since "[d]ecisions about the welfare of future children must be left to the parents who conceive, bear, support, and raise them rather than to the employers who hire those parents."[79] Thus, the employer was barred from using its employment policy to protect fetal health.

Furthermore, the Court found that concerns about "the welfare of the next generation" could not be considered to be a part of the essence of the employer's business. Citing Judge Easterbrook's dissent in *Johnson Controls,* the Court stated that "[i]t is a word play to say that 'the job' at Johnson is to make batteries without risk to fetuses in the same way 'the job' at Western Air Lines is to fly planes without crashing."[80] The majority contended that since only a small minority of women bear children while exposed to lead, and an even fewer number of women have children with elevated blood levels, the employer was unable to demonstrate that "all or substantially all women would be unable to perform safely and efficiently the duties of the job involved."[81] Thus, the employer was unable to prove that concerns about fetal health were part of the essence of Johnson Controls' business.

After finding that the fetal protection policy was impermissible under Title VII, the Court addressed the issue of tort liability and the increased cost of employing fertile women. The Court mentioned the dissenting opinion of Circuit Judge Posner, which stated that potential tort liability for fetal injury might at some point become large enough to constitute a bfoq. In his dissent, Posner contended that "liability for a potential injury to a fetus is a social cost that Title VII does not require a company to ignore."[82] While the Court conceded that Title VII did not "prevent the employer from having a conscience," it held that the statute did bar exclusionary employment policies like fetal protection policies. The Court contended that these two aspects of Title VII were not in conflict.[83] According to the Court, it would be unlikely that a responsible employer, who complied with OSHA regulations, and warned its female employees about potential reproductive risks, would be held liable for prenatal injuries. The Court suggested that existing OSHA lead regulations, which established a series of mandatory protections that aimed at minimizing the risk of fetal harm, eliminated the need for fetal protection policies.[84]

Thus, the Supreme Court rejected Johnson Controls' contention that fetal protection policies were necessary to protect employers from tort liability. The Court stated that Title VII barred employers from dodging their responsibility for occupational health and safety by adopting exclusionary policies. In addition, the Court stated that concerns about tort damages, which "reflect[ed] a fear that hiring fertile women will cost more,"[85] did not constitute an affirmative defense to a Title VII claim. The Court's analysis of the tort liability claim was based upon its understanding that potential liability would not "be so prohibitive as to threaten the survival of the employer's business."[86] Interestingly, the Court's decision appears to have left open the question of whether gender-based employment policies would be permissible where potential tort damages threatened the solvency of the business.

While the Court distinguished those cases where potential liability might be so excessive as to make the continued functioning of the business impossible, it suggested that, in the vast majority of cases, fetal protection policies would be impermissible under Title VII. In its conclusion, the Court cited *Muller v. Oregon,* stating that "[c]oncern for a woman's existing or potential offspring historically has been the excuse for denying women equal employment opportunities."[87] The Court held that Congress enacted the Pregnancy Discrimination Act to bar discrimination based upon a woman's ability to become pregnant. According to the Court, the PDA prohibited employers from "decid[ing] whether a woman's reproductive role is more important to herself and her family than her economic role." Instead, the PDA placed this choice squarely with the woman.

Thus, the fetal protection policy at issue in *Johnson Controls* violated Title VII as amended by the PDA. The majority holding suggests that the Court would be quite hesitant to find that a gender-based employment policy based upon potential tort liability would pass muster under Title VII. It bears noting, however, that the majority opinion appears to have left open two critical issues. First, Justice Blackmun suggested that gender-neutral policies, that is, policies that bar both men and women from certain jobs on the basis of their reproductive capacity, did not have to meet the same rigorous standards under Title VII as do sex specific policies like that at issue in *Johnson Controls.*[88] Instead, a gender-neutral policy would be evaluated under the business necessity standard.

Second, Blackmun's opinion left open the possibility, however remote, that potential tort liability might constitute a bfoq of sterility where this liability threatened the solvency of the business. The Court makes this suggestion nearly at the end of its decision. In discussing the application of the bfoq defense, the majority cryptically notes:

> We, of course, are not presented with, nor do we decide, a case in which costs would be so prohibitive as to threaten the survival of an employer's business. We merely reiterate our prior holdings that the *incremental* cost of hiring women cannot justify discrimination against them.[89] (emphasis added)

Thus, Blackmun's majority opinion leaves open two important questions: first, whether sex-neutral policies that bar workers on the basis of reproductive capacity may be justified under disparate impact/business necessity; and second, whether a bfoq of sterility justifies barring women where tort liability threatens to bankrupt a business. The future adjudication of cases involving gender-based distinctions will reveal how lower federal and state courts will interpret these two important issues.

As has been noted, while the nine Justices were unanimous in their decision that Johnson Controls' policy constituted per se discrimination under Title VII, and that the bfoq exception did not apply to this policy, they disagreed about the breadth of the bfoq exception. While the majority opinion held that the bfoq defense was extremely narrow, and that it would almost always be inapplicable to a fetal protection policy, the concurrences in this case suggested that a fetal protection policy might fall within the bfoq exception under certain circumstances.

Concurring Opinions. There were two concurrences in this case: one was written by Justice White and joined by Chief Justice Rehnquist and Justice Kennedy; the other was written by Justice Scalia. The opinion by Justice White rejected much of the majority opinion's interpretation of Title VII and the bfoq exception. In fact, the White opinion stated that it concurred with the majority opinion, which reversed the decisions of the lower appellate and district courts, mainly because the lower court cases had been decided on the basis of summary judgment. According to Justice White, the *Johnson Controls* case could not be decided on the basis of summary judgment.

The most serious disagreement between the majority opinion and the opinion written by Justice White concerned the scope of the bfoq defense. While the majority opinion held that Johnson Controls' policy was not permissible under the bfoq exception, and was circumspect about the legality of any fetal protection policies in the future, Justice White contended that the bfoq defense might justify the use of a fetal protection policy in certain circumstances. White contended that concerns about tort liability arising from fetal harm might form the basis for a bfoq defense and, thus, might validate a fetal protection policy.

Justice White criticized the majority for its reluctance to consider the possibility that concerns about tort liability might constitute a valid bfoq. According to White, prior court holdings supported the view that cost considerations might form the basis for a bfoq defense.[90] White contended that the Supreme Court's decisions in *Dothard v. Rawlinson* and *Western Air Lines, Inc. v. Criswell* supported the view that the bfoq defense could be founded upon concerns about cost and third-party safety. Moreover, White contended that the holdings in these two cases "[made] clear that avoidance of substantial safety risks to third parties is *inherently* part of both an employee's ability to perform a job and an employer's 'normal operation' of its business."[91] White not only found that a fetal protection policy might be permissible under the bfoq defense, he also suggested that a worker's capacity to reproduce could be integrally related to their ability to perform a job. Thus, White implied that fertility, or rather, infertility, could be a job requirement in much the same way as are education, skill, and experience.

Although Justice White's opinion concurred with the majority's decision to reverse the Seventh Circuit's holding in *U.A.W. v. Johnson Controls,* the White opinion is much closer conceptually to the circuit's decision than it is to that of the majority. Both the White concurrence and the Seventh Circuit opinion contended that third-party safety was part of the "essence" of nearly all businesses. In addition, both opinions asserted that fertile women were not similar in their ability or inability to work as male workers if their employment imposed substantial safety and liability costs as a result of fetal exposure to occupational hazards.

Justice White suggested that some fetal protection policies might be permissible under the bfoq defense. His opinion concurred with that of the majority, however, mainly because he believed that this case was inappropriate for summary judgment. According to White, serious issues of fact existed at the time of trial, and, for this reason, the case should not have been decided by summary judgment.[92] Despite the existence of these factual issues, White indicated that fetal protection policies that were narrowly drawn to ensure the safe and efficient operation of a business might be lawful under Title VII.

Justice Scalia also filed a concurrence in this case. While Scalia agreed with White that considerations of cost and liability might form the basis of a bfoq exception, he approached the other relevant issues much differently than did either the majority opinion or the White concurrence. At the outset, Scalia stated that he agreed with the majority's analysis of the fetal protection issue; however, his understanding of the relevance of scientific evidence demonstrating the effects of paternal exposure to occupational hazards diverged sharply from that of the majority.

In his concurrence, Justice Scalia contended that evidence about the effects of lead exposure on the reproductive functions of male workers was irrelevant to the fetal protection issue. As may be recalled, evidence about the effects of paternal exposure had been used to demonstrate the discriminatory manner in which employers utilized these policies. Scalia asserted, however, that evidence about male transmission was irrelevant, since the Pregnancy Discrimination Act expressly barred employers from discriminating against women on the basis of pregnancy, regardless of the source of fetal harm. Scalia stated that "[b]y reason of the Pregnancy Discrimination Act, it would not matter if all pregnant women placed their children at risk in taking these [hazardous] jobs, just as it does not matter if no men do so."[93] Thus, Justice Scalia contended that the worker alone should make the choice about whether to expose his or her fetus to occupational harm. Title VII and the PDA barred employers from making this choice for them.[94]

Justice Scalia's contention that it is the worker, and not the employer, who should determine whether or not to perform a certain job clearly links his opinion with that of the majority. Both opinions held that an employer was not permitted to bar an employee from a particular job solely on the basis of concerns about fetal health. Instead, the worker had to be apprised of the risk and had to make the decision about whether to be exposed to such toxins. Ironically, the delegation of this decision to the worker may have serious repercussions for worker and fetal health. It is possible that, by barring employers from enacting these policies that aim, at least in part, at protecting fetal health, we are dissuading employers from taking action to protect fetal and reproductive health.[95]

Many analysts have argued that exclusionary policies like those employed by Johnson Controls, which barred women from certain jobs, did not serve fetal health since they removed the incentives for employers to make the workplace safe for employees and their fetuses. In some situations, however, the workplace cannot be made safe for either workers or their fetuses. It is in these difficult situations that employer policies that would allow men or women to choose to opt out of certain jobs that endanger fetal or reproductive health might be helpful.

Thus, while all nine justices concurred in the decision in *U.A.W. v. Johnson Controls,* there was substantial divergence among the justices about the permissibility of these policies under Title VII. The majority opinion asserted that cost-based considerations did not render fetal protection policies permissible under the bfoq exception to Title VII. The majority did not rule out the possibility, however, that these policies might be legal if enacted to guard against insolvency. The concurring opinions expressly stated that concerns about liability costs might, at some point, become serious enough to justify making infertility a bona fide occupational qualification. Both the majority and the concurring opinions left open the possibility, however slim, that lower courts may interpret *Johnson Controls* to allow a fetal protection policy, especially one that is used to protect against bankruptcy.

Conclusions

Throughout the 1980s and early 1990s, the federal and state courts treated fetal protection policies differently than they treated other sex-based employment policies. Fetal protection policies clearly constituted per se discrimination, since they explicitly classified employees on the basis of their sex; however, nearly all the federal and state courts that examined these policies analyzed them under the much less rigorous disparate impact framework. Moreover, all but one of the federal appellate courts to have adjudicated a fetal protection policy altered traditional bfoq analysis to include concerns about fetal health and safety. In so doing, the courts granted fetuses special protections, separate from those of women. This modification of the bfoq exception to include employer concerns about fetal health and safety constituted a radical departure from the legislative history of Title VII and from settled Title VII caselaw.

Moreover, while the Supreme Court found that the fetal protection policy at issue in *U.A.W. v. Johnson Controls* was barred under Title VII, it left the door open as to whether concerns about tort liability might at some point become large enough to justify these policies under the bfoq exception. Again, this categorization of tort liability as falling within the bfoq exception was a departure from settled caselaw and from the legislative history of Title VII and the PDA. By leaving open to question of whether tort liability might justify a bfoq of sterility, the Court's decision makes it unclear whether the fetal protection issue has been definitively decided.

Courts frequently engage in policymaking and the appellate courts and, in particular, the Supreme Court were the lead policymakers in the area of fetal protection in the 1980s and early 1990s. There were three components of this court-formulated policy on fetal protection. First, the courts tended to treat fetal protection policies differently than they would have other forms of disparate treatment. In large part, this differential treatment was a result of the court's conceptions of women's roles in society and of fetal rights. All of the lower courts that considered this issue based their holdings on what they considered to be common-sensical notions about motherhood, pregnancy, and fetal rights. All but one of the federal appellate courts considered fetal rights to be a part of Title VII analysis, and all of the courts, including the Supreme Court, engaged in a balancing of fetal rights against women's employment rights.

Moreover, the debate over abortion, with its contraposition of women's rights with fetal rights, played out in the fetal protection controversy. All the courts that considered these policies employed a zero-sum calculus, pitting women against their potential fetuses. The Seventh Circuit in *Johnson Controls* described these potential fetuses as individuals, and expressly elevated concerns about the "unborn" over the employment rights of women. The Supreme Court in *Johnson Controls* stepped back from this view of fetal rights. It based its decision on its understanding of women's rights under Title VII and pointedly ignored calls to grant fetuses independent rights. It bears noting, however, that, by leaving open the question of whether gender-neutral policies can be justified under the less rigorous disparate impact framework, the Court also left open the possibility that men's and women's employment rights might, at some time in the future, be subordinated to fetal rights.

This linkage between abortion and fetal protection is troubling, especially since it is conceivable that the adjudication of fetal protection cases in the 1980s and early 1990s might have been employed to restrict women's reproductive rights. By suggesting that fetuses have separate rights in the workplace, the courts in these fetal protection cases may have undermined *Roe v. Wade,* which held that the right of a woman to choose to have an abortion in the first or second trimester outweighed any fetal "rights" that the state might seek to assert during this period.

Thus, the first component of judicial policymaking in the area of fetal protection is the "special" consideration afforded these policies under Title VII. This first aspect overlaps with the second, in that the adjudication of these policies also functioned as a forum for the ongoing debate about gender equality in American society. By examining the holdings of the lower courts in this area, it becomes apparent that the debate over these policies was grounded in a disagreement about what women's roles in industrial society should be.

A third aspect of judicial policymaking in this area is the inability of the courts to comprehend complex scientific data. The court holdings in this area, particularly the holding of the Seventh Circuit in *Johnson Controls,* reveal that courts frequently miscomprehended the nature of the scientific method and the procedures used to evaluate occupational and environmental toxins.

Judicial policymaking is often problematic, as it appears to have been in the area of fetal protection. Quite simply, courts are not well-suited for policymaking. They lack the expertise to analyze complex scientific data and are not capable of implementing their decisions. In fact, the impact of the Court's holding in *Johnson Controls* on employer practices remains unclear. Nevertheless, judicial policymaking, with all of its shortcomings, seemed inevitable in the fetal protection debate after Congress and the administrative agencies began opting out.

Unfortunately, the judiciary's "policy" on fetal protection tended to reinforce cultural stereotypes of gender and sex. The judiciary's perception of sex roles was not unprecedented, rooted as it was in adjudication of state protective laws of the early 1900s and gender-based claims of the 1970s and 1980s. It was troubling, however. In the fetal protection debate, the courts, in their efforts to legitimate employer policies, frequently misconstrued scientific data on maternal and paternal transmission of toxins, and also miscomprehended the nature of the scientific method itself. Moreover, on their way to legitimating these policies, the courts ignored statutory law and caselaw on gender discrimination in employment. As a result, the courts sacrificed not only women's employment rights, but, quite possibly, occupational health and safety in general, in order to reinforce a notion of the sexes as fundamentally different, and a conception of fetuses as having rights separate from those of the woman.

8. Fetal Protection Policies and Gender Equality: Some Conclusions

Fetal protection policies, which excluded fertile women from certain workplaces out of a concern about fetal health, were a disturbing development in employment relations. These policies barred women who worked in traditionally male-dominated workplaces from a large number of jobs, thus exacerbating the existing sex segregation of the work force. In addition, by allowing employers to bar susceptible workers instead of cleaning up dirty workplaces, these policies undermined efforts to make the workplace safer.

While fetal protection policies were harmful to employees and potential employees because of their direct influence on gender segregation and occupational safety and health, they were perhaps even more damaging because of their impact on gender roles. The policies were based on a view of women as potentially pregnant workers for whom work force participation is of secondary importance. This view elevated women's reproductive function while denigrating their work-force contribution. Fetal protection policies "rank ordered" women's roles, safeguarding the childbearing role at the expense of the worker role.

These policies were, in many ways, anomalous. At a time when the discriminatory practices of employers were becoming more subtle and the statistical models for proving discrimination were becoming more complex, fetal protection policies stood out as a striking example of explicit, per se discrimination. Employers justified their exclusion of women by relying on both moral and pragmatic rationales. Not only did they contend that they had a strong moral obligation to protect fetuses from toxic substances in the workplace, they also claimed that the exclusion of women was necessary to limit their potential tort liability. The extent to which employers adopted these policies for benevolent or even benign motives is open to question, since employers "protected" the offspring of women only, even where men were also exposed to potential embryotoxins and fetotoxins.

It is impossible to determine whether employers' motives in adopting these policies were benevolent or malevolent, and, for the purposes of this book, such a determination is almost irrelevant. What is important is how governmental entities, charged with ensuring equal employment opportunity and safeguarding occupational safety and health, responded to this view of women as marginal workers who could be barred from the workplace on grounds of protecting the health of their potential fetuses. Policymakers had the statutory authority to bar these policies under existing employment discrimination law and to require employers to make workplaces safe for *both* workers and their offspring. Unfortunately, they did neither. This non-response had as much to do with the government's conceptions of sex and gender roles as it did with the peculiar characteristics of fetal protection policies. For much of this nation's history, governmental decision-makers have demonstrated a startling ambivalence in dealing with gender issues. American policymakers, and the public as well, have shown that they have difficulty distinguishing between sex, which is based solely upon one's biology, and gender, which is derived not only from physical characteristics but from socially and culturally contrived features as well. The governmental response to fetal protection policies may seen as symptomatic of this continuing confusion.

Fetal protection policies, which implicated the most permanent and immutable of sex characteristics, the capacity to become pregnant, raised fundamental questions about women's "basic nature," women's responsibility for childbearing, and women's ability to control their reproduction. These policies used strong cultural images of motherhood and pregnancy to foster a view of women as fundamentally different from men by virtue of their childbearing potential. The policies derived from the perception that women had a "special" role in the propagation of the race, and that this role overrode all other activities that women might seek to engage in. At the heart of the debate over these policies were differing views of the nature of sex characteristics and of the implications deriving from the fact that women alone bear children.

The fetal protection controversy may be seen as a microcosm of the larger debate over equality that has divided not only biological determinists and cultural determinists but feminists as well. On the one hand, biological determinists and special treatment feminists have argued that men and women are fundamentally different and that these differences necessitate different treatment, especially where childbearing is at issue. On the other hand, cultural determinists and equal treatment feminists have emphasized the similarities between the sexes, minimized the differences, and contended that pregnancy and childbearing can be analogized to other physical conditions that are experienced by both men and women. Debate among these groups has focused on the significance of physical differences, reproductive characteristics in particular, and has examined the need for and desirability of formulating gender-based laws and policies.

Fetal protection policies fit neatly into the ongoing equality debate, since they are based on a view of the sexes as fundamentally different by virtue of women's childbearing capabilities. These policies derive from the perception that women alone are responsible for the well-being of their offspring and that this procreative role must be protected, even at the expense of other aspects of women's lives.

In evaluating the response of governmental institutions to fetal protection policies, perhaps one should not expect the government to vigorously oppose these gender-based policies. Our government, operating according to a view of the sexes as fundamentally different, has frequently permitted laws and policies that have a negative impact on women. Throughout the twentieth century, the federal and state legislatures and courts have formulated policies that have resulted in women being treated differently than men solely on the basis of primary and secondary sex characteristics. In fact, the governmental response to fetal protection policies may be seen as part of a larger trend toward disregarding or, at best, discounting claims based on sex discrimination.

Throughout the nineteenth and twentieth centuries, our federal and state governments have taken a lax approach to combating gender discrimination. In the early part of this century, most state legislatures formulated some kind of "protective" legislation barring women from working in certain occupations and also set maximum-hours limitations. The Supreme Court upheld the use of these laws, finding them necessary to protect women's childbearing and childrearing roles. In fact, there is a striking similarity between the state protective laws of the early 1900s and the fetal protection policies of the 1980s. Both elevated women's procreative role above all other functions and imposed restrictions to protect and foster this role. In addition, both succeeded in convincing governmental organizations that the laws or policies were necessary to promote a greater good.

Governmental activities in the fetal protection debate also paralleled the governmental response to contemporary gender-based laws. The ultimate demise of the ERA was at least in part a result of the perception by many legislators that all culturally based distinctions between men and women had their basis in physical differences. Similarly, the U.S. Supreme Court's decision in *Rostker v. Goldberg*, which upheld the all-male draft, relied on a view of sex differences as encompassing not only biological characteristics but sociological differences also. In the contemporary era, both Congress and the Court have interpreted sex equality in such a way that laws were permitted to stand that were based not only on biological differences but on stereotypical notions of sex roles also.

The fetal protection controversy brought to a head many of the questions about gender equality and women's role in industrial society that had been simmering just below the surface of public debate. Proponents of these policies manipulated cultural images of motherhood and pregnancy in an effort to win support for the policies. The volatile nature of the gender equality debate, especially when coupled with the symbolic imagery used to support fetal protection policies, probably made the government more hesitant to tackle the complex issues raised by these policies. In addition, the controversy over abortion spilled over to further complicate the response of decision-makers to fetal protection policies.

Even though Congress and the regulatory agencies were charged with ensuring equality of employment opportunity and protecting worker health, little governmental activity was actually aimed at regulating the use of fetal protection policies. Congress failed to provide either new legislation for dealing with these policies or effective oversight of those administrative agencies having responsibility for ensuring equal employment opportunity and occupational safety and health. The administrative agencies themselves failed to formulate or implement coherent guidelines for regulating the use of these policies, and they failed to utilize existing case law, statutory law, and agency policy to regulate the policies.

The little activity that did occur was centered in the administrative agencies and was characterized by a tendency to treat fetal protection policies differently than other facially discriminatory policies. Moreover, agency activity was frequently inconsistent with caselaw, statutory law, and agency policy in the areas of equal employment opportunity and occupational safety and health. For example, the Equal Employment Opportunity Commission created a separate category for dealing with these policies, contending that they were different from other forms of disparate treatment, without spelling out the grounds for this distinction. The Occupational Safety and Health Administration refused to attempt to regulate these policies under its general duty clause, despite the fact that the policies appear to have been governed under this clause. In fact, OSHA's failure to promulgate new standards for reproductive and fetal toxins, together with its lax enforcement of existing standards, shifted the responsibility for protection against occupational exposure to toxins from the employer to the female employee. Fetal protection policies also dictated how the costs of occupational exposure to toxins should be borne, deciding that women should shoulder most of these costs.

These agencies engaged in a subtle balancing of fetal rights and women's rights, in an effort that was very similar to the government's approach to abortion in the 1980s. The EEOC's policy did not bar fetal protection policies under Title VII's disparate treatment framework; rather, it permitted the policies under disparate impact, provided employers could show that they had marshalled sufficient evidence about the workplace hazard. Similarly, after the D.C. Circuit's opinion in *American Cyanamid,* OSHA did not prohibit fetal protection policies under its general duty clause; instead, it required that employers meet certain, albeit minimal, standards of workplace safety. Unfortunately for women, the balancing approach of the EEOC and OSHA, and by association, of the OFCCP and the EPA, was one that greatly advantaged the fetus or potential fetus. So great was this advantage that these agencies effectively disregarded the fact that their primary duty was to workers, not fetuses.

Like the administrative agencies, Congress also shirked its oversight responsibilities in the areas of equal employment and occupational safety and health. In large part, this failure may be the result of a perception by the largely self-interested legislators that the fetal protection issue was a "hot potato" and that any stated position on this issue would end up costing them votes at reelection time. Legislators had begun to recognize that abortion was a costly issue in terms of electoral consequences, and that the fetal protection and abortion controversies were connected, if only in their discourse about fetal rights.

It bears noting that the language of "fetal protection" was employed early in the abortion debate. Anti-abortion activists, who sought to make abortions less accessible, were successful in lobbying for state legislation mandating that physicians performing abortions attempt to preserve fetal life.[1] While these "fetal protection" regulations were struck down by the Supreme Court in cases heard in the 1970s through mid-1980s, the Court ultimately permitted such a regulation in its 1989 decision in *Webster v. Reproductive Health Services*.[2]

A heightened sensitivity about the connection between abortion and fetal protection likely diminished the resolve of legislators to act decisively in the fetal protection debate. Congress only considered taking action after the Seventh Circuit issued its highly unpopular decision in *Johnson Controls*. Even then, it could not be said that Congress acted decisively; its response to this holding was to question OSHA about its role in regulating fetal protection policies, and to formulate, but not introduce, the 1991 Employee Protection Act.

Thus, effective regulation of fetal protection policies by Congress and the regulatory agencies was hampered by the controversial nature of this issue. Legislators were concerned about taking a stance on an issue for which the electoral consequences were uncertain. Similarly, administrators, many of whom had limited staff or budget to deal with this issue, chose to overlook the problems raised by these policies. In large part, this institutional failure was the result of a lack of consensus over what was required by the principle of equality, as the debate over fetal protection brought into conflict competing views of gender equality. Administrators and legislators may have been uncertain about whether employers were in fact barred by anti-discrimination laws from distinguishing among workers on the basis of childbearing capacity. Although this issue was settled by the Pregnancy Discrimination Act, these legislators and agency heads may have continued to be uncertain about whether these policies were, or should have been, barred under this legislation.

The institutional willpower to oppose fetal protection policies was further weakened by the manipulation of cultural images relating to women's physical capacities and childbearing and by the fetal rights discourse. Those who supported fetal protection policies, and these included not only employers but also religious groups and New Rightists, were very skillful at using these themes to gain support among both governmental officials and the public at large. In Congress and the administrative agencies the use of these stereotypical images appear to have had some effect. It was in the courts, however, that the manipulation of these images had the greatest impact.

In the vacuum left by the inaction of Congress and the regulatory agencies, the judiciary was left with the primary responsibility for evaluating fetal protection policies. It is generally well-accepted that courts engage in policymaking: the separation of powers is often blurred to allow an overlap of functions by governmental entities. As a result, courts sometimes act as "political" institutions, formulating policies to deal with controversial issues. Judicial decisions in fetal protection cases have had a significant impact on women and have reinforced stereotypical notions of gender roles and sex differences. In evaluating the judicial response to fetal protection policies, this book has had two principal foci. First, it has aimed at interpreting the policy formulated by the courts in their efforts to evaluate fetal protection policies. Second, it has attempted to assess the impact of judicial decisions in this area.

While there was some inconsistency among the federal and state courts as to the proper disposition of fetal protection policies, certain trends in the adjudication of these policies had become apparent by the late 1980s and early 1990s. All the courts that adjudicated these policies, from the federal and state appeals courts to the U.S. Supreme Court, came to consider the relationship between Title VII and the "right" of the fetus to be free from workplace exposures. While the Supreme Court considered fetal rights in a cursory fashion, stating only that the workplace at issue in *Johnson Controls* did not necessitate a bfoq of infertility, it left open the possibility that tort liability for fetal harm might at some point become large enough to allow such a bfoq.

Other courts that considered this issue were less circumspect about the significance of fetal rights than was the Supreme Court. In upholding the fetal protection policy at issue in *Wright v. Olin,* the Fourth Circuit took into account the effects of toxic exposure on the "unborn child." The Seventh Circuit espoused an even more radical view of fetal rights. In *U.A.W. v. Johnson Controls,* the Seventh Circuit held that the fetus was an "independent individual" with rights separate from those of the woman.[3] Thus, while there was wide variation among courts, one element of the judicial policy on this issue has been a preoccupation with the rights of fetuses and a willingness to balance these rights against the employment rights of women. Again, the uncertainty surrounding the adjudication of abortion cases and the increased willingness of courts to allow more extensive restrictions on access to abortion probably had an impact on the litigation of fetal protection cases.

Like the legislatures and the agencies, the judiciary tended to decide fetal protection cases on the basis of stereotypical notions of women and the physical differences between the sexes. The federal appellate courts and state courts that decided these cases carved out a special niche for these policies, deciding them differently than other cases involving disparate treatment of a protected class. In sidestepping those prior holdings, these courts relied upon common-sensical notions about the importance of wage-earning for women, the responsibility of women for the well-being of their fetuses and, in some cases, their families, and the differing susceptibility of fetuses to maternal and paternal exposure to occupational toxins.

In most cases, these conceptions about the importance of gender in determining work-force participation had to be "teased out" of the language of the court's decision; in some cases, however, these stereotypical conceptions of sex roles were made explicit.[4] For example, in *Johnson Controls,* the Seventh Circuit held the following:

> More is at stake in this case . . . than an individual woman's decision to weigh and accept the risks of employment. Since they have become a force in the workplace as well as in the home *because of their desire to better the family's station in life, it would not be improbable that a female employee might somehow rationally discount this clear risk* in her hope and belief that her infant would not be adversely affected from lead exposure.[5] (emphasis added)

For this court, women were not serious workers. They did not get jobs outside the home because they needed to work; instead, their incomes were merely "extra" money used to make the family more comfortable. This myth of "pin money" is not a novel one. Throughout the first half of the 1900s, many individuals in government and the private sector espoused this view in an attempt to limit women's work-force participation.

Thus, the disposition of fetal protection policies by the courts had two key elements. First, all courts that considered this issue, including the Supreme Court, weighed the rights of fetuses to be free from workplace exposures against the rights of women to choose their employment. The concern about fetal well-being that underlay this balancing approach is noteworthy, especially given the expansion of fetal rights in the areas of criminal, tort, and property law. Moreover, this concern for fetal rights may have continuing importance for the abortion debate, because it establishes the principle that embryos and fetuses, even those in the first or second trimesters of development, may have rights separate from those of the woman.

The second element of judicial policymaking in the area of fetal protection is the grounding of many of these decisions in stereotypical notions of women's relative physical weaknesses, their primary responsibility for the well-being of their families, and their role as secondary participants in the paid work force. Many of these ideas have lingering significance for the ongoing debate over gender equality. In fact, these decisions may be seen as reinforcing a view of women as substantially different from men by virtue of their procreative capacity. The adjudication of fetal protection policies by the federal and state courts clearly contributes to this debate by giving support to the views of biological determinists and special treatment feminists, who contend that the sexes may be treated differently where reproduction is at issue.

By examining the governmental response to fetal protection policies, this book has aimed at assessing the manner in which institutions of government deal with questions of sex difference. As has been demonstrated, the government has had difficulty in responding effectively to issues involving reproductive differences between men and women. The manipulation of symbolic images of motherhood and pregnancy by advocates of these policies confused the issue of biological difference, making it difficult, if not impossible, to separate the fetal protection issue from wider questions involving gender differences.

In large part because of these wider ramifications, the governmental institutions were unable, or unwilling, to take action aimed at regulating fetal protection policies. Congress and the administrative agencies charged with enforcing anti-discrimination and occupational safety and health legislation did little to deal with either the fetal protection policies or the problem of reproductive hazards more generally. As a result, aggrieved workers were forced to utilize the state and federal court systems. These courts, however, were not disinterested arbiters of these policies. Throughout the nineteenth and twentieth centuries, the judiciary has interpreted gender equality in such a way as to emphasize the differences between the sexes and, on the basis of these differences, permit disparate treatment. In adjudicating fetal protection policies, nearly all the federal district and appellate courts, as well as the state courts, used conceptions of gender difference to allow employers to bar women on the basis of concerns about fetal health.

The institutions of our government failed to respond effectively to private employer policies that had a significant impact on women's employment opportunities. At a time when women are widely perceived as having achieved equality in the workplace and at home, this institutional failure may be startling. In light of the government's record in the area of gender discrimination and sexual equality, however, this failure should come as no real surprise. Government in the U.S. has long operated according to certain assumptions about the nature of gender equality and about the importance of sex characteristics in determining rights in the public spheres, so that fetal protection policies did not emerge in a landscape free from sex discrimination. Since *Bradwell v. Illinois* and *Muller v. Oregon,* our governmental institutions have viewed women as fundamentally different from men and have used this conception of difference to justify the disparate treatment of women. The use of fetal protection policies, and the failure of governmental institutions to bar these policies, may be seen as simply another manifestation of this longstanding pattern.

It remains to be seen whether the Supreme Court's holding that these policies are barred under Title VII will have any real impact. If Congress and the administrative agencies continue to refuse to regulate these policies, the implementation of the Court's decision will be dependent upon further litigation. This is indeed a troubling prospect, given the expense, time, and uncertainty inherent in a strategy of continued reliance upon judicial policymaking. The principles of equal employment opportunity and occupational safety and health would clearly be better met by the effective oversight of private employer policies and practices by those institutions of government best equipped to provide such oversight, namely, the legislature and the administrative agencies.

In the future, the simmering controversy over abortion will likely continue to boil over into debates like this one. As a nation, we remain divided over the very questions that were at the heart of the fetal protection debate: namely, the establishment of fetal rights and the extent to which reproduction, or reproductive capacity, should determine one's role in society. One might reasonably expect that these issues will continue to be played out in various arenas and that the debate over fetal protection has not been definitively resolved.

Notes
References
Index

Notes

Preface

1. As Zillah R. Eisenstein has noted, "[The] viewing of women as mothers makes them their bodies . . . They are weaker and less intelligent than men; they are dominated by their reproductive functions" (Eisenstein, *The Female Body and the Law* [Berkeley: University of California Press, 1988], 83).

2. Margaret Atwood, *The Handmaid's Tale* (New York: Fawcett Crest, 1985), 284.

Chapter 1. Introduction

1. Wendy W. Williams, "Firing the Woman to Protect the Fetus: The Reconciliation of Fetal Protection with Employment Opportunity Goals Under Title VII," *The Georgetown Law Journal* 69 (1980–81): 647.

2. Mary E. Becker, "From *Muller v. Oregon* to Fetal Vulnerability Policies," *The University of Chicago Law Review* 53 (1986): 1226.

3. U.S. Office of Technology Assessment, United States Congress, *Reproductive Hazards in the Work Place* (Washington, D.C.: Government Printing Office, 1985), 19.

4. Maureen Paul, Cynthia Daniels, and Robert Rofosky, "Corporate Response to Reproductive Hazards in the Work Place: Results of the Family, Work, and Health Survey," *American Journal of Industrial Medicine* 16 (1989): 279–80.

5. Paul et al., "Corporate Response," 267.

6. Becker, "From *Muller v. Oregon*," 1226.

7. Joan E. Bertin, "Reproductive Hazards in the Workplace," in Sherrill Cohen and Nadine Taub, eds., *Reproductive Laws for the 1990s* (Clifton, NJ: Humana Press, 1989), 279.

8. Bertin, "Reproductive Hazards," 279.

9. Bureau of National Affairs, Inc., "Awareness of Fetal Risks in Workplace 'An Emerging Issue,'" *Occupational Safety and Health Reporter* 20 (1990): 25.

10. Becker, "From *Muller v. Oregon*," 1238–39.

11. Paul et al., "Corporate Response," 273.

12. Becker, "From *Muller v. Oregon*," 1238–39.

13. Michael J. Wright, "Reproductive Hazards and 'Protective' Discrimination," *Feminist Studies* 5 (1979): 304–5.

14. Wendy Kaminer, *A Fearful Freedom: Women's Flight from Equality* (Reading, MA: Addison-Wesley, 1990), 136. A recent study conducted by the National Institute for Occupational Safety and Health found that pregnant women who work at video terminals all day were not at greater risk of having miscarriages. The results of this study are not viewed as dispositive on the issue of vdt's and reproductive health, however; many scientists believe that other studies need to be done before vdt use may be ruled out as a potential reproductive hazard ("Major U.S. Study Finds No Miscarriage Risk from Video Terminals," *New York Times,* 14 March 1991, sec. A).

15. In January 1987, several manufacturers of semiconductor chips announced that they would limit the employment of women in response to a study that showed that women employed in the manufacture of these chips had a higher rate of miscarriage. Prior to this, women had been excluded only in industries in which they were a distinct minority. The majority of employees in this industry, however, are women. Joan Bertin, an attorney with the ACLU Reproductive Rights Project, contends that recent developments in the semiconductor industry suggest that women are always marginal workers, and that "their rights and interests in employment must always yield to their paramount responsibility as childbearers" (Bertin, "Reproductive Hazards," 278).

16. Becker, "From *Muller v. Oregon*," 1240. The "Family, Work, and Health" survey, undertaken in the late 1980s in Massachusetts indicated that while unionization was not associated with better health and safety training, unionized firms were "more likely to restrict women and disallow transfers" than were nonunionized firms (Paul et al., "Corporate Response," 278).

17. U.S. Office of Technology Assessment, 19.

18. U.S. Office of Technology Assessment, 19.

19. W. Williams, 1980–81, "Firing the Woman," 644.

20. U.S. Office of Technology Assessment, 27.

21. There is some basis for this fear of tort liability. For example, in 1982, the Manville Corporation, faced with a potential liability of over two billion dollars as a result of suits brought by more than 16,500 former employees who had contracted asbestos-related diseases, claimed that it was compelled to file for bankruptcy because of this liability.

22. U.S. Office of Technological Assistance, 27; U.S. Congress, House of Representatives, Majority Staff of the Committee on Education and Labor, *A Report on the Equal Employment Opportunity Commission, Title VII, and Workplace Fetal Protection Policies in the 1980s,* 101st Cong., 2d sess. (1990), 10, note 28.

23. Throughout the 1980s, OSHA maintained a "no inspection" policy for employers who demonstrated compliance with occupational safety and health standards. Employers may have believed that regulatory agencies would see these policies as being the "solution" to the problem of reproductive hazards and would choose not to impose additional regulations.

24. It is not necessary that one adopt a "conspiracy theory" of employer actions in order to accept that employers often have less than benevolent motives in enacting these policies. Under Edmund Phelps and Kenneth Arrow's model of statistical discrimination an employer need not act malevolently in formulating discriminatory policies. Phelps and Arrow contend that sex segregation results from imperfect information about the relative abilities of job applicants. In their view, risk-adverse employers "statistically discriminate" against female applicants if they "believe them to be less qualified, reliable, long-term, etc. on the average . . . than are men" (cited in Paulette Olson, "The Persistence of Occupational Segregation: A

Critique of Its Theoretical Underpinnings," *Journal of Economic Issues* 24 [1990]: 161). According to Phelps and Arrow, employers who "statistically discriminate" against women do not act out of any malicious intent or sexist motivation; instead, they act out of "'rational' expectations concerning the productivity of women in comparison with men" (Olson, 161).

25. Christine Jannett and Randal G. Stewart, *Three Worlds of Inequality: Race, Class and Gender* (South Melbourne, Australia: Macmillan of Australia, 1987), 299, note 1.

26. Barbara Sinclair Deckard, *The Women's Movement: Political, Socioeconomic and Psychological Issues*, 3d ed. (New York: Harper and Row, 1983), 109; Nancy E. McGlen and Karen O'Connor, *Women's Rights: The Struggle for Equality in the Nineteenth and Twentieth Centuries* (New York: Praeger, 1983), 244; Victor R. Fuchs, *Women's Quest for Economic Equality* (Cambridge and London: Harvard University Press, 1988), 32.

27. McGlen and O'Connor, *Women's Rights*, 244; Deckard, *The Women's Movement*, 97.

28. Becker, "From *Muller v. Oregon*," 1229.

29. House Report on the EEOC, 6–7.

30. McGlen and O'Connor, *Women's Rights*, 217.

31. For a more extensive discussion, see Barbara Hinkson Craig and David M. O'Brien, *Abortion and American Politics* (Chatham, NJ: Chatham House, 1993).

Chapter 2. Gender and the American Mind

1. While equal treatment is required by the federal Constitution, most state constitutions, and various statutes, the contours of this equality are only vaguely understood. This ambiguity is perhaps most pronounced in the area of gender equality.

2. As evidence of this, Darwin claimed that, "Man is more courageous, pugnacious, and energetic than woman and has a more inventive genius . . . [while] [w]ith women the powers of intuition, of rapid perception, and perhaps of imitation, are more strongly marked than in man; but some, at least, of these faculties are characteristic of the lower races, and therefore of a past and lower state of civilization" (Charles Darwin, *The Descent of Man* [New York: Merrill and Baker, 1890], 587).

3. Kaminer, *Fearful Freedom*, 44.

4. Marion Lowe and Ruth Hubbard, *Women's Nature: Rationalizations of Inequality* (New York: Pergamon, 1983), 4–5. Hubbard points out that this view was not held of poor women, whose ability to work and bear many children was considered "'evidence' of their animal-like, less-evolved nature."

5. Margaret Forster, *Significant Sisters: The Grassroots of Active Feminism: 1839–1939* (London: Secker and Warburg, 1984), 241.

6. Lowe and Hubbard, *Women's Nature*, 5.

7. Joan Smith, "Feminist Analysis of Gender: A Mystique," in Lowe and Hubbard, *Women's Nature*, 89.

8. Steven Goldberg, author of "The Inevitability of Patriarchy," contends that, by nature, women can never be the equals of men either in society or in the home. Men must always be in the leadership position. As support for this position, Goldberg contends that there has never been a society in which women were dominant, and he claims that this "suggestive fact" can be explained by men's inherent drive for dominance. Like other sociobiologists, Goldberg claims that higher levels of the hormone testosterone drive men to dominance (Philip Green, *The Pursuit of Inequality*. New York: Pantheon Books, 1981. 127).

9. Michael Levin, *Feminism and Freedom* (New Brunswick and Oxford: Transaction Books, 1987), 3.

10.   Levin offers this "empirical data" for his contention that women are inherently better parents: women bond with their newborns within the first few hours after birth; breast-feeding produces pleasant hormonal changes; women learn "baby talk" without being taught—by this Levin means that there is an increase in the pitch of their voices, they stress vowels, repeat syllables, and add "ie" to the words, without being instructed to do so (Levin, *Feminism and Freedom,* 270).

11.   Lowe and Hubbard, *Women's Nature,* ix; Eisenstein, *The Female Body,* 109. Neoconservatives and New Rightists disagree, however, about the nature of women's "difference" from men. Members of the New Right believe that God and nature intended that women's primary function was to bear and rear children; men were supposed to provide for and protect their wives and children. Unlike New Rightists, neoconservatives do not contend that women are different because of their role as wife and mother. As Eisenstein has noted, neoconservatives assert that "women's 'difference' from men requires a notion of equality that does not presume sameness" (121). While neoconservatives see efforts to assure equality of opportunity as acceptable, they oppose efforts to enforce what is known as equality of outcome, which presumes a "sameness" between men and women.

12.   Eisenstein, *The Female Body,* 82.

13.   Fuchs, *Women's Quest,* 41.

14.   Fuchs, *Women's Quest,* 43.

15.   Michael Walzer, *Spheres of Justice: A Defense of Pluralism and Equality* (New York: Basic Books, 1983), 241.

16.   Elizabeth H. Wolgast, *Equality and the Rights of Women* (Ithaca and London: Cornell University Press, 1980), 25.

17.   Masako N. Darrough and Robert H. Blank, eds., *Biological Differences and Social Equality: Implications for Social Policy* (Westport, CT, and London: Greenwood Press, 1983), 123.

18.   Deckard, *The Women's Movement,* 98.

19.   Eisenstein, *The Female Body,* 3; Kate Millett, *Sexual Politics* (New York: Ballantine Books, 1969), 36; Deborah L. Rhode, *Justice and Gender: Sex Discrimination and the Law* (Cambridge and London: Harvard University Press, 1989), 3; Walzer, *Spheres of Justice,* 241; Wolgast, *Equality,* 136.

20.   Lowe and Hubbard, *Women's Nature,* 7.

21.   Millett, *Sexual Politics,* 36.

22.   Simone de Beauvoir's *The Second Sex* was a seminal work in this area.

23.   Eisenstein, *The Female Body,* 2.

24.   *California Federal Savings and Loan Association v. Guerra* 479 U.S. 272; 107 S.Ct. 683 (1987).

25.   497 U.S. 272, 276; 107 S.Ct. 683, 687.

26.   In her article about the effects of *California Federal,* Hannah Arterian Furnish contends that the Supreme Court's holding in this case had a direct bearing on the controversy over fetal protection policies. According to Furnish, fetal protection policies may be permissible under this case's standard for interpreting the PDA. Furnish contends that "*California Federal's* thrust and tone suggest that employment distinctions are compatible with the PDA if they are based solely on the physical reality of pregnancy and childbirth and if such distinctions actually advantage rather than penalize pregnant women" (Furnish, "Beyond Protection: Relevant Difference and Equality in the Toxic Work Environment," *University of California at Davis Law Review* 21 [1987]: 11–17).

27.   Kaminer, *Fearful Freedom,* 23; Eisenstein, *The Female Body,* 204. The ACLU brief

drew a parallel between the California law and past protective legislation, claiming that the California law "supports the notion that women's place is in the home" (Eisenstein, 204).

28.   *California Federal Savings and Loan Association v. Guerra* 758 F.2d 390, 396.

29.   479 U.S. 272, 285; 107 S.Ct. 683, 691.

30.   479 U.S. 272, 288; 107 S.Ct. 683, 693.

31.   479 U.S. 272, 297; 107 S.Ct. 683, 698. The concurring opinion of Justice Stevens also voices uncertainty about how much preferential treatment may be afforded to pregnant women. Stevens contends that preferential treatment will only be permissible if it is consistent with the goals of Title VII.

32.   479 U.S. 272, 300; 107 S.Ct. 683, 699.

33.   Carol Gilligan, *In a Different Voice: Psychological Theory and Women's Development* (Cambridge: Harvard University Press, 1982), 171. According to Gilligan, men and women have distinct modes of language and thought: women use a "language of responsibility," that "provides a weblike imagery of relationships," while men use a "language of rights" that hierarchically orders these relationships.

34.   Rhode, *Justice and Gender,* 306.

35.   Susan Lehrer, *Origins of Protective Labor Legislation for Women: 1905–1925* (Albany: State University of New York Press, 1987), 239.

36.   Wolgast, *Equality,* 14–15.

37.   Wolgast, *Equality,* 27.

38.   Wolgast, *Equality,* 16.

39.   Lucinda M. Finley, "Transcending Equality Theory: A Way Out of the Maternity and the Workplace Debate," *Columbia Law Review* 86 (1986): 1153.

40.   Finley, "Transcending Equality," 1181.

41.   One of the strengths of special treatment is that it challenges these male norms, and serves as a critique of what Joan C. Williams has termed "possessive individualism" (J. Williams, "Deconstructing Gender," *Michigan Law Review* 87 (1989): 797). Williams contends that special treatment feminism, or the feminism of difference, is based on a belief in the "transformative potential" of women. According to this belief, women are able to achieve equality not by "playing by men's rules" but by "transforming the world in women's image" (810).

42.   Wendy Kaminer claims that the growing conservatism of the 1980s compelled some feminists to "retreat from egalitarianism, which challenge[s] the ideology of sexual difference, and reviv[es] [the concept of] protectionism, which invoke[s] it" (Kaminer, *Fearful Freedom,* 5). Egalitarians explain that some feminists were disheartened by the fact that gender discrimination remained, in spite of federal anti-discrimination legislation, and that women found it difficult to balance the pressures of home and work.

43.   Finley, "Transcending Equality," 1145.

44.   Wendy W. Williams, "Equality's Riddle: Pregnancy and the Equal Treatment/Special Treatment Debate," *New York University Review of Law and Social Change* 13 (1984–85): 380.

45.   J. Williams, "Deconstructing Gender," 813.

46.   As Kaminer states, "Protectionism, and the determinism it reflects, exploits and engenders hopelessness, resignation to the status quo, and distrust of social freedom, as its history makes clear" (Kaminer, *Fearful Freedom,* 59).

47.   J. Williams, "Deconstructing Gender," 806; Kaminer, *Fearful Freedom,* 62. Kaminer further states that we should reject protectionism because it "is based on a belief that women (and men) are defined by their reproductive roles, that their potential to bear children (whether or not fulfilled) shapes women's temperaments, talents, and ideals. It reflects an assumption that

support for maternity—special protections for mothers, or what some call special rights—matters more than fundamental rights of choice that acknowledge women's integrity as individuals" (215).

48. Eisenstein, *The Female Body*, 104–6.

49. W. Williams, "Equality's Riddle," 327.

50. W. Williams, "Equality's Riddle," 327.

51. W. Williams, "Equality's Riddle," 356.

52. W. Williams, "Equality's Riddle," 352.

53. W. Williams, "Equality's Riddle," 326. As Deborah Rhode has noted, the rhetoric of the relational feminists "is easily appropriated by right-wing leaders who have always know that 'you girls think differently'" (Rhode, *Justice and Gender*, 310).

54. Lehrer, *Origins*, 6.

55. Rhode, *Justice and Gender*, 3.

Chapter 3. Gender Discrimination Past and Present

1. *Lochner v. New York*, 198 U.S. 45 (1905).

2. 198 U.S. 45.

3. 198 U.S. 45, 57; 25 S.Ct. 539, 543.

4. *Muller v. Oregon* 208 U.S. 412 (1908).

5. Sheila B. Kamerman, Alfred J. Kahn and Paul Kingston, *Maternity Policies and Working Women* (New York: Columbia University Press, 1983), 32.

6. *Bradwell v. Illinois* 83 U.S. 130; 16 Wall. 130 (1873).

7. 83 U.S. 130, 141.

8. According to the Court, "The right of a state to regulate the working hours of women rests on the police power and the right to preserve the health of the women of the state, and is not affected by other laws of the state granting or denying to women the same rights as to contract and the elective franchise as are enjoyed by men" (208 U.S. 412).

9. 208 U.S. 421.

10. Ronnie Ratner contends that the *Muller* decision is in part a result of the public's perception that women and children were not regarded as the legal equivalents of adult males and thus were not subject to the laissez-faire doctrine ushered in by *Lochner* (Department of Labor, *Time of Change: 1983 Handbook on Women Workers* [Washington, D.C.: Government Printing Office, 1983], 177).

11. 208 U.S. 422–23.

12. 208 U.S. 421.

13. Judith A. Baer, *The Chains of Protection: The Judicial Response to Women's Labor Legislation* (Westport, CT: Greenwood Press, 1978), 66–67.

14. Kaminer, *Fearful Freedom*, 68.

15. Kaminer, *Fearful Freedom*, 69.

16. Kaminer, *Fearful Freedom*, 70.

17. Kaminer, *Fearful Freedom*, 70.

18. *Adkins v. Children's Hospital*, 261 U.S. 525 (1923). The Court in *Adkins* distinguished its holding from that in *Muller v. Oregon* by stating that: "In view of the great changes which have taken place since [*Muller*] . . . culminating in the nineteenth amendment, it is not unreasonable to say that [gender] differences have now come almost, if not quite, to the vanishing point . . . [W]e cannot accept the doctrine that women of mature age . . . require or

may be subjected to restrictions upon their liberty of contract which could not lawfully be imposed in the case of men under similar circumstances."

According to the Court, since women had the right to vote, there was no further need for protective legislation governing minimum wages. The Court believed that women were to be treated as the functional equals to men, with regard to employment matters.

19. *West Coast Hotel v. Parrish,* 300 U.S. 379 (1937).

20. 300 U.S. 394–95.

21. *West Coast Hotel Company v. Parrish* was decided with five Justices joining the majority opinion of Chief Justice Hughes, and four Justices dissenting. Justice Sutherland's dissenting opinion for this case is quite interesting. The dissent urged the majority to not allow its concern about present economic conditions to undermine settled constitutional doctrine (300 U.S. 379, 402). Furthermore, the dissent, while appearing to agree that women, as a class, have less bargaining power than men, rejected the majority's contention that this difference is the result of physical characteristics. In the dissent's view, "The ability to make a fair bargain, as everyone knows, does not rest on sex" (300 U.S. 413). Thus, the dissent implies, gender-based classifications are unwarranted.

22. *Radice v. New York,* 264 U.S. 292 (1924).

23. 264 U.S. 295.

24. Baer, *Chains,* 101. Moreover, Baer contends that the Court's decision in *Radice* was even a stronger affirmance of the state's power to "determine that women's differences justified different treatment" than was its decision in *Muller* (87–88).

25. *Goesart et al. v. Cleary et al.,* 335 U.S. 464 (1948).

26. 335 U.S. 465–66.

27. 335 U.S. 466.

28. The Court states only that "[t]he Constitution does not require legislatures to reflect sociological insight, or shifting social standards, any more than it requires them to keep abreast of the latest scientific standards" (335 U.S. 466).

29. Wendy Kaminer points out that *Goesart* was decided in the same term that *Shelly v. Kramer* was decided. In *Shelly,* a landmark race discrimination case, the Court held that a municipality could not deny black families the right to live in white neighborhoods on the basis of a belief that the presence of these families might create racial tensions (Kaminer, *Fearful Freedom,* 26). Kaminer points out an interesting inconsistency in the Court's approach to race and sex discrimination claims.

30. 335 U.S. 464, 467 (1948).

31. The district court that heard *Goesart v. Cleary* explained the distinction in this way: "The legislature may . . . have reasoned that a graver responsibility attaches to the bartender who has control of the liquor supply than to the waitress who merely receives prepared orders of liquor from the bartender for service at a table" (*Goesart v. Cleary,* 74 F. Supp. 739 [E.D. Mich. 1947]).

32. As Herma Kay Hill has stated, "The conception of 'protection' in *Goesart* is not one of improving work conditions for a class of workers, but rather of 'protecting' one class of workers (men) from competition from another class (women)" (Herma Kay Hill, "Models of Equality," *University of Illinois Law Review* 1 [1985]: 259).

33. Lehrer, *Origins,* 228; Nancy C. Cott, *The Grounding of Modern Feminism* (New Haven and London: Yale University Press, 1987), 135.

34. Department of Labor, 178. One analyst contends that minimum wage legislation harmed women by making them "more expensive employees." Employers who were obligated to pay

women a minimum wage might opt instead to employ men, for whom a minimum wage was not mandated until 1938 (Rhode, *Justice,* 121).

35. Lehrer, *Origins,* 228.

36. McGlen and O'Connor, *Women's Rights,* 376.

37. States ratifying the ERA for these years are as follows: 1973, 30; 1974, 3; 1975, 1; 1976, 0; 1977, 1.

38. The ERA was reintroduced in the House of Representatives in January 1983; however, it fell six votes short of the two-thirds quorum required for passage. As Sharon Whitney notes, some representatives who voted against the ERA stated that they would have supported it if it had had an anti-abortion amendment tagged on to it (Sharon Whitney, *The Equal Rights Amendment: The History and the Movement* [New York: Franklin Watts, 1984], 96).

39. Whitney, *Equal Rights,* 48.

40. Whitney, *Equal Rights,* 30. In her book, *Why We Lost the ERA,* Jane Mansbridge claims that these polls were misleading. Mansbridge contends that there were serious problems with the methods used in polling, and, consequently, with the data (Jane J. Mansbridge, *Why We Lost the ERA* [Chicago: University of Chicago Press, 1986], 17).

41. Whitney, *Equal Rights,* 70–71.

42. Mansbridge, *ERA,* 2.

43. Deckard, *The Women's Movement,* 179.

44. Mansbridge, *ERA,* 34. Among those individuals who opposed the amendment were the following: "suburban homemakers; working women from offices and factories; politicians (like Jesse Helms) from the South; members of religious groups who strictly interpret scripture and church rules—fundamentalist Christians, orthodox Jews, and conservative Roman Catholics; some lawyers; and members of special groups opposed to progressive ideas and legislation" (Whitney, *Equal Rights,* 56).

45. Whitney, *Equal Rights,* 28. The anti-ERA movement succeeded because it was "privileged" in Mancur Olson's sense of the term. The movement was headed by relatively few people; thus, it was based upon a few, relatively simple precepts which remained consistent throughout the ratification campaign (McGlen and O'Conner, *Women's Rights,* 372–73).

46. McGlen and O'Conner, *Women's Rights,* 33; Whitney, *Equal Rights,* 84.

47. ERA supporters contended that the draft would enable poor women to obtain job skills that they would otherwise not be able to obtain; in addition, women in combat would be entitled to veterans' benefits (Deckard, *The Women's Movement,* 181).

48. Mansbridge, *ERA,* 13.

49. Whitney, *Equal Rights,* 62. Also, see the Supreme Court's decisions in *Griswold v. Connecticut* 381 U.S. 479 (1965), *Eisenstadt v. Baird* 405 U.S. 438 (1972), and *Roe v. Wade* 410 U.S. 113 (1973).

50. Mansbridge, *ERA,* 86.

51. Mansbridge, *ERA,* 20.

52. Whitney, *Equal Rights,* 34–35.

53. Mansbridge, *ERA,* 61–62.

54. *Reed v. Reed* 404 U.S. 71 (1971).

55. Court citing its 1920 decision in *Royster Guano Co. v. Virginia* 253 U.S. 412, 415 (1920).

56. In a concurring opinion, three of the Justices explained why the Court had decided to use the rational relationship standard, rather than the strict scrutiny test. These Justices reasoned that such a judicial holding would be unnecessary if the ERA were to be passed, since, under the ERA, sex distinctions would be inherently suspect (Wolgast, *Equality,* 83).

57. *Sail'er Inn, Inc. v. Kirby* 485 P.2d 529, 540 (1971). While the Supreme Court's decision in *Goesart v. Cleary* remained on the books, the California court disregarded it, holding that "[a]lthough *Goesart* has not been overruled, its holding has been the subject of academic criticism . . . and its sweeping statement that the states are not constitutionally precluded from 'drawing a sharp line between the sexes' has come under increasing limitation." Moreover, the state court held that it "need not, however, speculate as to the continuing validity of *Goesart.* The rationale for upholding the statute in that case cannot sustain [its] statute" (485 P.2d 529, 543).

58. 485 P.2d 529, 539.

59. 485 P.2d 529, 541.

60. *Frontiero v. Richardson* 411 U.S. 677; 93 S.Ct. 1764 (1973).

61. 411 U.S. 677, 683; 93 S.Ct. 1764, 1768.

62. *Craig v. Boren* 429 U.S. 190; 97 S.Ct. 451 (1976).

63. 429 U.S. 190, 197; 97 S.Ct. 451, 457.

64. Wendy W. Williams, "The Supreme Court and Sex Equality," in Sheilah L. Martin and Kathleen E. Mahoney, eds., *Equality and Judicial Neutrality* (Toronto: Carswell Publishers, 1987), 117.

65. W. Williams, "Supreme Court," 117. Furthermore, Williams suggests, "[T]he U.S. Supreme Court is significantly more ambivalent in its commitment to sex equality than race equality . . . This ambivalence is expressed not only in its adoption of an 'intermediate' standard of review, but also in its tenuous commitment even to that standard." Williams contends that the changed composition of the Court in the years since *Craig* was decided makes it unclear as to whether the majority of Justices would apply this standard if a sex-based classification came before the Court (119).

66. Catherine MacKinnon, feminist legal scholar, has proposed an alternative standard for adjudicating sex-based classifications. MacKinnon suggests that the test be whether "the policy or practice in question integrally contributes to the maintenance of an underclass or a deprived position because of gender status" (cited in W. Williams, "Supreme Court," 121). Some feminists, among them Wendy Williams, have rejected this test, claiming that it will not be adopted and cannot work because it "is too nakedly substantive and political to a judiciary deeply invested in viewing itself as neutral and non-interventionist" (W. Williams, "Supreme Court," 122).

67. Kaminer, *Fearful Freedom,* 33; Sylvia A. Law, "Rethinking Sex and the Constitution," *University of Pennsylvania Law Review* 132 (1984): 998; W. Williams, "Supreme Court," 117.

68. Reva Siegel, "Reasoning from the Body: A Historical Perspective on Abortion Regulation and Questions of Equal Protection," *Stanford Law Review* 44 (1991–92): 261, 265.

69. The Fifth Amendment due process clause has been interpreted as imposing the same requirements on the federal government as the equal protection clause of the Fourteenth Amendment imposes on states.

70. *Rostker v. Goldberg* 453 U.S. 57; 101 S.Ct. 2646 (1981).

71. 453 U.S. 64–65.

72. 453 U.S. 78.

73. 1980 Senate Report cited in *Rostker v. Goldberg* 453 U.S. 57, 77; 101 S.Ct. 2646, 2658.

74. Senate Report cited in Marshall dissent, 453 U.S. 57, 92.

75. 453 U.S. 57, 86.

76. The dissenting opinions of both Justices Marshall and White focus upon the distinction between conscription and registration. Both Justices contend that even if women are not allowed in combat, they can make a substantial contribution to military preparedness by being registered for non-combat positions (453 U.S. 85–90). In reality, in a time of combat, only about

two-thirds of those drafted would require combat skills; the other one-third would be needed in non-combat positions (Rhode, *Justice and Gender,* 99). Moreover, the substantial contribution made by women in non-combat positions in the Persian Gulf War suggests that Justices Marshall and White were right about this issue.

77. In the period since the Gulf War, however, this tendency appears to be changing. Through executive action by both the Bush and Clinton administrations, a significant number of jobs, albeit termed "non-combat" positions, have been opened to women.

78. Rhode, *Justice and Gender,* 101.

79. Rhode, *Justice and Gender,* 101.

80. Rhode, *Justice and Gender,* 3–5.

Part 2. The Governmental Response to Fetal Protection Policies

1. Reproductive hazards generally refer to those toxicants that contribute to or cause certain disorders of reproduction; among these are infertility, impotence, menstrual disorders, spontaneous abortion, low birth weight, birth defects, congenital mental retardation, and various genetic disorders (U.S. Department of Health and Human Services, Centers for Disease Control, National Institute for Occupational Safety and Health, *Proposed National Strategy for the Prevention of Disorders of Reproduction* [Washington, D.C.: Government Printing Office, 1989], 2). These toxicants may result in impairment to an individual's procreative capacity or alteration of the normal development of an embryo or fetus.

According to the National Institute on Occupational Safety and Health Registry of the Toxic Effects of Chemical Substances, which has entries for over 79,000 chemicals, 15,000 of these entries, or more than 20 percent, cite data on reproductive effects. Over 2,800 chemicals have been studied for teratogenicity and 38 percent of these have been found to have some teratogenic potential (U.S. Department of Health and Human Services, 2). The National Institutes on Occupational Safety and Health rank reproductive impairment as sixth among the ten leading work-related diseases and impairments. This ranking is based upon the number of workers believed to be exposed to known or suspected reproductive toxicants (U.S. Office of Technology Assessment, 10).

Furthermore, occupational reproductive hazards may have an even greater effect on reproductive outcome than has been suspected previously. The cause of 60–80 percent of birth defects is unknown: only 20–25 percent of congenital abnormalities are believed to be the result of inherited genetic traits and chromosomal abnormalities, and only 10 percent are attributed to environmental factors such as drugs, alcohol, maternal infections, metabolic disorders, or nutritional deficiencies ("Research on Birth Defects Shifts to Flaws in Sperm," *New York Times,* 1 January 1991, sec. A1; U.S. Deparment of Health and Human Services, 3). In addition, at least 10–15 percent of American couples are infertile, meaning that they cannot conceive after having unprotected intercourse for at least one year. Many scientists suspect that the occurrence of both birth defects and infertility may be the result of exposure to occupational toxins ("Research on Birth Defects," 1; U.S. Department of Health and Human Services, 2).

As the GAO has noted, as a field of research, reproductive and developmental toxicity is only forty years old, and it lags behind other areas of research, like cancer, by several decades (U.S. General Accounting Office, *Reproductive and Developmental Toxicants: Regulatory Actions Provide Uncertain Protection* [Washington, D.C.: Government Printing Office, 1991], 13.

2. U.S. General Accounting Office (1991), 44.

3.   Mark A. Rothstein, *Medical Screening of Workers* (Washington, D.C.: Bureau of National Affairs, 1984), 65.

4.   U.S. Department of Health and Human Services, 6.

5.   U.S. Department of Health and Human Services, 6.

6.   U.S. Department of Health and Human Services, 9. It is difficult, however, to prove a causal connection between adverse reproductive outcome and workplace conditions. As NIOSH has noted, this assessment is "confounded by occupational exposure to mixed agents, by nonoccupational factors (like age, personal habits and hobbies), and by the need to evaluate any association relative to the background incidence of the outcomes studied" (U.S. Department of Health and Human Services, 6).

7.   Among these chemicals are arsenic, benzene, carbon disulfide, carbon monoxide, chloroprene, dibromochloropropane (DBCP), ethylene oxide (EtO), fluorocarbon 22, formaldehyde, glycol ethers, lead, mercury, organic mercury, methotrexate, methylene chloride, non-ionizing radiation, tetrachloride, toluene, trichloroethane, and vinyl chloride. This list was derived from a number of sources: among them, the survey conducted by the U.S. General Accounting Office, which examined the activities of four agencies charged with regulating occupational reproductive toxins (U.S. General Accounting Office [1991]); Bureau of National Affairs, "Awareness of Fetal Risks in Workplace An Emerging Issue," *Occupational Safety and Health Reporter* 20 [1990], 26; U.S. Office of Technology Assessment, 8; and W. Williams, "Firing the Woman," 648).

8.   This list was derived from the OSHA response to the GAO survey on the regulation of reproductive toxins. In conversations I have had with them, epidemiologists at OSHA have stressed that reproductive effects are but one consideration in OSHA's regulation of these materials. Moreover, the implication has been that this aspect is neither the overriding concern nor even a major concern in the regulation of these agents.

9.   U.S. General Accounting Office, 47.

10.   It does make sense, however, that the EPA should have regulated DBCP. Although it was restricted because of its adverse reproductive effects upon workers who used it, it could have been released for use by the public. Moreover, there was some question about the environmental effects of this chemical. Thus, evidence indicated that DBCP was both an occupational and an environmental hazard.

11.   For example, a survey conducted in 1980 revealed that 17 percent of female workers with children work in jobs that could involve exposure to teratogens, which are agents that may harm a developing fetus (Rothstein, *Medical Screening*, 65).

It is also widely accepted that fetuses are susceptible to toxins at lower levels of exposure than are women. For this reason, NIOSH warns that pregnant women who are exposed to workplace toxins are more likely to suffer spontaneous abortions or still births, or to have a child with low birth weight, birth defects, or developmental handicaps than are women who are not exposed to these toxins (Report in a *Daily Labor Report* article, cited in Furnish, "Beyond Protection," 18, note 82).

12.   W. Williams, "Firing the Woman," 661.

13.   Part of the problem is that data on adverse reproductive outcomes frequently do not accurately reflect the incidence of spontaneous abortion. Thus, where an embryo is aborted early in the term because of chromosomal or genetic abnormalities, which may be the result of abnormal sperm morphology, the woman may not even be aware that she was pregnant.

14.   "Research on Birth Defects," 1.

15.   "Research on Birth Defects," 1.

16.   Among these agents are alcohol, opiates such as heroin and methadone, waste anes-
thetic gases, benzene, lead, pesticides, polyvinyl chloride, and solvents ("Research on Birth
Defects," 36; Wendy Chavkin, "Occupational Hazards to Reproduction: A Review Essay and
Annotated Bibliography," *Feminist Studies* 5 [1979]: 313; Michael J. Wright, "Reproductive
Hazards and 'Protective' Discrimination," *Feminist Studies* 5 [1979]: 303); Williams, "Firing
the Woman," 657–59; U.S. Department of Health and Human Services, 8).

17.   These studies indicate that there is a greater incidence of birth defects among the
children of welders, fire fighters, and workers exposed to radiation ("Research on Birth Defects," 36; Bertin, "Reproductive Hazards," 280).

18.   Moreover, the most recent research suggests that birth defects may result from paternal exposure prior to conception. Scientists hypothesize that certain toxins can alter sperm
morphology or cause genetic mutations, and that these alterations become manifest in birth
defects and in an increased incidence of spontaneous abortions and stillbirths (Felissa Cohen,
"Paternal Contributions to Birth Defects," *Nursing Clinics of North America* 21.1 [1986]: 52,
62; "Research on Birth Defects," 1).

A more controversial theory is that paternal exposure to occupational hazards may harm a
developing fetus after conception. It is generally accepted that hazardous toxins can be transmitted to the fetus by the mother via the placental membrane; the idea that paternal exposure
places the fetus or child at risk after conception, however, is less well accepted. According to
this theory, paternal transmission to a child or a fetus may occur in two possible ways: the man
may transport hazardous materials from work to home on his clothing, shoes, or hair and thus
expose a child to these materials; or an exposed man may transmit toxic substances to a fetus
through vaginal absorption of those substances that are present in his seminal fluid (W. Williams, "Firing the Woman," 657).

19.   Some epidemiologists even argue that men are more susceptible to workplace toxins.
They claim that pre-conception paternal exposure may ultimately be more dangerous than
post-conception maternal exposure (U.S. Congress, Report on the EEOC, 7-8; Rothstein,
Medical Screening, 63). These scientists contend that sperm are more sensitive to the mutagenic effects of some substances than are ova (U.S. Congress, Report on the EEOC, 7-8). For
example, sperm have been shown to be more sensitive to the mutagenic effects of ionizing
radiation than have ova (Rothstein, *Medical Screening,* 63). Moreover, the rapid cell division
that occurs during sperm production is especially sensitive to mutagenesis, the production of
genetically altered sperm (63). For this reason, paternal exposure to workplace toxins may have
multigenerational effects.

20.   Two governmental research-gathering agencies have considered the scientific basis
for these policies and both have rejected the differential treatment of female workers. The
National Institute on Occupational Safety and Health has concluded that "neither sex can be
said to be more vulnerable" to occupational toxins, and the Office of Technology Assessment
has stated that "scientific evidence generally fails to [either] confirm or disconfirm a need for
differential exposure standards for men and women based on reproductive effects" (U.S.
Department of Health and Human Services, 4; U.S. Office of Technology Assessment, 26).

Chapter 4. Congress, Title VII, and Fetal Protection Policies

1.   Title VII is applicable to employers with fifteen or more employees, to employment
agencies, and to labor organizations (42 U.S.C.A. 2000 e–1 [b]).

2. Sheila B. Kamerman, Alfred J. Kahn, and Paul Kingston, *Maternity Policies and Working Women* (New York: Columbia University Press, 1983), 39; Whitney, *Equal Rights,* 19.

3. Baer, *Chains,* 136.

4. At first, the function of the EEOC was to interpret Title VII; it did not have the power to bring a suit independently of the injured party. In the early years, however, the EEOC failed even to issue guidelines for interpreting Title VII. During this period, the agency was intended to investigate and conciliate claims prior to the commencement of individual suits. By the early 1970s, NOW and other groups were lobbying Congress to give the EEOC the power to bring suits independent of the individual employee. Congress agreed to this request, and, in 1972, Title VII was amended to allow the EEOC to bring a suit after finding that a violation had occurred.

5. 42 U.S.C.A. 2000e–2 (e).

6. EEOC Guidelines on Discrimination Because of Sex, *Federal Register,* 29 Code of Federal Regulations 1604.2, vol. 37, no. 66, 4/5/72.

7. United States Department of Labor, Women's Bureau, *Time of Change: 1983 Handbook on Women Workers* (Washington, D.C.: Government Printing Office, 1983), 178.

8. The EEOC's stance on state protective laws began to change in the late 1960s. In 1968, the EEOC filed an amicus curiae, or "friend of the court," brief on behalf of the plaintiffs in *Rosenfeld v. Southern Pacific Co.,* which was pending before the Court of Appeals for the Ninth Circuit. In this case, the EEOC alleged that California's law prohibiting women from lifting weights or working overtime violated Title VII. The appellate court ruled that the employer could not use the state protective law as a bfoq defense to sex discrimination (519 F.2d 527 [1975]).

9. EEOC Guidelines on Discrimination Because of Sex, *Federal Register,* 29 Code of Federal Regulations 1604.2, vol. 37, no. 66, 4/5/72.

10. *Dothard et al. v. Rawlinson et al.* 433 U.S. 321 (1977).

11. According to the regulation, a sex restriction would be placed on a job where it was found:

A. That the presence of the opposite sex would cause disruption of the orderly running and security of the institution;

B. That the position would require contact with the inmates of the opposite sex without the presence of others;

C. That the position would require patrolling dormitories, rest rooms, or showers while in use, frequently, during the night or day (*Dothard,* 334).

12. 433 US 334.

13. 433 US 336, note 23.

14. In dicta that has been used by later courts to invalidate bfoqs, the Court held that: "In the usual case, the argument that a particular job is too dangerous for women may appropriately be met by the rejoinder that it is the purpose of Title VII to allow the individual woman to make that choice for herself" (433 U.S. 335).

15. 433 US 336.

16. 433 US 335.

17. In addition to the gender classification system, the Alabama Board of Corrections also had a separate height/weight requirement. The majority opinion struck down this height/

weight requirement as violative of Title VII. The majority opinion offers no rationale for its decision to give greater weight to one classification than it does to the other. Since the Alabama gender classification scheme is based in whole upon the psychological impact on prisoners of allowing women to be correctional officers, it is not clear why a height/weight requirement is violative of Title VII, while an explicitly sex-based classification is not.

18. 433 U.S. 335.

19. 433 U.S. 342, 346–47.

20. This study is based upon an examination of those cases which appeared in the Commerce Clearing House series for the years from 1976–89. These 28 cases involved the exclusion of one sex from the jobs of correctional officer, police officer, and sheriff; however, the majority of cases arose in conjunction with the job of correctional officer. Of these 28 cases, the courts allowed the bfoq in only six cases (Commerce Clearing House, *Employment Practices Decisions* [Chicago: Commerce Clearing House, 1975–91]; vol. 16, case 8263, p. 5364; vol. 17, case 8445, p. 6330; vol. 23, case 30935, p. 15824; vol. 47, case 38265, p. 53544; vol. 47, case 38266, p. 54175; vol. 48, case 38392, p. 54175). In 21 cases, the courts distinguished the holding in *Dothard,* contending that the conditions of the penal system in question did not justify the exclusion of either men or women (Commerce Clearing House, *Employment Practices Decisions* [Chicago: Commerce Clearing House, 1975–91]; vol. 14, case 7632, p. 5210; vol. 17, case 8362, p. 5880; vol. 18, case 8723, p. 4942; vol. 18, case 8770, p. 5128; vol. 18, case 8899, p. 5707; vol. 19, case 9012, p. 6238; vol. 19, case 9042, p. 6492; vol. 22, case 30564, p. 14042; vol. 22, case 30797, p. 15087; vol. 23, case 30935, p. 15824; vol. 30, case 33006, p. 26796; vol. 30, case 33176, p. 27646; vol. 31, case 33482, p. 29211; vol. 31, case 33564, p. 29604; vol. 34, case 34431, p. 33788; vol. 42, case 36887, p. 46202; vol. 43, case 37161, p. 47590; vol. 45, case 37765, p. 50915; vol. 47, case 38252, p. 53473; vol. 49, case 38902, p. 56805; vol. 51, case 39352, p. 59428).

21. The plaintiff establishes this prima facie case by showing that: (a) he belongs to a class that is protected under Title VII; (b) he applied for and was qualified for a job for which the employer was seeking applicants; (c) that despite his qualifications, he was rejected; and (d) that after his rejection, the job remained open and the employer continued to seek applicants.

22. In *Griggs v. Duke Power Company,* the first case in which the Supreme Court utilized the disparate impact framework, an employer policy that required that a prospective employee have either a high school diploma or pass a general intelligence test was found to violate Title VII. The Court held that, even though this requirement was neutral, in that it was not expressly directed against a protected group, it nevertheless had a differential impact on African-Americans since it disqualified them from employment at a substantially higher rate than it excluded white applicants (401 U.S. 424; 91 S.Ct. 849 [1971]).

23. Michael J. Zimmer, Charles A. Sullivan, and Richard F. Richards, *Cases and Materials on Employment Discrimination* (Boston and Toronto: Little, Brown and Co., 1988), 215.

24. Zimmer, *Cases,* 215.

25. The definition of "business necessity" has frequently been at issue in disparate impact cases. In *Robinson v. Lorillard Corp. et al.,* the Fourth Circuit Court of Appeals held that the business necessity test could be satisfied only where "there exists an overriding legitimate business purpose such that the practice is necessary to the safe and efficient operation of the business" (444 F.2d 798 [1971]). Moreover, the court determined that "while considerations of economy and efficiency will often be relevant to determining the existence of business necessity, dollar cost alone is not determinative" (444 F.2d 799, note 8).

26. For example, the Supreme Court's 1989 decision in *Wards Cove Packing Co., Inc. v.*

Atonio made it substantially more difficult for a plaintiff to prevail in these cases. In *Wards Cove*, the Court held that "[while] mere insubstantial justification will not suffice . . . there is no requirement that the challenged [business] practice be 'essential' or 'indispensable' to the employer's business" in order to meet the business necessity test (490 U.S. 642, 659). Thus, after *Wards Cove*, it was much more difficult for a plaintiff to establish a violation on the basis of disparate impact.

27. It remains uncertain whether employers must prove that the business justification serves an important or compelling interest. Moreover, it is unclear whether employers must consider all alternatives that are less discriminatory or only those which do not impose additional costs.

28. *Geduldig v. Aiello* (417 U.S. 484; 94 S.Ct. 2485 [1974]).

29. 417 U.S. 484, 496–97; 94 S.Ct. 2485, 2491–92.

30. 417 U.S. 496–97, note 20.

31. As Reva Siegel has noted, the Court's decision in *Geduldig* demonstrates that it was unwilling to accept that pregnancy discrimination distinguishes the sexes not only biologically but socially as well. As Siegel has noted, "Judgments about women's capacity to bear children play a key role in social definitions of gender roles and thus in the social logic of 'discrimination' based on gender as such" (Siegel, "Reasoning," 269).

32. *General Electric Co. v. Gilbert* 429 U.S. 125; 97 S.Ct. 401 (1976).

33. 429 U.S. 125, 138–39; 97 S.Ct. 401, 409.

34. 429 U.S. 125, 136; 97 S.Ct. 401, 408.

35. In a case decided later in the 1976 term, which involved a company's policy of denying accumulated seniority to female workers returning from pregnancy leave, the Court held that such a denial did violate Title VII. Even though the affected class was that of pregnant women, and even though nonpregnant women were unaffected by this policy, the Court distinguished its holdings in *Geduldig* and *General Electric,* holding that the policy "did not merely refuse to extend to women a benefit that men could not and did not receive but imposed on female employees a substantial burden that men need not suffer and thus such policy, in absence of proof of any business necessity for it, constituted an unlawful employment practice" (*Nashville Gas Co. v. Satty,* 985 S.Ct. 349 [1977]).

36. Kamerman et al., *Maternity Policies,* 40–41.

37. W. Williams "Firing the Woman," 682.

38. For example, see Senate 542-10; 413–19.

39. For example, one Senate report stated that:

> The Supreme Court's decision . . . in *Gilbert* came as a deep disappointment to working women across the nation. It constituted a serious setback to women's rights and to the development of anti-discrimination law under Title VII of the Civil Rights Act of 1964. But far more important, this decision poses a serious threat to the security of the family unit. (Senate 542-10, Legislative History, 1)

> Another Report stated that the function of the PDA was to change the definition of sex discrimination in Title VII to "reflect the 'commonsense' view and to insure that working women are protected against all forms of employment discrimination based on sex." (Senate 413-19, 3)

40. Senate 542-10, 149.

41. For example, Wendy W. Williams echoed these concerns about women being viewed as marginal workers, stating that "because of their capacity to become pregnant, women have been viewed as marginal workers not deserving the full benefits of compensation and advancement granted to other workers" (Senate 542-10, 61).

42. Senate 542-10, 151.

43. Senate 542-10, 153.

44. Senate 542-10, 168.

45. Senate 413-19, 3.

46. Senate 542-10, 40–41.

47. Brief Amicus Curiae in Support of Petitioners by the Equal Rights Advocates et al., filed in the Supreme Court of the United States, October Term 1990, *International Union, United Auto Workers v. Johnson Controls,* 4–5. The ERA asserted that: "From the opening days of the Congressional hearings, Congress was on notice that the largest U.S. association of business and professional organizations believed that the second clause of the PDA prohibited a policy virtually identical to the Johnson Controls policy, and that the Chamber opposed the bill for that reason" (ERA amicus brief, *International Union v. Johnson Controls,* 5).

48. ERA amicus brief, *International Union v. Johnson Controls,* 1.

49. For example, see Brief Amicus Curiae in Support of Respondents by the U.S. Catholic Conference, filed in the Supreme Court of the United States, October Term 1990, *International Union, United Auto Workers v. Johnson Controls,* 24–26.

50. For example, see Brief Amicus Curiae in Support of Respondents by the Chamber of Commerce, filed in the Supreme Court of the United States, October Term 1990, *International Union, United Auto Workers v. Johnson Controls,* 16.

51. Chamber of Commerce amicus brief, *International Union v. Johnson Controls,* 18.

52. For example, see ERA amicus brief, *International Union v. Johnson Controls,* 11–13.

53. Letter from Pat Williams to other members of House of Representatives regarding Employee Protection Act, March 1990.

54. John Weintraub, aide to Representative Williams stated that the bill had about 40 co-sponsors, and that these sponsors wanted to begin hearings on the issue, but that it was decided they should wait until the Supreme Court's decision in *Johnson Controls.* After this decision, the sponsors of the bill would be able to determine "which legal holes are in need of filling" to protect the rights of men and women in the workplace (interview with John Weintraub, staff of Pat Williams, U.S. House of Representatives, Washington, D.C., 18 December 1990).

55. It is worth noting that there was little activity in Congress on reproductive hazards until the Seventh Circuit decided *Johnson Controls.* In 1982, Representative Al Gore chaired hearings on the issue of reproductive hazards in the workplace; however, no further action was taken to deal with this problem. One epidemiologist interviewed stated that it was "conceivable that *another* decade could go by without progress" (interview with agency personnel, General Accounting Office, Inter-Agency Project, Washington, D.C, 26 November 1990).

56. One epidemiologist at the GAO stated that the survey was intended to provide an accounting of standards that have been set up to deal with substances that are mutagenic or teratogenic, or that may result in infertility. The survey was sent to officers at the Occupational Safety and Health Administration, the Environmental Protection Agency, the Food and Drug Administration, and the Consumer Products Safety Commission.

57. Notes from GAO-OSHA meeting, 5/23/90.

58. U.S. General Accounting Office, 47.

59. Interview with Greg Watchman, General Counsel for Majority Staff, U.S. House of Representatives, Committee on Education and Labor, Washington, D.C., 3 December 1990.

60. Congress's hesitancy in taking action to counter these Court decisions was at least partly the result of recommendations by influential civil rights groups who did not want Congress to include the more controversial provisions on fetal protection and comparable worth in the proposed legislation. These groups believed, with good reason, that including these provisions would undercut support for the civil rights bill.

61. More specifically, the Order applies to contractors and subcontractors of government employers in any of these categories: contractors or subcontractors who provide the federal government with more than $10,000 in supplies, services, or work; contractors or subcontractors that have had more than $10,000 of government business in any twelve-month period; anyone who has government bills of lading in any amount; any firm that serves as an issuing or paying agent of U.S. savings bonds and notes; any firm that serves as a depository of federal funds in any amount; contractors or subcontractors who hold federally assisted contracts in excess of $10,000, including those who employ construction workers in either a non-federal or non-federally assisted construction site. In addition, contractors with fifty or more employees who also have a contract of $50,000 or more must develop a written affirmative action program.

Chapter 5. Equality in Employment

1. In particular, a number of analysts have contended that under the Reagan and Bush Administration the EEOC failed to enforce Title VII effectively. For example, Wendy Kaminer has argued that, beginning in the early 1980s, the EEOC "stopped living up to its rules" (Kaminer, *Fearful Freedom*, 124). For further discussion of this, see Rhode, *Justice and Gender*, 162; Kaminer, *Fearful Freedom*, 124).

2. The administrative Procedure Act established extensive rule-making procedures to govern the promulgation of legislative rules. These procedures, however, do not apply to interpretive rules or guidelines.

3. Ernest Gellhorn and Barry B. Boyer, *Administrative Law and Process* (St. Paul, MN: West Publishing, 1981), 249.

4. Cited in House Report on EEOC, 36.

5. OSH Reporter, 9880, p. 11,503.

6. House report on EEOC, 38; OSH Reporter 9880, p. 11,503.

7. Edmund D. Cooke, Jr., and Sally J. Kenney, "The View from Capitol Hill," in Cohen and Taub, 335; House Report on EEOC, 39.

8. *OSH Reporter*, vol. 9800, p. 11,503.

9. This aspect of the guidelines appears to have been prompted by earlier conflict between the EEOC and OSHA over the *American Cyanamid* case, which will be discussed at length in Chapter 6.

10. W. Williams, "Firing the Woman," 646.

11. House Report on EEOC, 15–16.

12. House Report on EEOC, 15.

13. U.S. Equal Employment Opportunity Commission, "Policy Guidance on Reproductive and Fetal Hazards" (Washington, D.C.: Government Printing Office, 10/7/88), 5.

14. EEOC Policy Guidance, 1988, 6–7.

15. EEOC Policy Guidance, 1988, 4; 4, note 11.

16. *Hayes v. Shelby Memorial Hospital* 726 F.2d 1543 (Eleventh Cir., 1984).

17. *Wright v. Olin* 697 F.2d1172 (Fourth Cir. 1982).

18. EEOC Policy Guidance, 1988, 9.

19. House Report on EEOC, 24.

20. House Report on EEOC, 24–25.

21. EEOC Policy Guidance, 1988, 10.

22. EEOC Policy Guidance, 1988, 8.

23. EEOC Policy Guidance, 1988, 8.

24. U.S. Equal Employment Opportunity Commission, "Policy Guidance on *U.A.W. v. Johnson Controls*" (Washington, D.C.: Government Printing Office, 1/24/90), 7, note 16.

25. EEOC Policy Guidance, 1988, 2.

26. *International Union, United Auto Workers v. Johnson Controls* 886 F.2d 871 (1989).

27. *Wards Cove Packing Co., Inc. v. Atonio* 490 U.S. 642, 109 S.Ct. 2115 (1989).

28. EEOC Policy Guidance, 1990, 6.

29. EEOC Policy Guidance, 1990, 9.

30. EEOC Policy Guidance, 1990, 9.

31. The commission contends that "Title VII and the institutions which enforce it were designed to eliminate employment discrimination, not to evaluate evidence concerning workplace safety . . . [since] [s]uch evaluations are better left to agencies with appropriate expertise such as OSHA or the EPA" (EEOC Policy Guidance, 1990, 10).

32. Furthermore, the commission argued that the court disregarded the extensive data compiled by OSHA when it formulated the 1976 lead standard, and contended that "[future] Commission investigations, in contrast, should defer to pertinent conclusions by appropriate governmental agencies" (EEOC Policy Guidance, 1990, 10).

33. EEOC Policy Guidance, 1990, 11. Obviously, the EEOC office responsible for the Seventh Circuit would continue to be bound by the circuit's opinion in *Johnson Controls*.

34. EEOC Policy Guidance, 1990, 12.

35. EEOC Policy Guidance, 1990, 12, note 14.

36. EEOC Policy Guidance, 1990, 12, note 14.

37. EEOC Policy Guidance, 1990, 12.

38. EEOC Policy Guidance, 1990, 13.

39. EEOC Policy Guidance, 1990, 13.

40. In the wake of the Supreme Court's decision in *U.A.W. v. Johnson Controls,* the EEOC is attempting to draft another set of guidelines to govern the disposition of fetal protection claims. In the interim, it appears that no cases have been filed with either the Office of Legal Counsel in Washington, D.C., or with the field offices. It will be interesting to see how the Commission will integrate the Supreme Court's decision into its new policy guidance on reproductive and fetal hazards.

41. House Report on EEOC.

42. House Report on EEOC, 16.

43. House Report on EEOC, 20.

44. House Report on EEOC, 18–19.

45. House Report on EEOC, 18–19.

46. House Report on EEOC, 16.

47. House Report on EEOC, 16–17.

48. EEOC letter to Majority Staff, in House Report on EEOC, 52.

49. EEOC letter to Majority Staff, in House Report on EEOC, 52.

50. EEOC letter to Majority Staff, in House Report on EEOC, 53.

51. Cooke and Kenney, "in Cohen and Taub," 336; House Report on EEOC, 17.

52. Interviews with Carolyn Wheeler, U.S. EEOC, Washington, D.C., 19 June 1991; and Diana Johnsen, 19 June 1991.

53. Throughout the 1970s, the Department of Justice actively advocated equal employment opportunity for women and minority men. When Assistant Attorney General William Bradford Reynolds was appointed, however, the agency's policies changed radically. Reynolds was openly hostile to affirmative action programs, and to other actions aimed at imposing what he termed a "radically egalitarian society" (Kaminer, *Fearful Freedom*, 128–29).

54. House Report on EEOC, 26.

55. Interview with Carolyn Wheeler, U.S. EEOC, 29 November 1990. It is unusual for the Department of Justice to file an amicus brief in litigation in the federal district or appellate courts. Typically, the DOJ files briefs only in the U.S. Supreme Court. Furthermore, the EEOC may not file an amicus brief by itself at the Supreme Court level; instead, the DOJ must file on its behalf.

56. Within the EEOC, there continued to be serious disagreement as to which dissenting opinion was correct. There were a number of individuals within the commission who were opposed to Judge Easterbrook's opinion, which implied that the employer could not legitimately consider the welfare of the fetus in formulating policies. Others in the Commission believed that Easterbrook's position correctly applied Title VII caselaw, and that the other opinions did not.

57. In fact, interviews with agency personnel suggest that the DOJ believed that "it was a step in the right direction to protect the fetus" (interview with Clifford Sloan, U.S. Department of Justice, Washington, D.C., 30 November 1990).

58. Interview with Carolyn Wheeler, U.S. EEOC, 29 November 1990.

59. *OSH Reporter,* vol. 28849, p. 38481.

60. Interview with Carolyn Wheeler, U.S. EEOC, 29 November 1991.

61. *Congressional Quarterly's Federal Regulatory Directory* (Washington, D.C.: Congressional Quarterly, 1986), 720. Some have argued that the Order is even more effective for halting discrimination than is Title VII. As one commentator has noted, contractors found in violation of the act can have their contract revoked. Thus, this analyst claims that the order has "enormous potential to bring about equality in employment" (Kenney, "Reproductive Hazards," 225).

62. Letter from Annie A. Blackwell, Director, Division of Policy, Planning and Program Development, Office of Federal Contract Compliance, U.S. Department of Labor, 21 November 1990; interview with Jan Walstedt, Women's Bureau, Department of Labor, Washington, D.C., 24 June 1991; Congressional Quarterly, 720.

63. Letter from Blackwell, OFCCP, 21 November 1990; interview with Walstedt, Department of Labor, 24 June 1991. While agency personnel contended that these were the actions most frequently proposed by the OFCCP in sex discrimination cases, I was unable to determine whether these were the actions that were most frequently undertaken.

64. Letter from Blackwell, OFCCP, 21 November 1990.

65. Letter from Blackwell, OFCCP, 21 November 1990.

66. Letter from Blackwell, OFCCP, 21 November 1990.

67. Letter from Blackwell, OFCCP, 21 November 1990.

68. In the years 1986–88, the complaints issued by the OFCCP numbered as follows: 1986, 0; 1987, 4; 1988, 5.

69. Letter from Blackwell, OFCCP, 21 November 1990; interview with Walstedt, Department of Labor, 24 June 1991.

70. Letter from Blackwell, OFCCP, 21 November 1990.

71. Letter from Blackwell, OFCCP, 21 November 1990.

72. Interview with Walstedt, Department of Labor, 24 June 1991; letter from Blackwell, OFCCP, 21 November 1991.

73. *Congressional Quarterly,* 154. The EEOC also radically changed its position on some less innovative aspects of Title VII. For example, in the 1980s, the EEOC began to challenge the use of statistical evidence to establish disparate impact. Prior to this, the agency and the courts had increasingly used statistical evidence as a means of determining whether an employer had unlawfully discriminated against an individual or group.

74. Clarence Thomas served as an attorney for Monsanto Co. from 1977 to 1979, and he was chair of the EEOC from 1982 to 1990. He served as a judge of the D.C. Circuit from 1990 to 1991 and in June 1991 was nominated to replace Justice Thurgood Marshall on the U.S. Supreme Court.

75. Clarence Thomas, "The Equal Employment Opportunity Commission: Reflections on a New Philosophy," *Stetson Law Review* 15 (1985): 32–33.

76. Clarence Thomas, "Current Litigation Trends and Goals at the Equal Employment Opportunity Commission," *Labor Law Journal* 34 (1983): 210.

77. Thomas, "Equal Employment," 36.

78. Thomas, "Equal Employment," 36.

79. In oral argument, Circuit Court Judge Thomas asked the attorney for the F.C.C.: "What diversity is accomplished by a policy preference to women? What are women's issues? . . . I am at a loss as to what the difference is [between programming by male owners and programming by female owners]" (Clarence Thomas, "Promoting Diversity for Diversity's Sake," *Legal Times* 17 [7/15/91]: 12).

80. Kaminer, *A Fearful Freedom,* 126–27.

81. U.S. Congress, House of Representatives, Committee on Education and Labor, Subcommittee on Employment Opportunities, "Oversight Hearings on the OFCCP's Proposed Affirmative Action Regulations," 4/15/83.

82. Changes in the Department of Justice during the early years of the Reagan Administration, especially the ascent of Attorney General Edwin Meese and Civil Rights Division head Bradford Reynolds likely affected the course of EEOC and OFCCP activities in the area of gender discrimination. Both Meese and Reynolds made repeated attempts to dismantle Executive Order 11246 and other affirmative action programs.

83. This pattern of poor enforcement of equal employment opportunity statutes and regulations is perhaps not surprising, given Lenahan O'Connell's finding that administrative agencies do not perform optimally in the area of equal employment opportunity.

Chapter 6. Fetuses and the Workplace Health and Safety

1. Stephen A. Bokat and Horace A. Thompson III, *Occupational Safety and Health Law* (Washington, D.C.: Bureau of National Affairs, 1988), 679.

2. Prior to this, employers in those states without occupational safety and health laws were often able to operate with a larger margin of profit than were those in states with comprehensive laws.

3. 29 U.S.C. 651.

4. 29 U.S.C. 651 (1).

5. 29 U.S.C. 652 (5). The only private employers excluded under the act were businesses regulated under the 1954 Atomic Energy Act and businesses regulated under job safety rules other than the Department of Labor.

6. U.S. Office of Technology Assessment, 16.

7. 29 U.S.C. 651 (1)–(13).

8. 29 U.S.C. 654.

9. Cited in Bokat and Thompson, *Occupational Safety*, 108–9.

10. Wendy A. Cherner-Maneval, "Occupational Safety and Health—Employer Policy Excluding Fertile Female Workers Permitted Under the Occupational Safety and Health Act—*Oil, Chemical and Atomic Workers International Union v. American Cyanamid*," *Temple Law Quarterly* 58 (1985): 955.

11. A violation of the OSH Act occurs where there has been both noncompliance with an OSHA standard and the endangerment of one or more employees as a result of this noncompliance. Section 666 (a) of the OSH Act established the types of violations and penalties for these violations. The type of violation that has occurred is determined by the gravity of the employer's culpability (for further discussion, see Bokat and Thompson, *Occupational Safety*, 257). Violations may be either willful, serious or non-serious, and the penalties range from $10,000 to up to $300 per violation. OSHA may only propose penalties against recalcitrant employers; it does not have the authority to assess these penalties. Instead, another agency, usually the Occupational Safety and Health Review Commission, reviews the amount and determines whether it should be assessed.

12. Section 655 of the act established extensive guidelines for the promulgation of these standards. In part, this section holds that: "The Secretary . . . shall set the standard which most adequately assures, to the extent feasible, on the basis of the best available evidence, that no employee will suffer material impairment of health or functional capacity even if such an employee has regular exposure to the hazard dealt with by such a standard for the period of his working life" (29 U.S.C. 655).

13. Cited in Bokat and Thompson, *Occupational Safety*, 63–64.

14. The emergency temporary standard is rarely used. In part this is because courts have been extremely reluctant to allow OSHA to issue these standards (U.S. Office of Technology Assessment, 16).

15. The substances are asbestos, coal tar pitch volatiles; 4-nitrobiphenyl; alpha-naphthylamine; 4,4' methylene bis; methyl choloromethyl ether; 3,3'-dichlorobenzidine; bis-chloromethyl ether; beta-naphthylamine; benzidine; 4-aminodiphenyl; ethylenimine; beta-propiolactone; 2-acetylaminofluorene; 4-dimethylaminozobenzene; n-nitrosomdimethylamine; vinyl chloride; inorganic arsenic; lead; benzene; coke oven emissions; cotton dust; 1,2-dibromo-3-chloropropane; acrylonitrile; ethylene oxide (Hearing Conservation Amendment to the Noise Standard).

16. Carolyn Bell, "Implementing Safety and Health Regulations for Women in the Workplace," *Feminist Studies* 5 (1979): 291.

17. 29 U.S.C. 651 (b) (11); Bokat and Thompson, *Occupational Safety*, 682.

18. 29 U.S.C. 667.

19. 29 U.S.C. 667. When these state standards are applied to products that are distributed or used in interstate commerce, they must meet an additional requirement: they must be "required by compelling local conditions and they must not unduly burden interstate commerce" (29 U.S.C. 667).

20. OSHA does retain the authority to periodically review the administration and enforcement of a state plan, and, even after final approval, OSHA may reconsider or withdraw approval of a plan.

21. These states or territories are Alaska, Arizona, California, Connecticut (for state employees), Hawaii, Indiana, Iowa, Kentucky, Maryland, Michigan, Minnesota, Nevada, New Mexico, New York (for state employees), North Carolina, Oregon, Puerto Rico, South Carolina, Tennessee, Utah, Vermont, Virginia, the Virgin Islands, Washington, and Wyoming.

22. Warren Freedman, *The Law and Occupational Injury, Disease, and Death* (New York: Quorum Books, 1990), 97.

23. Cynthia Ruggerio, "Referral of Toxic Chemical Regulation Under the Toxic Substances Control Act: EPA's Administrative Dumping Ground," *Boston College Environmental Affairs Law Review* 17 (1989): 75–122. 84.

24. David Bollier, "The Emasculation of OSHA," *Business and Society Review* 51 (1984): 40.

25. In fact, the agency began to abandon the use of the targeting program in late 1985. In its place, it began to issue an unprecedented number of record-keeping violations. These violations are essentially procedural in nature; however, OSHA classified these as "willful" violations, and assessed extremely large fines against employers. These fines were almost always contested, and as a result, OSHA found itself embroiled in litigation of many of these violations. In fact, many of the "mega-fines" assessed against employers for both substantive and procedural violations were diminished through employer appeals. For a more extensive discussion of OSHA use of fines during the Reagan era, see Willis J. Goldsmith, "OSHA's Hazard Communication Standard: The Early Returns," *Employee Relations Law Journal* 12 (1989) 639–41.

26. In fact, Nicholas Ashford, a member of the National Advisory Committee on Occupational Safety and Health, stated that "it's fairly well understood that no new health standards will be promulgated voluntarily by the Reagan Administration" (cited in James Crawford, "The Deregulation of Worker Health," *Business and Society Review* 40 [1981–82]: 11–14).

27. A number of these standards regulated exposure to carcinogenic substances; among these were ethylene oxide, benzene, ethylene dibromide, and asbestos. In addition, in 1984 a federal court ordered OSHA to issue a field sanitary standard for migrant farm workers.

28. Sidney A. Shapiro and Thomas O. McGarity, "Reorienting OSHA: Regulatory Alternatives and Legislative Reform," *Yale Journal on Regulation* 6 (1989): 15–16.

29. For further discussion, see Shapiro and McGarity, "Reorienting OSHA."

30. Shapiro and McGarity, "Reorienting OSHA," 6.

31. Ruggerio, "Referral," 82.

32. Shapiro and McGarity, "Reorienting OSHA," 12.

33. As Stephen Shapiro has noted, OSHA has either no standards or inadequate standards for more than one half of the 110 chemicals that have been identified by the National Cancer Institute as confirmed or suspected carcinogens. Shapiro contends that this failure to regulate many known workplace carcinogens is "perhaps the best indicator of OSHA's failure" (Shapiro and McGarity, "Reorienting OSHA," 2).

34. *Oil, Chemical and Atomic Workers v. American Cyanamid Co.* 741 F.2d 444 (D.C. Cir. 1984).

35. Apparently, in speaking with employees about sterilization, the company doctor and nurse down-played the seriousness of the procedure, describing it as a "buttonhole surgery" (741 F.2d 446).

36. In January 1980, 13 female employees and the Oil, Chemical, and Atomic Workers Union filed a class-action suit against American Cyanamid in the federal district court in West Virginia. The women and their union contended that Cyanamid's fetal protection policy consti-

tuted unlawful sex discrimination and was barred under Title VII. This suit was later settled out of court after the plaintiffs accepted an offer of judgment by Cyanamid.

37. The citation classified the violation as willful, stated that the policy should immediately be terminated, and proposed a penalty of $10,000 (741 F.2d 447).

38. Cited in Richard Lewis, "OCAW v. American Cyanamid: The Shrinking of the Occupational Safety and Health Act," *University of Pennsylvania Law Review* 133 (1985): 1168.

39. Cited in Bokat, and Thompson, *Occupational Safety*, 126.

40. The Secretary of Labor contended that the fact that employees needed to be sterilized to work in certain high-risk areas was evidence that the workplace was not safe. Furthermore, the Secretary asserted that the policy "destroyed human resources in that it led to a loss of workers' reproductive capacities" (cited in Lewis, "OCAW," 1183).

41. 741 F.2d 447.

42. In an interesting passage, the commission held that: "An employee's decision to undergo sterilization in order to gain or retain employment grows out of economic and social factors which operate primarily outside the workplace. The employer neither controls nor creates these factors" (741 F.2d 447).

43. In addition to the fact that these policies did not fall within the scope of the general duty clause, OSHRC contended that there was another reason that OSHA did not have jurisdiction over fetal protection policies. In its opinion, OSHRC stated that the general duty provisions of the OSH Act did not apply where another agency had jurisdiction to act in the area. It contended that since the Equal Employment Opportunity Commission had authority to regulate these policies under the Pregnancy Discrimination Act, OSHA was precluded from taking action (Commerce Clearing House, Labor and Employment Series, Topical Law, *Secretary of Labor v. American Cyanamid Co.* 240.36, p. 394).

44. One of the other two judges who were sitting on the court was Circuit Court Judge Antonin Scalia.

45. 741 F.2d 448.

46. 741 F.2d 444.

47. 741 F.2d 450.

48. When Judge Bork was asked about his opinion in this case at the Senate confirmation hearings on his nomination to the Supreme Court, he stated, "I suppose the five women who chose to stay on that job with higher pay and [who] chose sterilization—I suppose that they were glad to have the choice" (cited in Joni F. Katz, "Hazardous Working Conditions and Fetal Protection Policies: Women Are Going Back to the Future," *Boston College Environmental Affairs Law Review* 17 [1989]: 229, note 231).

49. 741 F.2d 446.

50. For example, see Lewis, "OCAW," 1176–77; Cherner-Maneval, "Occupational Safety," 963.

51. Lewis, "OCAW," 1177.

52. House Report on EEOC, cited in Lewis, "OCAW," 1177.

53. Prior to the appellate decision, OSHA had issued guidelines on fetal protection policies. The guidelines provided temporary removal protections for men and women planning a pregnancy. Many groups, including the Oil, Chemical, and Atomic Workers Union, criticized these guidelines and suggested that they might undermine worker rights. As a result of this criticism, the guidelines were withdrawn just before the court announced its decision (Gary Z. Nothstein and Jeffrey P. Ayres, "Sex-Based Considerations of Differentiation in the Workplace: Exploring the Biomedical Interface Between OSHA and Title VII," *Villanova Law Review* 26.2 [1981]: 257–62).

54. Among these are arsenic, benzene, carbon disulfide, carbon monoxide, chloroprene, dibromochloropropane (DBCP), ethylene oxide (EtO), fluorocarbon 22, formaldehyde, glycol ethers, lead, mercury, organic mercury, methotrexate, methylene chloride, non-ionizing radiation, tetrachloride, toluene, trichloroethane, and vinyl chloride.

55. 29 C.F.R. 1910.1047 (the Ethylene Oxide Standard).

56. U.S. General Accounting Office (1991).

57. U.S. General Accounting Office (1991), 61.

58. For further discussion of the possible reasons that OSHA and the other agencies have failed to promulgate regulations to protect reproductive and developmental health, see U.S. General Accounting Office (1991), 66–70.

59. Interviews with OSHA officials suggest that the agency recognizes that these standards are not stringent enough to protect worker and fetal health absolutely. As one epidemiologist at OSHA noted, "The 1978 Lead Standard isn't stringent enough . . . [I]t bottomed out on economic feasibility, not [absolute] safety" (interview with Peter Infante, Epidemiologist, Occupational Safety and Health Administration, Washington, D.C., 28 November 1990.

60. U.S. Department of Labor (1983), 154.

61. One OSHA employee stated that "OSHA has not initiated rulemaking on this issue . . . possibly because there is no pressure [to do so] from the public" (interview with OSHA official, Policy Formulation Office, Washington, D.C., 15 October 1990).

62. "Proposed Guidelines for Assessing Female Reproductive Risk," and "Proposed Guidelines for Assessing Male Reproductive Risk and Request for Comments," 53 *Fed. Reg.* 126, 30 June 1988, 24,883–47 and 24,849–69.

It bears noting that OSHA and NIOSH have had significant coordination problems. NIOSH was created to research occupational safety and health issues and to develop criteria to be used by OSHA in formulating standards. In the past, however, OSHA has not had the personnel to review NIOSH research, and relations between the two agencies have been strained. In addition, because OSHA and NIOSH are housed in different departments, OSHA in the Department of Labor and NIOSH in its own department, there has been no single administrator to resolve coordination problems. As a result, the two agencies coexist in what one commentator has termed "an uneasy, and sometimes unproductive, relationship" (Shapiro and McGarity, "Reorienting OSHA," 58–59).

63. Text of Subcommittee Hearing, provided by OSHA official.

64. Text of Subcommittee Hearing, provided by OSHA official.

65. In attempting to assess the activities of those states with state plans for occupational safety and health in effect, I sent questionnaires to the states and then followed up the questionnaires with telephone interviews. The phone interviews helped to "flesh out" the state regulations by providing background information about both the state plan and whatever other activities the state might have undertaken to deal with reproductive hazards in the workplace. The results of this survey were in some ways predictable, but they were also interesting. Of the 25 states and territories with state plans in effect, 24 answered my questionnaire. The Puerto Rico Occupational Safety and Health Office did not respond to the preliminary questionnaire. It can be safely assumed that it, like the Virgin Islands, the other territory with a state plan in effect, has adopted regulations that are identical to the federal OSHA.

66. It bears noting, however, that the New York State Department of Labor was the first agency to urge employers to stop using dimethylformamide (DMF), a substance used by leather workers which was found to cause testicular cancer.

67. In fact, industry wanted OSHA to adopt a hazard communication standard because

they believed that a federal law would be less rigorous than were most of the state right-to-know laws. For a more extensive discussion of this: see Robert D. Moran, *OSHA Handbook,* 2d ed. (Rockville, MD: Government Institutes, 1989); Daniel Marcus, "OSHA's Expanding Hazard Communication Requirements," *Natural Resources and Environment* 4 (1990): 19–21, 49–50; and Willis J. Goldsmith, "OSHA's Hazard Communication Standard: The Early Returns," *Employee Relations Law Journal* 12 (1986–87): 313–18.

68. Paul, et al., "Corporate Response," and "Bureau of National Affairs," "Awareness," 26.

69. Toxic Substances Control Act, 2(a)(2).

70. Emily Buss, "Getting Beyond Discrimination: A Regulatory Solution to the Problem of Fetal Hazards in the Workplace," *Yale Law Review* 95 (1986): 592–93; Ruggerio, "Referral," 106.

71. William H. Rodgers, Jr., *Environmental Law: Pesticides and Toxic Substances* (St. Paul, MN: West Publishing, 1988), 408.

72. Under one provision of the act, the EPA was authorized to "compile and keep current" a list of chemicals which were suspected of being hazardous. This list does exist, but it is not in any accessible or definitive form (Rodgers, *Environmental Law,* 411).

73. Buss, "Discrimination," 593.

74. Toxic Substances Control Act 4 (b)(2)(a).

75. One of the more interesting provisions of the TSCA is that manufacturers, importers, and processors of chemicals are required to ensure that this testing is performed and must bear the cost of the testing.

76. This notification was to include information on the "identity, use, anticipated production or importation volume, workplace hazards, and disposal characteristics of the substance" (*U.S. Environmental Laws* [Washington, D.C.: Bureau of National Affairs, 1988], 145).

77. Section 9 of the TSCA states: "[Where] such risk may be prevented or diminished to a sufficient extent by action taken under a Federal law not administered by the Administrator, the Administrator shall submit to the agency which administers such law a report which describes such risk and includes in such description a specification of the activity or combination of activities."

78. One commentator has written that "Congress inten[ded] that TSCA serve as a supplementary regulatory mechanism to provide enforcement strength where OSHA is weak, without completely undercutting the OSH Act" (Ruggerio, "Referral," 92).

79. U.S. Office of Technology Assessment, 15.

80. For example, Hayes claims that in the last two or three years the EPA has begun "flexing the statute's enormous information-gathering muscle" (David J. Hayes, "TSCA: The Sleeping Giant is Stirring," *Natural Resources and Environment* 4 [1990]: 3).

81. Richard N. L. Andrews, "Deregulation: The Failure at EPA, in Norman J. Vig and Michael E. Kraft, eds., *Environmental Policy in the 1980s: Reagan's New Agenda* (Washington, D.C.: Congressional Quarterly, 1984), 166.

82. As one commentator has noted, "Such a policy [of budget reductions] could be interpreted only as a back door repeal of statutory responsibilities through administrative tactics, and as such it fundamentally corroded the legitimacy of the administration's programs in the eyes of Congress and the public" (Andrews, "Deregulation," 173).

83. U.S. Office of Technology Assessment, 18; Nina G. Stillman and John R. Wheeler, "The Expansion of Occupational Safety and Health Law," *Notre Dame Law Review* 62 (1987): 982–83.

84. For a more extensive discussion of the "unreasonable risk" requirement, see Stillman and Wheeler, "Expansion," 982–83; Rodgers, *Environmental Law,* 372–75.

85. TSCA 2608(d), cited in Ruggerio, "Referral," 92.

86. According to Cynthia Ruggerio, the EPA has avoided regulatory responsibility under TSCA by utilizing the section 9 referral provision in at least six instances, in the regulation of 4,4'-methylenedianiline, 1,3-butadene, glycol ethers, tolenediamine, 4,4'-methylene bis, and formaldehyde (Ruggerio, "Referral," 99–105).

87. Ruggerio, "Referral," 77.

88. In addition, the preemption provisions of the TSCA place even more responsibility in the hands of the EPA, or, through referral, OSHA. Although the TSCA seems to favor non-preemption of state and municipal ordinances, in practice, it is difficult for states and municipalities to legitimate their ordinances. Thus, federal regulations governing the manufacture, use and disposal of chemicals often override state and municipal provisions. For a more extensive discussion of this, see Rodgers, *Environmental Law*, 495–97.

89. Ruggerio, "Referral," 122, and Shapiro and McGarity, "Reorienting OSHA," 17.

90. Buss, "Discrimination," 595.

91. Buss, "Discrimination," 598.

92. One commentator has suggested that EPA action under TSCA be supplemented by traditional tort law protection (Buss, "Discrimination," 597–98).

Chapter 7. Courts, BFOQs, and Fetal Rights

1. *United Auto Workers v. Johnson Controls, Inc.* 499 U.S. 187; 111 S.Ct. 1196 (1991).

2. *Zuniga v. Kleberg City Hospital* 692 F.2d 986 (5th Cir. 1982).

3. *Wright v. Olin Corporation* 697 F.2d 1172 (4th Cir. 1982).

4. *Hayes v. Shelby Memorial Hospital* 726 F.2d 1543 (11th Cir. 1984).

5. *Grant v. General Motors Corporation* 908 F.2d 1303 (6th Cir. 1990).

6. *Johnson Controls, Inc. v. California Fair Employment and Housing Commission* 267 Cal. Rptr. 165 (California Court of Appeals, 4th Dst, 1990).

7. 692 F.2d 988. It is significant to note that the disposition of this case was not governed by the Pregnancy Discrimination Act because Zuniga was fired before the effective date of the act. It is possible that the court would have utilized the disparate treatment or the per se frameworks had the PDA been operative.

8. The court held that: "Even if the business necessity defense does extend to the preservation of fetal health or the avoidance of tort liability, we find that Zuniga has effectively revealed the alleged business necessity to be a mere pretext for discrimination by showing that the Hospital failed to utilize an available, alternative, less discriminatory means of achieving its business purpose" (*Zuniga v. Kleberg County Hospital,* 692 F.2d 992).

9. 697 F.2d 1182.

10. OSHA's lead standard has the same permissible exposure levels for both men and women. Despite this, the Olin Corporation issued informal, verbal warnings about lead to men, but written, formal warning to women.

11. 697 F.2d 1182. The Fourth Circuit also stated that disparate treatment was "wholly inappropriate" because the employer had already conceded that it was discriminating against women.

12. 697 F.2d 1189. The Fourth Circuit is also credited with having formulated a test for evaluating fetal protection policies under Title VII. This test was used by subsequent federal district courts and courts of appeals that have considered fetal protection policies. While it would appear that it is somewhat difficult to satisfy these requirements, most of these courts

have held that fetal protection policies were valid under this test. According to the Fourth Circuit, the employer has the burden of proof for establishing that:

(1) there is a significant risk of harm to fetuses as a result of the mother's continued exposure to certain workplace hazards;

(2) this risk to fetal health does not arise out of exposure to male employees;

(3) the exclusion of women employees is effective in eliminating the risk of harm to fetuses;

(4) scientific evidence rises to the level of "a general consensus within the scientific community," must be used to support the policy;

(5) there are no acceptable alternatives that would eliminate the risk of fetal harm with less differential impact between male and female employees. (1191)

13. *Wright v. Olin Corporation, Employment Practices Decisions,* vol. 35, p. 34877.

14. *Employment Practices Decisions,* vol. 35, p. 34881.

15. 726 F.2d 1548.

16. If the employer failed to prove that its fetal protection policy was neutral, the court stated that it had to prove that the policy was a bona fide occupational qualification. In this situation, the traditional per se/bfoq framework applied: an employer asserting the bfoq defense had to show that fertile or pregnant women were unable to perform the job in question. The court conceded that the hospital would be unable to satisfy the bfoq requirement, since there was no indication that Hayes was unable to perform her duties as an X-ray technician.

17. The court remarked that the policy would likely be ineffective in protecting a fetus, since "[t]he evidence suggests that the greatest danger of fetal damage from radiation occurs during the earliest days of pregnancy" (726 F.2d 1551, note 13). In remarks that seem to be purely gratis, the court stated that, since the policy applied only to pregnant women, it could not protect an embryo/fetus in the earliest stages of development. The court stated that "[d]uring the time before Hayes's pregnancy was discovered, serious injury could have occurred to her fetus," and that this policy, that was designed to "redress th[is] danger" was "largely ineffective in protecting the fetus" (726 F.2d 1552). Thus, the court seems to have implied that a broader policy, one that excluded pregnant women, women planning to have a child, and women *capable of having a child,* might pass muster under the business necessity test.

18. 726 F.2d 1552.

19. 726 F.2d 1553, note 15. The court stated that it "simply recognize[d] fetal protection as a legitimate area of employer concern to that the business necessity defense extends" (726 F.2d 1152).

20. 726 F.2d 1554. In laying out a blueprint for acceptable fetal protection policies, the Eleventh Circuit reiterated the test established by the earlier *Wright* court. Under this test, a policy that excluded one sex in the interest of fetal health did not violate Title VII if the employer could show that: (a) there was a substantial risk of harm to a fetus; (b) this harm was transmitted by only one sex; and (c) the employee was unable to show that there were no acceptable alternatives that would have had a lesser impact on the excluded sex.

21. The court contended that employers could protect themselves against potential lawsuits by purchasing insurance and by complying with governmental health and safety mandates. In addition, an employer could discharge an employee who failed to comply with health and safety procedures. The court contended, however, that the employer had to focus on ensuring workplace safety, not on avoiding litigation.

22. 886 F.2d 886.

23. 886 F.2d 888.

24. The court contended: "It is interesting to note that the U.A.W. has not presented any medical evidence in the record of any human study scientifically documenting genetic defects in human beings resulting from male lead exposure. It is this lack of convincing scientific data that the plaintiffs attempt to gloss over and cast aside in ignoring the differences between the effect of lead on the human and animal reproductive systems" (886 F.2d 889).

25. 886 F.2d 889–90. According to the court, the animal studies upon which the data on paternal exposure were based did "not present the type of solid scientific data necessary for a reasonable fact finder to reach a non-speculative conclusion that a father's exposure to lead presents the same danger to the unborn child as that resulting from a female employee's exposure" (886 F.2d 889–890).

26. The majority contended that because of procedural reasons, the union was precluded from addressing this issue at the appellate level because it failed to raise it at the district court level. Nonetheless, the court held that even if the union had preserved this issue for appeal, it still would have been unable to demonstrate that there were acceptable alternatives available to the employer (886 F.2d 891). In large part this was because the Supreme Court's 1989 decision in *Wards Cove Packing Co. v. Atonio* made it substantially more difficult for a plaintiff to present acceptable alternatives, by requiring that the alternatives satisfy a number of rigorous requirements.

27. 886 F.2d 886.

28. 886 F.2d 887. The majority opinion began by cataloguing Johnson Controls' "long pattern of laudable health and safety practices, [that] originate from its longstanding corporate concern for the danger lead poses to the health and welfare of employees, their families, and the general public" (886 F.2d 875). Judge Coffey contended that Johnson Controls adopted its fetal protection policy because there were no other alternatives that adequately protected fetuses from lead exposure. Judge Coffey accepted the assertion by Johnson Controls that its voluntary policy had been ineffective, and that alternative policies, which restricted only pregnant women or women who were attempting to become pregnant, did not sufficiently safeguard the interests of fetuses (886 F.2d 878). In particular, Coffey contended that limiting the policy in this way would fail to account for "one of the exigencies of life, the frequency of unplanned or undetected pregnancies" (886 F.2d 878). Judge Coffey thus concluded that a policy barring all fertile women from lead-exposed jobs was the only way to safeguard fetal health.

29. 886 F. 2d 893.

30. 886 F.2d 894.

31. 886 F.2d 894–97.

32. In addition, the court drew a parallel between the "businesses" of the employers in *Dothard* and *Torres*, on the one hand, and that of *Johnson Controls* on the other. *Dothard* and *Torres* involved the employment of men and women in prisons, while *Johnson Controls* involved employment in a battery manufacturing plant. Judge Coffey held that, like *Dothard* and *Torres*, the workplace in *Johnson Controls* was "unique" because it presented real health and safety concerns. As has been said, *Dothard* and *Torres* were decided on the basis of concerns about prison security and prisoner rehabilitation. The majority in Johnson Controls contended that this safety interest is "every bit as critical to the mission of Johnson's battery manufacturing business as rehabilitation of prisoners is the mission of the prison facility in *Torres*" (886 F.2d 894). Moreover, the "uniqueness" of this workplace required the employer to innovate to

ensure workplace safety. What is perhaps most important about *Johnson Controls*, however, is that these concerns are based upon *fetal* safety, rather than the safety of the workers.

33.   886 F.2d 897.

34.   In justifying these policies, Judge Coffey contended that society has an interest in shielding fetuses from workplace toxins. He stated that the risks to a fetus from lead exposure "are also shared by society in the form of government financed programs to train or maintain a handicapped child in a non-institutional or institutional environment and provide training necessary to overcome mental and physical harm attributed to lead exposure" (886 F.2d 898). Coffey seems to have implied that since society must ultimately come up with funds to care for children harmed by exposure to toxins, it may permit employers to restrict the employment of women in these high-risk areas. While fetal hazards might be minimized by more effective regulation of the workplace, or by the banning of toxic materials altogether, Judge Coffey does not address these larger issues.

35.   886 F.2d 897–901.

36.   In a footnote, the court explained that in these cases a court would appoint a guardian for the child who has the authority to consent to the transfusion. The court will also hold a hearing to decide whether the refusal of the parents to consent to the procedure constitutes medical neglect (886 F.2d 897, note 38).

37.   This example, and the implications drawn from it, are suggestive of the difficulties inherent in treating a fetus in the same way as one might treat a child. At present, *Roe v. Wade* is still the law, and the right of woman to choose to have an abortion outweighs the rights of an embryo or fetus, at least in the first two trimesters. The majority's decision in *Johnson Controls*, however, undermined this right by giving the fetus certain rights independent of those of the mother.

38.   Much of Judge Posner's decision addressed the insufficiency of the trial record in this case. Posner contended that the fact that this case was decided by summary judgment necessitated the remand of this case back to the district court. As has been said, a court grants a motion for summary judgment where there are no significant questions of fact at issue. Posner pointed out that in this case there exist unresolved factual questions, among these being the effects of paternal exposure on fetal health, the extent of the employer's vulnerability to tort liability, and the feasibility of warnings as a substitute for the blanket exclusion of women (886 F.2d 907).

39.   886 F.2d 903.

40.   886 F.2d 905.

41.   886 F.2d 904.

42.   Judge Posner states: "We know from the controversy over abortion that many people are passionately protective of fetal welfare, and they cannot all be expected—perhaps they cannot be required—to park their passions at the company gate" (886 F.2d 905). According to Posner, employers might have strong reservations about exposing fetuses to any workplace toxins.

43.   886 F.2d 903–4; 906.

44.   In a statement that has been cited by both opponents and supporters of fetal protection policies, Easterbrook asserted: "This is the most important sex-discrimination case this circuit has ever decided. It is likely the most important sex-discrimination case in any court since 1964, when Congress enacted Title VII" (886 F.2d 920).

45.   886 F.2d 908.

46.   886 F.2d 914.

47.   886 F.2d 921.

48.   886 F.2d 920.

49.   886 F.2d 921. Judge Easterbrook also warned about the use of scientific data by the courts. He stated that "[s]cientists formulate hypotheses, collect data, and apply statistical methods to assess them; judges and jurors find this process alien" (886 F.2d 916).

50.   908 F.2d 1308.

51.   908 F.2d 1308–9.

52.   908 F.2d 1308.

53.   908 F.2d 1309.

54.   908 F.2d 1309.

55.   908 F.2d 1310.

56.   908 F.2d 1303, 1311.

57.   *Johnson Controls v. California Fair Employment and Housing Commission* 267 Cal. Rptr. 165 (California Court of Appeals, 4th Dst.).

58.   267 Cal. Rptr. 170.

59.   The state court rejected the use of the business necessity defense, contending that the defense was available only where the policy or practice was facially neutral. According to the court, the fetal protection policy constituted overt discrimination (267 Cal. Rptr. 163).

60.   267 Cal. Rptr. 163.

61.   267 Cal. Rptr. 170. The court held that: "Whatever Congress' intent in enacting Title VII, the plain language of the California FEHA mandates a finding that women . . . may only face employment discrimination where it is necessary for the very operation of the business" (174).

62.   267 Cal. Rptr. 173.

63.   267 Cal. Rptr. 173–74. The state court claimed that each of the federal courts that had addressed the issue of fetal protection policies had "manifested great legal skill in refusing to answer the plain language of Title VII" (267 Cal. Rptr. 170).

64.   267 Cal. Rptr. 174.

65.   267 Cal. Rptr. 168.

66.   267 Cal. Rptr. 178.

67.   267 Cal. Rptr. 177.

68.   On 18 May 1990, the California Supreme Court denied certiorari in this case. Thus, the holding of the lower appellate court stands.

69.   Interviews cited in bibliography.

70.   In one interesting exchange, Justice Scalia stated, "The workplace is full of risks. How is a court to determine how careful the employer may be without violating Title VII? How many deformities is worth letting women work in the department? . . . How are we [the courts] to determine what the proper balance of risk to fetus and freedom for the women to work in the marketplace is?" (Official transcript, Proceedings before the Supreme Court of the United States, *International Union, United Auto Workers v. Johnson Controls, Inc.*, oral argument, 10 October 1990, 41–43).

71.   499 U.S. 187–88; 111 S.Ct. 1198.

72.   499 U.S. 199; 111 S.Ct. 1203.

73.   The Court held that "[t]he beneficence of an employer's purpose does not undermine the conclusion that an explicit gender-based policy is sex discrimination under 703(a)" (499 U.S. 200; 111 S.Ct. 1204).

74.   The Court held that this conclusion accords with the policy of the EEOC. The Court cited the EEOC's 1990 Policy Guidance as evidence of the EEOC's conclusion that bfoq is the

proper approach to evaluating fetal protection policies (499 U.S. 200; 111 S.Ct. 1204). As was discussed in Chapter 5, the EEOC's stance on fetal protection policies has been inconsistent; as late as 1988, it contended that these policies could be evaluated under the disparate impact/ business necessity framework.

75.   499 U.S. 201; 111 S.Ct. 1204.

76.   499 U.S. 202; 111 S.Ct. 1205.

77.   499 U.S. 203–4; 111 S.Ct. 1206.

78.   499 U.S. 204–5; 111 S.Ct. 1206.

79.   499 U.S. 206–7; 111 S.Ct. 1207.

80.   499 U.S. 207; 111 S.Ct. 1207.

81.   499 U.S. 207; 111 S.Ct. 1208.

82.   499 U.S. 208; 111 S.Ct. 1208.

83.   499 U.S. 208; 111 S.Ct. 1208.

84.   The Court cites 43 Fed. Reg. 52952, 52966 (499 U.S. 208; 111 S.Ct. 1208).

85.   499 U.S. 210; 111 S.Ct. 1209.

86.   499 U.S. 210–11; 111 S.Ct. 1209.

87.   499 U.S. 211; 111 S.Ct. 1210.

88.   499 U.S. 187, 197–99; 111 S.Ct. 1202–4.

89.   499 U.S. 210–11; 111 S.Ct. 1209.

90.   499 U.S. 211; 111 S.Ct. 1210.

91.   499 U.S. 216–17; 111 S.Ct. 1213 (emphasis in original). White agreed with the finding of the Seventh Circuit that third-party safety is part of the "essence" of many, if not all, businesses (499 U.S. 217, note 5; 111 S.Ct. 1213, note 5).

92.   Among these issues were the level of risk-avoidance that was part of the normal operation of Johnson Controls' business; the question of whether the fetal risks associated with battery-manufacturing substantially increased after 1982, thus necessitating a mandatory fetal protection policy; and the question of whether fetal harm could be transmitted through paternal exposure (499 U.S. 220; 111 S.Ct. 1215).

93.   499 U.S. 223; 111 S.Ct. 1216.

94.   Justice Scalia cited Judge Easterbrook's dissenting opinion in *Johnson Controls*, which holds that "Title VII gives parents the power to make occupational decisions affecting their families. A legislative forum is available to those who believe that such decisions should be made elsewhere" (499 U.S. 223; 111 S.Ct. 1216).

95.   For further discussion of the impact of the Court's opinion on occupational safety and health, see Robert H. Blank, *Fetal Protection in the Workplace: Women's Rights, Business Interests, and the Unborn* (New York: Columbia University Press, 1993).

Chapter 8. Fetal Protection Policies and Gender Equality

1.   For further discussion of these statutes, see Craig and O'Brien, *Abortion,* 83.

2.   For example, see *Planned Parenthood of Central Missouri v. Danforth* 428 U.S. 552 (1976); *Colautti v. Franklin* 439 U.S. 379 (1979); *Thornburgh v. American College of Obstetricians and Gynecologists* 476 U.S. 747 (1986); and *Webster v. Reproductive Health Services* 492 U.S. 490 (1989).

3.   This contention that a fetus, ostensibly one that was less than a trimester gestational age, had rights independent of the woman was clearly in conflict with *Roe v. Wade*. This

landmark case held that before the third trimester the fetus's "right" to life could be overridden by the woman's right to choose abortion.

4. For example, in other cases, like *Johnson Controls,* the Supreme Court was more circumspect about which conception of gender roles it was relying upon. For a fuller discussion of the litigation of fetal protection policies, see Chapter 7.

5. *International Union, United Autoworkers v. Johnson Controls,* 886 F. 2d 897 (7th Cir. 1989).

References

Interviews

Bertin, Joan. American Civil Liberties Union, Reproductive Rights Project, New York, New York. 14 December 1990.

Bokat, Stephen. National Chamber Litigation Center, Washington, D.C. 19 December 1990.

Chapman, Barbara. General Accounting Office, Inter-Agency Project, Washington, D.C. 26 November 1990.

Chopko, Mark. United States Catholic Conference, Washington, D.C. 7 December 1990.

Daniel, Margo. Occupational Safety and Health Administration, Policy Formulation Office, Washington, D.C. 15 October 1990, 20 November 1990, 29 November 1990.

Depoy, Marilyn. American Federation of State, County, and Municipal Employees, Washington, D.C. 15 January 1991.

Foote-Soiza, Anne. Washington State Department of Labor, Olympia, Washington. 27 December 1990.

Frumin, Eric. Amalgamated Clothing and Textile Workers Union, New York, New York. 17 January 1991.

Govan, Reggie. General Counsel for Majority Staff, House of Representatives Committee on Education and Labor, Washington, D.C. 29 August 1991.

Hostadler, Kathleen. Oil, Chemical, and Atomic Workers Union, Legal Department, Toledo, Ohio. 7 February 1991.

Infante, Peter. Occupational Safety and Health Administration, Washington, D.C. 28 November 1990.

Johnsen, Diana. Equal Employment Opportunity Commission, Washington, D.C. 19 June 1991.

Johnson, Randy. Minority Staff, House of Representatives Committee on Education and Labor, Washington, D.C. 20 November 1990.

Krekel, Sylvia. Oil, Chemical, and Atomic Workers Union, Toledo, Ohio. 15 January 1991.

Lado, Marianne Engelman. National Association for the Advancement of Colored Persons, Legal Defense and Educational Fund, Inc., Washington, D.C. 1 November 1990.

LaGrande, Dave. Communications Workers of America, New York, New York. 27 December 1990.

Mirer, Franklin. International Union of United Auto Workers, Washington, D.C. 16 January 1991.

Oskan, Milo. Connecticut State Department of Labor, Division of Occupational Safety and Health, Hartford, Connecticut. 21 December 1990.

Scott, Judy. United Mine Workers, Washington, D.C. 15 January 1991.

Sloan, Clifford. U.S. Department of Justice, Washington, D.C. 30 November 1990.

Snyder, Jeffrey. Occupational Safety and Health Administration, Health Standards Office, Washington, D.C. 27 February 1991.

Uhlar, Richard. International Chemical Workers Union, Washington, D.C. 15 January 1991.

Walstedt, Jan. Department of Labor, Women's Bureau, Washington, D.C. 24 June 1991.

Watchman, Gregory. Majority Staff, U.S. House of Representatives, Committee on Education and Labor, Washington, D.C. 3 December 1990.

Weeks, James. United Mine Workers, Washington, D.C. 15 January 1991.

Weinreib, John. Staff, Pat Williams (Democrat-Montana), U.S. House of Representatives, Washington, D.C. 20 December 1990.

Wheeler, Carolyn. U.S. Equal Employment Opportunity Commission, Washington, D.C. 29 November 1990, 19 June 1991.

Books and Articles

Abramovitz, Mimi. *Regulating the Lives of Women: Social Welfare Policy from Colonial Times to the Present.* Boston: South End Press, 1989.

Andrews, Richard N. L. "Deregulation: The Failure at the EPA." In Norman J. Vig and Michael E. Kraft, eds., *Environmental Policy in the 1980s: Reagan's New Agenda.* Washington, D.C.: Congressional Quarterly, 1984. 161–78.

Atwood, Margaret. *The Handmaid's Tale.* New York: Fawcett Crest, 1985.

Baer, Judith A. *The Chains of Protection: The Judicial Response to Women's Labor Legislation.* Westport, CT: Greenwood Press, 1978.

Becker, Mary E. "From *Muller v. Oregon* to Fetal Vulnerability Policies." *The University of Chicago Law Review* 53 (1986): 1219–73.

Bell, Carolyn. "Implementing Safety and Health Regulations for Women in the Workplace." *Feminist Studies* 5 (1979): 286–301.

Bertin, Joan E. "Reproductive Hazards in the Workplace." In Sherrill Cohen and Nadine Taub, eds., *Reproductive Laws for the 1990s.* Clifton, NJ: Humana Press, 1989.

Blank, Robert H. *Fetal Protection in the Workplace: Women's Rights, Business Interests, and the Unborn.* New York: Columbia University Press, 1993.

Bokat, Stephen A., and Horace A. Thompson III. *Occupational Safety and Health Law.* Washington, D.C.: Bureau of National Affairs, 1988.

Bollier, David. "The Emasculation of OSHA." *Business and Society Review* 51 (1984): 37–41.

Bureau of National Affairs. "Awareness of Fetal Risks in Workplace 'An Emerging Issue.'" *Occupational Safety and Health Reporter* 20 (1990): 25–26.

Bureau of National Affairs. "Employer Defends Its Fetal Protection Policy as 'Reasonably Necessary' Before the High Court." *Occupational Safety and Health Reporter* 20 (1990): 280–81.

Bureau of National Affairs. "Union Attacks Fetal Protection Policy as Fundamentally Biased Against Women." *Occupational Safety and Health Reporter* 20 (1990): 39–40.

Burstein, Paul. *Discrimination, Jobs, and Politics: The Struggle for Equal Employment Oppor-*

tunity in the U.S. since the New Deal. Chicago and London: The University of Chicago Press, 1985.

Buss, Emily. "Getting Beyond Discrimination: A Regulatory Solution to the Problem of Fetal Hazards in the Workplace." *Yale Law Review* 95 (1986): 577–98.

Carle, Susan D. "A Hazardous Mix: Discretion to Disclose and Incentives to Supress Under OSHA's Hazard Communication Standard." *Yale Law Journal* 97 (1987–88): 581–601.

Chavkin, Wendy. "Occupational Hazards to Reproduction: A Review Essay and Annotated Bibliography." *Feminist Studies* 5 (1979): 310–25.

Cherner-Maneval, Wendy A. "Occupational Safety and Health—Employer Policy Excluding Fertile Female Workers Permitted Under the Occupational Safety and Health Act—*Oil, Chemical and Atomic Workers International Union v. American Cyanamid.*" *Temple Law Quarterly* 58 (1985): 939–75.

Cohen, Felissa. "Paternal Contributions to Birth Defects." *Nursing Clinics of North America* 21.1 (1986): 49–64.

Cohen, Sherrill, and Nadine Taub, eds. *Reproductive Laws for the 1990s.* Clifton, NJ: Humana Press, 1989.

Cooke, Edmund D., Jr., and Sally J. Kenney. "The View from Capitol Hill." In Sherrill Cohen and Nadine Taub, eds., *Reproductive Laws for the 1990s.* Clifton, NJ: Humana Press, 1989. 331–39.

Commerce Clearing House. *Employment Practices Decisions.* Chicago, IL: Commerce Clearing House, 1975–91.

Commerce Clearing House. *Employment Safety and Health Guide: Developments 1989.* Chicago, IL: Commerce Clearing House, 1989.

Cott, Nancy C. *The Grounding of Modern Feminism.* New Haven and London: Yale University Press, 1987.

Craig, Barbara Hinkson, and David M. O'Brien. *Abortion and American Politics.* Chatham, NJ: Chatham House, 1993.

Crawford, James. "The Deregulation of Worker Health." *Business and Society Review* 40 (1981–82): 9–14.

Darrough, Masako N., and Robert H. Blank, eds. *Biological Differences and Social Equality: Implications for Social Policy.* Westport, CT, and London: Greenwood Press, 1983.

Deckard, Barbara Sinclair. *The Women's Movement: Political, Socioeconomic and Psychological Issues.* 3d ed. New York: Harper and Row, 1983.

Dube, Lawrence E., Jr. "OSHA's Communication Standard: 'Right to Know' Comes to the Workplace." *Labor Law Journal* 36 (1985): 696–701.

Duran, Rowena M. "The Employer's Dilemma: The Implications of Occupational Safety and Health in the Arbitral Process—Conflicting Contractual and Statutory Commands." *Syracuse Law Review* 34 (1983): 1067–1105.

Edley, Christopher F., Jr., *Administrative Law: Rethinking Judicial Control of the Bureaucracy.* New Haven: Yale University Press, 1990.

Eisenstein, Zillah R. *The Female Body and the Law.* Berkeley: University of California Press, 1988.

"Environmental Protection Agency Proposed Amendments to Developmental Risk Guidelines." *Federal Register* 54 (1989): 9386.

Epstein, Lee. *Conservatives in Court.* Knoxville: University of Tennessee Press, 1985.

"Equal Employment Opportunity Commission Guidelines on Discrimination Because of Sex." *Federal Register* 37 (1972): 66.

Evans-Stanton, Sherri. "Gender Specific Regulations in the Chemical Workplace." *Santa Clara Law Review* 27 (1987): 353–76.

Finley, Lucinda M. "Transcending Equality Theory: A Way Out of the Maternity and the Workplace Debate." *Columbia Law Review* 86 (1986): 1118–82.

Fishkin, James S. *Justice, Equal Opportunity and the Family.* New Haven and London: Yale University Press, 1983.

Forster, Margaret, *Significant Sisters: The Grassroots of Active Feminism: 1839–1939.* London: Secker and Warburg, 1984.

Freedman, Warren. *The Law and Occupational Injury, Disease, and Death.* New York: Quorum Books, 1990.

Frug, Mary Joe. "A Postmodern Feminist Legal Manifesto." *Harvard Law Review* 105 (1992): 1045–75.

Frug, Mary Joe. "Securing Job Equality for Women: Labor Market Hostility to Working Mothers." *Boston University Law Review* 59 (1979): 55–104.

Fuchs, Victor R. *Women's Quest for Economic Equality.* Cambridge and London: Harvard University Press, 1988.

Furnish, Hannah Arterian. "Beyond Protection: Relevant Difference and Equality in the Toxic Work Environment." *University of California at Davis Law Review* 21 (1987): 1–43.

Gellhorn, Ernest, and Barry B. Boyer. *Administrative Law and Process.* St. Paul, MN: West Publishing, 1981.

Gilligan, Carol. *In A Different Voice: Psychological Theory and Women's Development.* Cambridge: Harvard University Press, 1982.

Ginsburg, Ruth Bader. "Some Thoughts on Autonomy and Equality in Relation to *Roe v. Wade*." *North Carolina Law Review* 63 (1985): 375–86.

Glass, Jennifer. "The Impact of Occupational Segregation on Working Conditions." *Social Forces* 63 (1990): 779–96.

Goldin, Claudia. "Maximum Hours Legislation and Female Employment: A Reassessment." *Journal of Political Economy* 96 (1988): 189–205.

Goldsmith, Willis J. "OSHA's Hazard Communication Standard: The Early Returns." *Employee Relations Law Journal* 12 (1986–87): 313–18.

Goldsmith, Willis J. "President Reagan's OSHA." *Employee Relations Law Journal* 14 (1989): 633–41.

Goldstein, Robert D. *Mother-Love and Abortion: A Legal Interpretation.* Berkeley: University of California Press, 1988.

Gunther, Gerald. *Individual Rights in Constitutional Law.* 4th ed. Mineola, NY: The Foundation Press, 1986.

Harrison, Cynthia. *On Account of Sex: The Politics of Women's Issues, 1945–1968.* Berkeley: University of California Press, 1988.

Hayes, David J. "TSCA: The Sleeping Giant is Stirring." *Natural Resources and Environment* 4 (1990): 3–5ff.

Hill, Herma Kay. "Models of Equality." *University of Illinois Law Review* 1 (1985): 1–85.

Horowitz, David L. *The Courts and Social Policy.* Washington, D.C.: The Brookings Institution, 1977.

Hunt, James W. *The Law of the Workplace: Rights of Employers and Employees.* Washington, D.C.: Bureau of National Affairs, 1984.

Jannett, Christine, and Randal G. Stewart. *Three Worlds of Inequality: Race, Class and Gender.* South Melbourne, Australia: MacMillan of Australia, 1987.

Johnson, Dawn E. "The Creation of Fetal Rights: Conflicts With Women's Constitutional Rights to Liberty, Privacy, and Equal Protection." *Yale Law Journal* 95 (1985–86): 599–625.

"Justices Listen to Arguments on Fetal Protection Policy." *New York Times*, 11 October 1990, sec. 1.

Kairys, David, ed. *The Politics of Law: A Progressive Critique*. 2d ed. New York: Pantheon, 1990.

Kamerman, Sheila B., Alfred J. Kahn, and Paul Kingston. *Maternity Policies and Working Women*. New York: Columbia University Press, 1983.

Kaminer, Wendy. *A Fearful Freedom: Women's Flight from Equality*. Reading, MA: Addison-Wesley, 1990.

Karst, Kenneth L. "Equal Citizenship under the Fourteenth Amendment." *Harvard Law Review* 91 (1977): 1–68.

Katz, Joni F. "Hazardous Working Conditions and Fetal Protection Policies: Women Are Going Back to the Future." *Boston College Environmental Affairs Law Review* 17 (1989): 201–30.

Kellough, J. Edward. "Federal Agencies and Affirmative Action for Blacks and Women." *Social Science Quarterly* 71 (1990): 83–91.

Kenney, Sally Jane. "Reproductive Hazards in the Workplace: A Comparative Study of Law and Public Policy in Britain and America." Ph.D. diss., Princeton University, 1989.

Klein, Ethel. *Gender Politics: From Consciousness to Mass Politics*. Cambridge: Harvard University Press, 1984.

Lavelle, Marianne. "A System of Failure." *National Law Journal* 11.33: 1.

Law, Sylvia A. "Rethinking Sex and the Constitution." *University of Pennsylvania Law Review* 132 (1984): 955–1040.

Lehrer, Susan. *Origins of Protective Labor Legislation for Women: 1905–1925*. Albany: State University of New York Press, 1987.

Levin, Michael. *Feminism and Freedom*. New Brunswick and Oxford: Transaction Books, 1987.

Lewis, Richard. "OCAW v. American Cyanamid: The Shrinking of the Occupational Safety and Health Act." *University of Pennsylvania Law Review* 133 (1985): 1167–91.

Lowe, Marion, and Ruth Hubbard. *Woman's Nature: Rationalizations of Inequality*. New York: Pergamon, 1983.

Lowi, Theodore J. *The End of Liberalism: The Second Republic of the United States*. 2d ed. New York: W.W. Norton, 1979.

Luker, Kirsten. *Abortion and the Politics of Motherhood*. Berkeley: University of California Press, 1984.

McGlen, Nancy E., and Karen O'Connor. *Women's Rights: The Struggle for Equality in the Nineteenth and Twentieth Centuries*. New York: Praeger, 1983.

McKeegan, Michelle. *Abortion Politics: Mutiny ir ᵢhe Ranks of the Right*. New York: The Free Press, 1992.

MacKinnon, Catherine A. *Toward a Feminist Theory of the State*. Cambridge: Harvard University Press, 1989.

Manna, John J., Jr. "The Extent of OSHA Preemption of State Hazard Reporting Requirements." *Columbia Law Review* 88 (1988): 630–46.

Mansbridge, Jane J. *Why We Lost the ERA*. Chicago: The University of Chicago Press, 1986.

Marcus, Daniel. "OSHA's Expanding Hazard Communication Requirements." *Natural Resources and Environment* 4 (1990): 19–21, 49–50.

Martin, Sheilah L., and Kathleen E. Mahoney, eds. *Equality and Judicial Neutrality*. Toronto: Carswell Publishers, 1987.

216   *References*

Maschke, Karen J. *Litigation, Courts, and Woman Workers.* New York: Praeger, 1989.

Millet, Kate. *Sexual Politics.* New York: Ballantine Books, 1969.

Minow, Martha. *Making All the Difference: Inclusion, Exclusion and American Law.* Ithaca and London: Cornell University Press, 1990.

Mirer, Franklin E. "Worker Participation in Health and Safety: Lessons from Joint Programs in the American Automobile Industry." *American Industrial Hygiene Association Journal* 50 (August 1989): 598–603.

Moelis, Laurence S. "Fetal Protection and Potential Liability: Judicial Application of the Pregnancy Discrimination Act and the Disparate Impact Theory." *American Journal of Law and Medicine* 11.3 (1985–86): 369–90.

Moran, Robert D. *OSHA Handbook.* 2d ed. Rockville, MD: Government Institutes, 1989.

Morgan, Robin. *Sisterhood is Powerful: An Anthology of Writings from the Women's Liberation Movement.* New York: Vintage, 1970.

Needleman, Herbert L., and David Bellinger. "Commentary: Recent Developments." *Environmental Research* 46 (1988): 190–91.

Nelkin, Dorothy, and Michael S. Brown. *Workers at Risk: Voices from the Workplace.* Chicago and London: The University of Chicago Press, 1984.

"The Civil Rights Act of 1991 and Less Discriminatory Alternatives in Disparate Treatment Litigation." *Harvard Law Review* 106 (1993): 1621–38.

Nothstein, Gary Z., and Jeffrey P. Ayres. "Sex-Based Considerations of Differentiation in the Workplace: Exploring the Biomedical Interface Between OSHA and Title VII." *Villanova Law Review* 26.2 (1981): 239–321.

Ocker, Kirsten. "OSHA's Hazard Communication Standard." *Idaho Law Review* 25 (1988–89): 619–29.

O'Connell, Lenahan. "Investigators at Work: How Bureaucratic and Legal Constraints Influence the Enforcement of Discrimination Law." *Public Administration Review* 51 (1991): 123–30.

O'Connor, Karen, and Lee Epstein. "The Rise of Conservative Interest Group Litigation." *Journal of Politics* 45 (1983): 479–88.

O'Connor, Karen, and Lee Epstein: "Sex and the Supreme Court: An Analysis of Judicial Support for Gender-Based Claims." *Social Science Quarterly* 64 (1983): 327–31.

Olson, Paulette. "The Persistence of Occupational Segregation: A Critique of Its Theoretical Underpinnings." *Journal of Economic Issues* 24 (1990): 161–69.

Olson, Susan M. "Interest Group Litigation in Federal District Court: Beyond the Political Disadvantage Theory." *Journal of Politics* 52 (1990): 854–81.

O'Reilly, James T. "Driving a Soft Bargain: Unions, Toxic Materials, and Right to Know Legislation." *Harvard Environmental Law Review* 9 (1985): 307–29.

Paul, Maureen, Cynthia Daniels, and Robert Rosofsky. "Corporate Response to Reproductive Hazards in the Workplace: Results of the Family, Work, and Health Survey." *American Journal of Industrial Medicine* 16 (1989): 267–80.

Petchesky, Rosalind. "Workers, Reproductive Hazards, and the Politics of Protection: An Introduction." *Feminist Studies* 5 (1979): 233–46.

Rabkin, Jeremy. *Judicial Compulsions: How Public Law Distorts Public Policy.* New York: Basic Books, 1989.

Radl, Shirley Rogers. *The Invisible Woman: Target of the Religious New Right.* New York: Delacorte Press, 1983.

Rae, Douglas. *Equalities.* Cambridge and London: Harvard University Press, 1981.

Rees, Joseph. *Reforming the Workplace: A Study of Self-Regulation in Occupational Safety.* Philadelphia: University of Pennsylvania Press, 1988.

Rempel, David. "The Lead-Exposed Worker." *Journal of the American Medical Association* 262.4 (1989): 532–34.

"Research on Birth Defects Shifts to Flaws in Sperm." *New York Times,* 1 January 1991, sec. 1.

Rhode, Deborah L. *Justice and Gender: Sex Discrimination and the Law.* Cambridge and London: Harvard University Press, 1989.

Rodgers, William H., Jr. *Environmental Law: Pesticides and Toxic Substances.* St. Paul, MN: West Publishing, 1988.

Rosenberg, Gerald N. *The Hollow Hope: Can Courts Bring About Social Change?* Chicago: The University of Chicago Press, 1991.

Rossi, Alice S., ed. *The Feminist Papers: From Adams to de Beavoir.* New York: Columbia University Press, 1973.

Rothstein, Mark A. *Medical Screening of Workers.* Washington, D.C.: Bureau of National Affairs, 1984.

Ruggerio, Cynthia. "Referral of Toxic Chemical Regulation Under the Toxic Substances Control Act: EPA's Administrative Dumping Ground." *Boston College Environmental Affairs Law Review* 17 (1989): 75–122.

"Rules on Video Display Terminals in Workplace Are Backed in San Francisco." *New York Times,* 18 December 1990, sec. 1.

Shapiro, Sidney A. and Thomas O. McGarity. "Reorienting OSHA: Regulatory Alternatives and Legislative Reform." *Yale Journal on Regulation* 6 (1989): 1–63.

Siegel, Reva. "Reasoning from the Body: A Historical Perspective on Abortion Regulation and Questions of Equal Protection." *Stanford Law Review* 44 (1991–92): 261–381.

Smith, Joan. "Feminist Analysis of Gender: A Mystique." In *Morion Lowe and Ruth Hubbard, eds., Women's Nature: Rationalizations of Inequality.* New York: Pergamon, 1983. 89–109.

Stillman, Nina G., and John R. Wheeler. "The Expansion of Occupational Safety and Health Law." *Notre Dame Law Review* 62 (1987): 969–1009.

Sunstein, Cass R. *After the Rights Revolution: Reconceiving the Regulatory State.* Cambridge: Harvard University Press, 1990.

"Supreme Court Hears 'Fetal Protection' Case." *The Washington Post,* 11 October 1990, sec. 1.

Thomas, Clarence. "Affirmative Action Goals and Timetables: Too Tough? Not Tough Enough!" *Yale Law and Policy Review* 5 (1987): 402–20.

Thomas, Clarence. "Current Litigation Trends and Goals at the Equal Employment Opportunity Commission." *Labor Law Journal* 34 (1983): 208–14.

Thomas, Clarence. "The Equal Employment Opportunity Commission: Reflections on a New Philosophy." *Stetson Law Review* 15 (1985): 29–36.

Thomas, Clarence. "The Higher Law Background of the Privileges and Immunities Clause of the Fourteenth Amendment." *Harvard Journal of Law and Public Policy* 12 (1989): 63–70.

Thomas, Clarence. "Promoting Diversity for Diversity's Sake." *Legal Times* 17 (1991): 10–12.

Toxic Substances Control Act Research Group. *The Toxic Substances Control Act: Overview and Evaluation.* Austin: Lyndon B. Johnson School of Public Affairs, University of Texas at Austin, 1982.

U.S. Congress, House of Representatives, Committee on Education and Labor, Subcommittee on Employment Opportunities. "Oversight Hearings on the OFCCP's Proposed Affirmative Action Regulations." 97th Cong., 1st Sess., 1983.

U.S. Congress, House of Representatives, Majority Staff of the Committee on Education and

Labor. *A Report on the Equal Employment Opportunity Commission, Title VII and Workplace Fetal Protection Policies in the 1980s.* 101st Cong., 2d sess., 1990.

U.S. Department of Health and Human Services, Centers for Disease Control, National Institute for Occupational Safety and Health. *Proposed National Strategy for the Prevention of Disorders of Reproduction.* Washington, D.C.: Government Printing Office, 1989.

U.S. Department of Labor. *State Labor Laws in Transition: From Protection to Equal Status for Women.* Washington, D.C.: Government Printing Office, 1976.

U.S. Department of Labor, Women's Bureau. *Time of Change: 1983 Handbook on Women Workers.* Washington, D.C.: Government Printing Office, 1983.

U.S. Environmental Laws. Washington, D.C.: Bureau of National Affairs, 1988.

U.S. Equal Employment Opportunity Commission. "Guidelines on Discrimination Because of Sex," *Federal Register* 29 Code of Federal Regulations 1604.2, vol. 37, no. 66, 5 April 1972.

U.S. Equal Employment Opportunity Commission. "Policy Guidance on Reproductive and Fetal Hazards." Washington, D.C.: Government Printing Office, 7 October 1988.

U.S. Equal Employment Opportunity Commission. "Policy Guidance on *United Auto Workers v. Johnson Controls.*" Washington, D.C.: Government Printing Office, 24 January 1990.

U.S. General Accounting Office. *Reproductive and Developmental Toxicants: Regulatory Actions Provide Uncertain Protection.* Washington, D.C.: Government Printing Office, 1991.

U.S. Office of Technology Assessment, United States Congress. *Reproductive Hazards in the Workplace.* Washington, D.C.: Government Printing Office, 1985.

"United States Opens a Drive to Wipe Out Lead Poisoning Among Children." *New York Times,* 20 December 1990, sec. 1.

Vig, Norman J., and Michael E. Kraft. *Environmental Policy in the 1980s: Reagan's New Agenda.* Washington, D.C.: Congressional Quarterly, 1984.

Walzer, Michael. *Spheres of Justice: A Defense of Pluralism and Equality.* New York: Basic Books, 1983.

Whitney, Sharon. *The Equal Rights Amendment: The History and the Movement.* New York: Franklin Watts, 1984.

Williams, Joan C. "Deconstructing Gender." *Michigan Law Review* 87 (1989): 797–845.

Williams, Wendy W. "Equality's Riddle: Pregnancy and the Equal Treatment/Special Treatment Debate." *New York University Review of Law and Social Change* 13 (1984–85): 325–80.

Williams, Wendy W. "The Supreme Court and Sex Equality." In Sheilah L. Martin and Kathleen E. Mohoney, eds., *Equality and Judicial Neutrality.* Toronto: Carswell Publishers, 1987. 117–30.

Williams, Wendy W. "Firing the Woman to Protect the Fetus: The Reconciliation of Fetal Protection with Employment Opportunity Goals under Title VII." *The Georgetown Law Journal* 69 (1980–81): 641–704.

Wolgast, Elizabeth H. *Equality and the Rights of Women.* Ithaca and London: Cornell University Press, 1980.

Wood, B. Dan. "Does Politics Make a Difference at the EEOC?" *American Journal of Political Science* 34 (1990): 503–30.

Wright, Michael J. "Reproductive Hazards and 'Protective' Discrimination." *Feminist Studies* 5 (1979): 302–9.

Zimmer, Michael J., Charles A. Sullivan, and Richard F. Richards. *Cases and Materials on Employment Discrimination.* Boston and Toronto: Little, Brown and Co., 1988.

Cases

Adkins v. Children's Hospital. 261 U.S. 525 (1923). U.S. Supreme Court.

Bradwell v. Illinois. 83 U.S. 130, 16 Wall. 130 (1873). U.S. Supreme Court.

Bunting v. Oregon. 243 U.S. 426 (1917). U.S. Supreme Court.

California Federal Savings and Loan Association v. Guerra. 479 U.S. 272, 107 S.Ct 683 (1987). U.S. Supreme Court.

Colautti v. Franklin. 439 U.S. 379, 99 S.Ct. 675 (1979). U.S. Supreme Court.

Criswell v. Western Airlines. 472 U.S. 400, 105 S.Ct. 2743 (1985). U.S. Supreme Court.

Diaz v. Pan American World Airways, Inc. 442 F.2d 385 (1971). Court of Appeals for Fifth Circuit.

Doerr v. B.F. Goodrich Co. 484 F. Supp. 320 (1979). N.D. Ohio.

Dothard et al. v. Rawlinson et al. 433 U.S. 321 (1977). U.S. Supreme Court.

Edwards v. Dept. of Corrections et al. 615 F. Supp. 804 (1985). M.D. Alabama.

Frontiero v. Richardson. 411 U.S. 677 (1973). U.S. Supreme Court.

Geduldig v. Aiello. 417 U.S. 484, 94 S.Ct. 2485 (1974). U.S. Supreme Court.

General Electric Co. v. Gilbert. 429 U.S. 125, 97 S.Ct. 401 (1976). U.S. Supreme Court.

Goesart et al. v. Cleary et al. 74 F. Supp. 735 (1947). E.D. Michigan.

Goesart et al. v. Cleary et al. 335 U.S. 464 (1948). U.S. Supreme Court.

Grant v. General Motors Corporation. 908 F.2d 1303 (1990). Court of Appeals for the Sixth Circuit.

Hayes v. Shelby Memorial Hospital. 726 F.2d 1543 (1984). Court of Appeals for the Eleventh Circuit.

International Union, United Autoworkers v. Johnson Controls. Employment Practices Decisions 680 F. Supp. 309 (E.D. Wis. 1988). E.D. Michigan.

International Union, United Autoworkers v. Johnson Controls. 886 F.2d 871 (1989). Court of Appeals for the Seventh Circuit.

International Union, United Autoworkers v. Johnson Controls. 499 U.S. 187, 111 S.Ct. 1196, 113 L.Ed. 2d 158 (1991). U.S. Supreme Court.

Johnson Controls, Inc. v. California Fair Employment and Housing Commission. 267 Cal. Rptr. 158 (1990). California Court of Appeals, 4th Dst.

Levin et al. v. Delta Air Lines, Inc. 730 F.2d 995 (1984). Court of Appeals for the Fifth Circuit.

Lochner v. New York. 198 U.S. 45 (1905). U.S. Supreme Court.

Muller v. Oregon. 208 U.S. 412 (1908). U.S. Supreme Court.

Nashville Gas Co. v. Satty. 985 S.Ct. 347 (1977). U.S. Supreme Court.

Oil, Chemical and Atomic Workers International Union, and Local 3-499, Oil, Chemical and Atomic Workers v. American Cyanamid Co. 741 Fed. Rptr. 2d. 444 (1984). Court of Appeals for the District of Columbia.

Phillips v. Martin Marietta Corp. 400 U.S. 542 (1971). U.S. Supreme Court.

Planned Parenthood of Central Missouri v. Danforth. 428 U.S. 552, 96 S.Ct. 2831 (1976). U.S. Supreme Court.

Planned Parenthood of Southeastern Pennsylvania v. Casey. 492 U.S. 490, 112 S.Ct. 2791 (1992). U.S. Supreme Court.

Radice v. New York. 264 U.S. 292 (1924). U.S. Supreme Court.

Reed v. Reed 404 U.S. 71 (1971). U.S. Supreme Court.

Robinson v. Lorillard Corp. et al. 444 F.2d 791 (1971). Court of Appeals for the Fourth Circuit.

Rostker v. Goldberg et al. 453 U.S. 57 (1981). U.S. Supreme Court.

Royster Girano Co. v. Virginia. 253 U.S. 412 (1920). U.S. Supreme Court.

Sail'er Inn, Inc. v. Kirby. 485 P.2d 529 (1971). California Supreme Court.

Steele v. Illinois Human Rights Commission et al. Employment Practices Decisions 37,883 (1987). Illinois Appellate Court.

Thornburgh v. American College of Obstetricians and Gynecologists. 476 (19XX). U.S. Supreme Court.

Wards Cove Packing Co., Inc. v. Atonio. 490 U.S. 642, 109 S.Ct. 2115 (1989). U.S. Supreme Court.

Webster v. Reproductive Health Services. 492 U.S. 490, 109 S.Ct. 3040 (1989). U.S. Supreme Court.

Weeks v. Southern Bell Telephone and Telegraph Co. 408 F.2d 228 (1969). Court of Appeals for the Fifth Circuit.

West Coast Hotel Company v. Parrish. 300 U.S. 379 (1937). U.S. Supreme Court.

Wright v. Olin Corporation. 697 F.2d 1172 (1982). Court of Appeals for the Fourth Circuit.

Zuniga v. Kleberg City Hospital. 692 F.2d 986 (1982). Court of Appeals for the Fifth Circuit.

Briefs

Brief for Petitioners. *International Union, United Autoworkers v. Johnson Controls, Inc*. Filed in the Supreme Court of the U.S., October Term 1990.

Brief for Respondents. *International Union, United Autoworkers v. Johnson Controls, Inc*. Filed in the Supreme Court of the U.S., October Term 1990.

Official Transcript Proceedings before the Supreme Court of the United States. *International Union, United Auto Workers v. Johnson Controls, Inc*. Oral Argument before the Supreme Court, 10 October 1990.

Index